The International Library of Sociology

THE SOCIAL BACKGROUND OF A PLAN

Founded by KARL MANNHEIM

The International Library of Sociology

URBAN AND REGIONAL SOCIOLOGY

In 13 Volumes

I	An Approach to Urban Sociology	*Mann*
II	City and Region	*Dickinson*
III	The City Region in Western Europe	*Dickinson*
IV	English Rural Life	*Bracey*
V	New Dubliners	*Humphreys*
VI	The Personality of the Urban African in South Africa	*de Ridder*
VII	The Regions of Germany	*Dickinson*
VIII	Revolution of Environment	*Gutkind*
IX	Rural Depopulation in England and Wales 1851 - 1951	*Saville*
X	The Social Background of a Plan	*Glass*
XI	The Sociology of an English Village: Gosforth	*Williams*
XII	The West European City	*Dickinson*
XIII	Westrigg	*Littlejohn*

THE SOCIAL BACKGROUND OF A PLAN

Edited by

RUTH GLASS

for

THE ASSOCIATION FOR PLANNING AND REGIONAL RECONSTRUCTION

Preface by

MAX LOCK

LONDON AND NEW YORK

First published in 1948 by
Routledge

Reprinted in 1998 (three times),1999, 2001
by Routledge
2 Park Square, Milton Park, Abingdon, Oxon, OX14 4RN
711 Third Avenue, New York, NY 10017

Transferred to Digital Printing 2007

Routledge is an imprint of the Taylor & Francis Group

First issued in paperback 2013

British Library Cataloguing in Publication Data
A CIP catalogue record for this book
is available from the British Library

The Social Background of a Plan
ISBN 978-0-415-17706-1 hbk
ISBN 978-0-415-86855-6 pbk
Urban and Regional Sociology: 13 Volumes
ISBN 978-0-415-17830-3
The International Library of Sociology: 274 Volumes
ISBN 978-0-415-17838-9

Publisher's Note

The publisher has gone to great lengths to ensure the quality of this reprint but points out that some imperfections in the original may be apparent

TABLE OF CONTENTS

Part III

EDUCATION SERVICES

Part IV

RETAIL TRADE

LIST OF TABLES

PART I. NEIGHBOURHOODS

PART II. HEALTH SERVICES

PART III. EDUCATION SERVICES

PART IV. RETAIL TRADE

APPENDICES

ILLUSTRATIONS IN POCKET AT END OF BOOK

Part I. The Pattern of Neighbourhoods

Part II. Health Services

Part III. Education Services

Part IV. Retail Trade

Appendix A. The Geographical and Economical Background

MIDDLESBROUGH: GENERAL INFORMATION

1. Location and Administrative Status

Middlesbrough is in the North Riding of Yorkshire. It is a County Borough, divided into eleven wards.

2. Population Growth

YEAR	POPULATION	SOURCE OF INFORMATION
1801	25	Census
1811	35	Census
1821	40	Census
1831	150	Census
1841	5,463	Census
1851	7,631	Census
1861	18,892	Census
1871	39,284	Census
1881	55,934	Census
1891	75,532	Census
1901	91,302	Census
1911	104,767	Census
1921	131,170	Census
1931	138,960	Census
1939	129,107	National Registration, September 1939.
1944 (Estimate A)	119,150	Based on Results of "Social Survey" Household Sample Enquiry.
1944 (Estimate B)	138,000	Based on Results of "Social Survey" Household Sample Enquiry.

Estimate A for 1944 shows the total resident population in June of that year. Estimate B includes all those who were temporarily absent, either in the Forces or on war work.

The 1939 National Registration figure excludes all those who were evacuated or on war service at that time.

Population in institutions is included in all the totals from 1801 to 1939, but excluded from the 1944 estimates.

3. Administrative Development

YEAR	STATUS
1801 . .	Township of Middlesbrough
1853 . .	Borough of Middlesbrough
1856 . .	Borough divided into wards
1858 . .	Borough extension
1866 . .	Borough extension
1874 . .	Borough extension
1891 . .	County Borough of Middlesbrough
1914 . .	Borough extension
1932 . .	Borough extension

PREFACE

The new Town and Country Planning Bill which has recently received the Royal Assent places the field of town and country planning in a new perspective. The responsibility of the planner is widened from the narrow limitations of individual action to the broader basis of team work. The plans of the civic designer now have their foundations in the work of the geographer, economist, sociologist, engineer and architect.

The Middlesbrough Corporation were in advance of legislation in fostering this approach and in providing the means for a thorough investigation of existing conditions as a basis for the preparation of their Masterplan.

Few social surveys undertaken in the past, were applied to practical planning proposals. Now that town planning ranks as a social science as well as a technical art, it is hoped that the student of sociology will find in this work a guide to the use of survey methods as a means to the achievement of planning ends.

Some planners seem to have invented a dividing line between social and physical planning, but none exists. From the social aspect, the "raw materials" of a plan are the citizens of the place. They are the planner's clients who must be consulted in the same way as the clients of an architect are consulted. But how to consult a population constitutes the planner's difficulty which is only met by the trained skill of the sociologist who can, by systematic enquiry, help to formulate a social plan based on the needs of the many varied groups within a town.

The conclusions to this book show that there seem to be three ways in which the science of sociology is indispensable to the planner.

1. *Pure Research.* Planners require to base their proposals on well established standards. Standards can only be reliably fixed after a number of investigations have been made on similar lines in a number of comparable towns. A great many social surveys are already contributing to this mass of information. But a great deal more work is required if planners are not to be over-influenced by mere whims and fashions. Standards, applied to the planning of neighbourhoods, of distribution of shops and shopping centres, of road design, of the economics of building, and of many other important aspects of civic design, require a solid factual basis before they can be accepted as authentic. The Universities and the research department of the Ministry of Town and Country Planning might become the chief agencies for basic research of this kind.

2. *Applied Research.* It is obvious that no two places have the same

problems and that a planning team can only do justice to its responsibility by studying all aspects of the town's social, economic and administrative life *on the spot.* Even supposing the planner has authentic standards to work upon, these must of necessity be modified by the peculiarities of the place with which he happens to be concerned. It is perhaps chiefly in this respect that the work undertaken by our sociologist at Middlesbrough has marked an advance in the technique of planning. In this work we were greatly assisted by the co-operation of the Ministry of Town and Country Planning who engaged the services of the Wartime Social Survey to undertake for us a sample investigation of the population of Middlesbrough. The results of this survey established such important facts as the distribution of households by size and by type, the catchment areas of shopping centres, the daily movements to work, the geographical distribution of income groups, and many other factors which strongly influenced the design and the refinements of the Masterplan. In this way we are satisfied that the planning proposals are neither capricious nor unduly biased. They are capable of implementation, provided that those entrusted with the carrying out of the Plan continue the same systematic method of relating the work of reconstruction to the needs of the people.

3. *Public Relations.* People will not make sacrifices to carry out plans which they have not in some way helped to make themselves. During the process of enquiry among the many groups of citizens that we encountered, a great deal of interest and enthusiasm was aroused. Although the sociologist's primary function is to obtain the facts upon which the Plan can be based, an indirect result is to be found in the confidence and public interest established between the people and the planners. We found that a scientific method of approach, far from keeping planning from the ordinary man and woman, in fact, brings it to their doorstep and identifies them with their Plan and in this way can be said to be not only scientific but democratic.

Although this book, as also the whole of the original work on the Middlesbrough Survey and Plan, which has been published separately by the Middlesbrough Corporation, will be of special interest to the people of Middlesbrough, both volumes have been issued for the benefit of the student of social studies at University, college and school, on the local Councils, in discussion groups and for those in any way concerned with the vital task of improving our towns. It is hoped that this publication will serve as a guide to other county boroughs and, in particular, to planning officers organising the surveys now required of them by the 1947 Town and Country Planning Act.

West Hartlepool, *August 1947.* MAX LOCK

INTRODUCTION

The social survey of Middlesbrough, which is presented here, belongs to a wider scheme. It is a part of the Middlesbrough Survey and Plan of 1944, which was directed by Max Lock in his capacity as Town Planning Consultant to the County Borough of Middlesbrough. The material here collected is published with the permission of the Middlesbrough Corporation.

The Survey and Plan had four stages. The first, that of field work, lasted from April to October 1944. The second stage, the tabulation, mapping and analysis of the results, and the writing of the survey reports, was completed in January 1945. Thirdly, on the basis of these reports and of subsequent discussions with the survey workers, the plan was prepared by the town planners and architects of the Middlesbrough team. The plan, and the evidence from which it was derived, were submitted to the Middlesbrough Council in October 1945, and it was accepted by the Council three months later. Previously, an exhibition of the Survey and Plan had been held in Middlesbrough.

At the outset, it had been decided that for the purpose of re-planning the town, not only its physical, but also its social and economic aspects had to be considered. Consequently, some division of labour was required, and during the first stage of this enterprise, enquiries were conducted simultaneously in three fields.

The survey of physical planning factors was directed by Max Lock, whose chief collaborators in this field were Jessica Albery and Justin Blanco-White. Their work was summarised in reports on housing, open spaces, transport and public utilities.

The geographical and economic survey was conducted by A. E. Smailes, who had the voluntary assistance of several geographers and economists.

The social survey of Middlesbrough was carried out by the Association for Planning and Regional Reconstruction, under my direction. The chief subjects considered were neighbourhood structure, health and education services and retail trade. In addition, a government research agency, the Wartime Social Survey, contributed a household sample enquiry, for which Dennis Chapman was responsible.

When the reports on the various social aspects of the Middlesbrough survey had been completed, it was realised that, while their motive was practical and specific, they were also of more general relevance. In theory, the necessity of interpreting people's needs and relationships in the physical design of town and countryside is now widely recognised; in practice few studies have as yet been undertaken for this purpose. Sociologists and town planners, though, in fact, near relations, have worked rather far apart from each other. Consequently, the social context of town planning still has to be explored; the contribution of social surveys to local planning schemes still has to be defined.

No single enquiry can fulfil these functions, but as the Middlesbrough social survey had a specific planning objective, it may be regarded as an experiment, the scope, the methods and the content of which, it might be worth while to examine.

Accordingly, it was decided to edit the reports on the various social aspects of the Middlesbrough survey so that they could be combined in one book. Originally, these reports had not been written from the point of view of general interest: they were detailed memoranda to the Town Planning Consultant from which specific proposals about, for instance, individual parts of the town, could be derived. In revising the reports, facts which were merely of local relevance were omitted, but it was still necessary to retain a good deal of descriptive material. The scope and the methods of the survey could not be outlined without telling the story of the town.

Although some time has elapsed since the survey was completed, conditions in Middlesbrough during the period of the enquiry, in the summer of 1944, are throughout described in the present tense.

The editing of the reports provided an opportunity to re-examine the facts which had been collected. The work had originally been done under considerable pressure of time and it was, therefore, useful to be able to extend the analysis of the data and to eliminate inaccuracies which had occurred. Some of the material which had been obtained incidentally was also included in order to round off the picture of Middlesbrough. While both the analysis and the presentation of the survey results were thus considerably revised, the conclusions, which had previously been reached, were again confirmed.

Of course, the picture of Middlesbrough is still incomplete since the survey itself had considerable shortcomings. Some of these are inevitable in every enquiry which is undertaken for immediate practical application: time is usually short and research facilities are limited. These restrictions are most noticeable when the survey, as in Middlesbrough, has to be largely improvised, that is, when it is not known in advance which aspects are most relevant and which methods are most appropriate.

In retrospect, it appears that, while the fields of enquiry were correctly chosen, the organisation of the survey could have been considerably improved. Survey and plan should not be considered as entirely separate stages. A preliminary enquiry should lead to an outline plan which, in turn, would indicate specific problems and areas which require further detailed investigations. When these have been completed, the final plan could be prepared.

As the survey continued without interruption in Middlesbrough and as its scope had to be experimental, some aspects were over-emphasised, while others had to be neglected. For instance, a detailed picture of institutional catchment areas was obtained for the whole town, but an intensive study of certain "problem" neighbourhoods had to be omitted. In future similar enquiries, it might be advisable first to demarcate neighbourhood boundaries, that is, to investigate the physical and social characteristics of the town's sub-divisions. It might then be sufficient to consider only the patterns of movement within and between those neighbourhoods which are likely to be subjected to considerable changes. At the same time, these neighbourhoods could, if necessary, be observed in considerable detail.

The altered procedure would also make it possible to co-ordinate the enquiries into the physical and the social aspects of the town far more closely. In fact, no clear line can be drawn between these two fields of investigation. The physical pattern of the town reflects and, in turn, perpetuates its social structure, and physical aspects have to be interpreted accordingly. Hence, while the techniques of investigation differ in these two fields, the territorial units of investigation should be identical. For instance, if the statistics on housing conditions are tabulated in terms of wards, but the statistics of social characteristics are presented in terms of neighbourhoods, it is difficult to relate the results of these two branches of the survey. At the beginning of the Middlesbrough survey, the method of compiling facts was deficient in this respect, but subsequently, an attempt was made to use, as far as possible, the same sub-divisions for all parts of the survey, and to use "natural", rather than administrative, sub-divisions, that is, neighbourhoods rather than wards.

Nevertheless, there are still inconsistencies which could not be avoided, as will be evident when the social survey is being examined. In addition to neighbourhoods, two other comparatively small territorial sub-divisions are referred to: wards, in the section on Health Services, and school districts, in the section on Education Services. Official statistics, for instance, birth rates and infant mortality rates, are usually given in terms of wards, and it would not be worthwhile to undertake a specific investigation for the purpose of regrouping the figures. The term "school district" is used since school catchment areas are not conterminous either with neighbourhoods or wards.

However, these inconsistencies disappear when the major territorial sub-divisions in the town are considered. Thus the "major areas" of Middlesbrough, which are referred to in the section on Health Services, and which are composed of groups of wards and housing estates, are roughly coincident with groups of school districts, and, in turn, also with the chief groups of neighbourhoods.

The list of sources and the methods of the social survey may be briefly summarised. Four major sources were used: published statistics; unpublished administrative records; general field work; and specific field enquiries.

Published statistics were chiefly derived from past censuses and from the annual reports of the various departments of the Middlesbrough County Borough. The unpublished records of these departments which we were allowed to consult were, on the whole, even more useful. Details, which had been filed for administrative purposes, were analysed and often also mapped: for instance, the distribution of births and infant deaths in the town; the use of school playing fields; and the origin of tenants on the new muncipal estates.

Material obtained from these sources was supplemented through general field work, that is, through interviews with officials and representatives of local organisations; and through visits to, and observations of, particular neighbourhoods and institutions. For instance, many discussions were held with the administrative officers and with the elected representatives of the County Borough; with teachers, doctors, trade-union officials and with the local clergy. The secretaries of political, social and trade organisations were consulted. Schools, clinics, welfare centres, wardens' posts and some of the industrial establishments were visited. Attendances at cafés, restaurants, cinemas and public houses were systematically observed. Several panels of local residents were formed. The general neighbourhood pattern of the town was discussed with one of these groups; others gave advice on the redevelopment of particular areas.

In addition, a number of specific field enquiries were organised. These were, first, detailed surveys of the location of institutions; secondly, studies of institutional catchment areas; and thirdly, questionnaire enquiries among particular groups in the Middlesbrough population.

The location of all non-residential buildings in Middlesbrough was established through the general land-use survey. Simultaneously, the distribution of clubs of different types and of shops was recorded in considerable detail. The majority of clubs were also visited, and their club leaders or representatives were interviewed. In the shop location survey, we distinguished between occupied and empty shops, and between shops of different trade types.

In order to obtain a picture of the spheres of influence of different types of institutions, special censuses of the school population, of club membership, and of the users of day-nurseries and infant welfare centres were taken.

The census of the elementary and secondary school population was carried out with the help of the education department, of the teachers, and, in particular, of the school children themselves. During the census week, every junior and every senior recorded on a special card his or her name, address, date of birth, school, department and class. For the infants, for the children in special schools, and for all those who were absent from school during the census week, the cards were completed by the teachers. On the basis of this information, the catchment area of each school could be mapped.

The club census covered 60 of the town's 71 Youth Clubs; the remainder were small sports clubs with less than 30 members. Every person visiting any of these clubs during a specified week recorded each day, on entering the club, his or her name, address, age, occupation, and the time of attendance. A similar, though not so detailed and comprehensive census was taken for adult clubs.

The addresses of all mothers who used wartime day-nurseries, and of those who attended infant welfare centres during a given period were obtained from the appropriate registers. The frequency of attendances at infant welfare centres was also noted.

The catchment areas of the three public libraries in the town were visible when a sample of library users had been taken. During a given week, the address of every fifth adult who borrowed books from the public libraries was recorded.

Additional material on the spheres of influence of other types of institutions was derived from the two questionnaire enquiries. The major purpose of the first of these, which was carried out separately by the Wartime Social Survey, was to obtain a picture of Middlesbrough's household structure. A sample of one in twenty-three of all households was chosen at random from the rating list. A questionnaire for housewives was drawn up, as well as another, slightly different one, for other adult members of their households. Altogether 1,387 housewives and 1,209 other adults were interviewed.

Three parts of this enquiry have been particularly useful in considering the social background of Middlesbrough's plan. The answers to the questions on household size and composition made it possible to prepare an estimate of Middlesbrough's housing requirements. The record of occupations, industries, places of work and incomes of chief wage earners, which was subsequently mapped, contributed to the picture of the neighbourhood pattern. Questions on shopping habits and on the use of post-offices, from the answers to which a series of maps was derived, were relevant both to the study of neighbourhoods and of retail trade.

While the local consumers were consulted through the household sample enquiry, the second questionnaire enquiry was carried out among the retailers themselves. Its chief purpose was to review the function and the degree of prosperity of the different shopping centres; to consider their location and lay-out problems, and the extent of their spheres of influence outside the town. As Middlesbrough is a service centre for the Tees-side and Cleveland area, this last point is of considerable importance.

The enquiry was designed to cover all retailers of commodities other than food, with the exception of certain categories of small cornershops in the town centre, chiefly tobacconists and newsagents. It appeared that the necessary information could most conveniently be obtained in that way since no census of retail distribution had yet been taken, and, therefore, a reliable shop sample could not be constructed. At the same time, a good deal was known already about the Middlesbrough foodshops, through the shop location survey, the household sample enquiry, and through additional data obtained from the food office.

In order to gauge the extent of wartime changes, many of the questions on the standardised schedule referred both to conditions in the summer of 1939 and in the summer of 1944. The visits to the shops also made it possible to observe the characteristics of their neighbourhoods, of their premises and of their customers. Altogether 337 retailers were interviewed, all of whom were pleased to have the opportunity of expressing their views. Indeed, during every phase of the social survey, the investigators made friends, and found helpers, among the people of Middlesbrough. Everywhere, they were most cordially received.

While the sources and methods of the social survey have been specifically described, the contribution of the physical survey to the picture of the social background of the plan should not be forgotten. For the study of neighbourhoods, in particular, all the relevant survey material, both physical and social, was considered. In fact the recognition of physical boundaries, and of variations in housing conditions, within the town was indispensable for the demarcation of neighbourhoods. Moreover, Middlesbrough's geographical and economic characteristics, to the study of which a separate section of the survey had been devoted, had constantly to be borne in mind.

The social survey was thus essentially a co-operative enterprise. The chief investigators were Griselda Rowntree and Barbara Foster Sutton. Miss Rowntree carried out the enquiry into, and wrote the reports on, Health and Education Services. Miss Foster Sutton's main subject was Retail Trade. She supervised the shop location survey, conducted all the interviews with retailers, and prepared the relevant draft report. Both contributed also to the investigation of Neighbourhoods, for the report on which I am responsible.

In addition, there were many other helpers. Jaqueline Tyrwhitt gave advice and collaborated both in the collection and in the mapping of survey material. Stella Johnstone carried out the survey of youth clubs. The British Institute of Public Opinion lent a member of their staff, Ian McFadyen, for the survey of adult clubs. Vera Hoyle and Mrs. Foster Sutton acted as part-time assistants, the latter in a voluntary capacity. The Hollerith Department of the Co-operative Wholesale Society in Manchester undertook the tabulation of the retail trade enquiry.

The architects and draughtsmen of the Middlesbrough team prepared all the original social survey maps, a number of which were later redrawn for this publication by the staff of the Association for Planning and Regional Reconstruction.

We are indebted to the Wartime Social Survey (now "The Social Survey") for their household sample enquiry which was directed by Dennis Chapman.

The contribution of Jessica Albery and Justin Blanco-White

should be especially acknowledged. They were responsible for the reports on Housing and Open Spaces respectively, which are frequently referred to, and they, together with Max Lock, applied the results of the social survey to the plan.

A. E. Smailes wrote the report on the Geographical and Economic Background, which is included in the Appendix. He was assisted in his investigation by S. G. Raybould, who also took part in the social survey, by E. P. Bramfit, Father Clifton and Madeline Linney.

At every stage, the survey team had the help of the Council and of the administrative officers of the Middlesbrough County Borough. All were always ready to give advice, to discuss our problems, and to give us access to their records. In particular, we should like to express our gratitude to the Mayor of Middlesbrough, Councillor R. Ridley Kitching, and to the Town Clerk, Mr. Preston Kitchen.

So many other people and organisations participated, that it is difficult to acknowledge all the individual contributions. Girls from the Kirby Secondary School carried out the shop location survey. Boys from Acklam Hall, another Secondary School, prepared most of the school catchment area maps. Among our constant advisers were Miss G. A. Prinn, the Warden of the Middlesbrough Settlement, and D. J. Longden, Area Officer of the Assistance Board.

We owe a great debt to the people of Middlesbrough, most of whom remained anonymous. It was their survey, and it is their job to carry out the plan.

September 1946. R.G.

PART I

THE PATTERN OF NEIGHBOURHOODS

I

AN INTRODUCTION TO MIDDLESBROUGH

Middlesbrough is the very prototype of a town born and reared during the past century. Hence all its defects and all its assets. Hence it is known chiefly for its iron and steel industry, for its mushroom growth, its grid-iron layout and its alleged ugliness. Instead of growing around a castle or a cathedral, as some of the old towns in the country, it has grown around coke-ovens and blast-furnaces. The founders of the great combines have been its Lords of the Manor. The scenery is marred by weird and giant industrial structures. The sky is obscured by the twin bursts of flame and smoke which emanate from industrial processes. The river is cut off from the town by the machinery of the docks and of the iron and steel works. Its bed is muddy. Its banks are littered with all the debris and the appurtenances of the works and the docks: vast slag heaps interspersed with railway lines, cranes, chimneys, furnaces and sheds. This core of Middlesbrough is still, as it was at the beginning of the century, "a place in which every sense is violently assailed all day long by some manifestation of the making of iron".[1]

To those who think of beauty and romance in terms of things rustic and antique, this place is indeed very ugly. Others differ. It is true that it lacks diversity and that it has no tradition, yet its very bleakness and impetuousness has a vigorous beauty of its own. The very fact that industry is all pervasive has its peculiar fascination. Battles have been and are fought here; battles for the organisation of the industry. Men have stood up daily, and still do so, against the physical dangers of production; accidents, diseases and exhaustion. They have faced the depletion of raw materials. They have been and are subjected to the economic hazards of the iron and steel trade. The imprint of courage and success is everywhere.

But there is also the imprint of failure. The rapid growth of the industry and of the town has entailed waste and neglect. The decay of the old town has kept pace with the expansion of the new. Hemmed in on the north by the Ironmasters' district, the docks and the River Tees, the town has sprawled southwards. The more prosperous a family became, the further out did it move, away from the original centre of the town. The poor people were left there, on either side of the railway, living in "rows and rows of little brown streets", in cottages which were cheaply and hastily built by the jerry builders of the second half of the last century. Whilst suburbia spread out, the old town deteriorated, so that by now most of it is a blighted area, urgently in need of reconstruction.

Industry has become dispersed and in part obsolete as well. The shifting of emphasis from iron to steel production; the exhaustion of the Cleveland ironstone mines; the vicissitudes of the post 1918 steel trade; all these have left gaps and derelict patches in the Ironmaster's district, in the docks and on the wharfs. On the other hand, new steel plants have been erected on both sides of the river outside the county borough boundary. The mighty I.C.I. works at Billingham have grown up, absorbing an increasing proportion of Middlesbrough's labour. In addition, some clothing and service industries have established themselves at scattered points within the residential area of the town.

This dispersal of housing and industry has divided the town and has made it rather amorphous in character. It has led to a sharp geographical division between the rich and the poor, to acute inequalities in the amenities of different areas of the town and to the lack of a common focus..

Going from north to south, there are three distinct residential belts in the town.

The very poor, unskilled workers and dock-labourers, live in the most northern area. The next residential belt is occupied by a more mixed group of artisans who, on the whole, have a higher grade of skill and are on a higher income level. Their district shades into one of varied housing development, on either side of and surrounding Albert Park. Many of the houses here were originally large and occupied by prosperous families. They were abandoned when the next southward move occurred. A large number of these houses are now sub-divided, let as furnished lodgings or used by several families. Others are occupied by clubs or offices. Hence an admixture of social groups is to be found in this particular intermediate area. Unless its deterioration is arrested, the slums of the next decade will be here.

The third belt at the southern end of the town belongs to the middle class. In Middlesbrough this is the highest social group as most of the people who belong to the upper class in terms of national standards have left the town altogether. The minor executives of industry, the professional people and prosperous tradesmen live in the centre of this area, in large, rather clumsy post-1918 houses. These are surrounded by smaller houses, also built after the last war by speculative builders for the type of owner-occupier who aspires to belong to the middle class.

There is also a fourth socio-geographical group in Middlesbrough, the new housing estates. Although geographically separate, they are fairly homogeneous in terms of physical and social characteristics.

The area in the extreme south, where Middlesbrough's most prosperous people live, is flanked on either side by a new municipal housing estate. A third housing estate is separated from the rest of the town; it is an isolated group of cottages at the north-eastern border.

But for the presence of the two housing estates at the south-eastern and the south-western fringe of the town, the pattern of socio-geographical differentiation in Middlesbrough is amazingly clear-cut. Walking from north to south you find a succession of distinct residential areas, each with its specific social and physical characteristics. Evidence of comparative prosperity increases steadily with every further move southward. The extremes of poverty and prosperity, in terms of the town's own standards, are on the northern and southern edge respectively. There are slums at one end; suburban villas at the other; the beginning of blight in the intermediate areas, which also bear the scars of the continued exodus southward of people who had advanced socially or wanted to advance. Here is the melting pot of the town, for the people who have just left the extreme north live here and also those who have not yet reached the stage of moving further south.

This segmentation of the town, this living apart of the different social groups, is accentuated by the unequal distribution of its amenities. All the specific urban amenities are in the north. All the breathing space is in the extreme south. In the north is the focus of transport: the railway station and the bus terminus. Here are the major churches; the chief shopping centres; clubs; cinemas; restaurants and pubs. The town hall; the general post-office; the theatre are in the north. All this was the necessary urban equipment according to the standards of the late 19th century. It was provided when Middlesbrough was in the early prime of townhood, according to these standards, and hence much of it is now outmoded. The principle of leaving reserves of the countryside within the town was not yet established. Moreover, fields and farms were still at its doorstep everywhere, except on the northern edge. And the town simply rushed forward in those days; there seemed to be no time to stop and consider its growth.

Albert Park, now the junction between the old and the new town, was opened in 1868. But all the other parks, playing fields and allotments are in, or at the edge of, the most recent southern suburbs. Here are some new shopping centres, and also the new schools, the only schools in Middlesbrough which provide the educational environment demanded by 1944 standards. But here is hardly anything else. There is a marked paucity of social institutions, for the suburbs are typical products of inter-war housing. They express the urge for an alliance of country and town. They also express the urge to defeat density by distance, by both physical and social distance between neighbours.

So the town is split; Albert Park divides the old part from the new. The difference between the two is striking although even the old town is quite young in years; it has grown old only through wear and tear. But the division is obvious because 19th and 20th century housing, as represented north and south of the Park respectively, differed markedly in their purpose as well as in their shortcomings. The first was primarily designed for the working class. Cheap and small houses were quickly built. The second was primarily intended for the middle class; the houses were supposed to be solid and substantial.

Thus the old part is crowded; an array of brick with hardly any green patches. But it is still the place for the most essential urban functions: work; trade; transport outlets; administration and entertainment. Its people are sociable. Here are the slums, and here is also the warmth of the town.

The new part is spacious and barren; not designed to draw people together, but rather to divide them from each other. It is free from the noise and the smoke of the old town. The countryside has been allowed to infiltrate here. There are some pleasant tree-lined streets, houses with gardens and open spaces. But there are few other urban amenities, apart from the most necessary schools and shops. These southern parts of Middlesbrough are shapeless, disjointed and frigid. Although dependent upon the old town, they have never fused with it. Hence they have never advanced beyond their status as suburbs.

The division between the southern and the northern parts of the town is not at once apparent from its map or from its history. Its size is fairly compact, both in terms of area and population. Its growth, throughout a single century, has been rapid and continuous. Suburbia appears to be rather out of place in such a town. Why has it not merged with the remainder?

It has not done so for a variety of reasons all of which are derived from one common cause: the social distinction between the northern and the southern areas. Because of it, their physical characteristics differed from the outset as well as their social habits. For the same reason, there was indifference to the decay of the north as long as there was expansion of the south, and both processes have accentuated the cleavage between 19th and 20th century Middlesbrough. People in the north live under conditions which almost compel them to be "matey"; people in the south have chosen conditions which make it possible for them to be secluded. As tastes differ, amenities differ and are rather ill-balanced between the two sections of the town.

Therefore, give and take between them is ill-balanced also. It is rather one-sided. The people from the new town continually pass through and use the amenities of the old, but there is much less movement in the opposite direction. For suburbia has only a few attractions: its playing fields and open spaces draw people from the north, particularly the school-children; a few also come to its clubs. Northerners pass through on their way to the country and to the hills. Otherwise they have hardly any reason for doing so, for all the chief urban amenities are within their own area, and these are used by the suburban people as well. Work, travelling, shopping, entertainment, all this can be done, and much of it can only be done, in and from the north. Thus the old town gives a great deal to the new but receives only little in return. This lack of reciprocity further emphasises the division between them.

Nor have the municipal housing estates on either flank of the suburbs yet acted as a link between the north and the south. On the contrary, so far, their presence there has led to further segmentation. The estates are clearly distinguished from suburbia proper; by their geographical position and by their lay-out; by the type of houses and by the type of people they contain. Although the children from the suburbs use the schools in the housing estates, and their mothers use the shops at their fringes, there is again very little movement in the opposite direction. Yet there is a close mutual friendship between the housing estates and the north, for it is from there that the majority of their tenants have come. They are still fond of their old streets and still frequent their old shops, churches and clubs. These visits are returned by Northerners who call on their relatives in the new council cottages and participate in some of their social activities. But such visits to the south are confined to the housing estates. There is no overspill of friendliness for the adjacent suburbs.

The bond between the new estates and their place of origin is particularly close because the estates are cut off from each other. Consequently, there is very little social intercourse either between the two housing estates in the south, or between them and the third, which occupies an entirely isolated position at the north-eastern fringe of Middlesbrough.

Thus the disjointedness of the town has been accentuated by inter-war housing. It is predominantly a working class town, but its working class settlements are too dispersed to admit of close social relationships between them. Only their rather ragged parent settlement, the old north, still stands out clearly and compactly. It is still their only common meeting ground.

The middle class minority live in an enclave of their own. But although their distinctiveness has thus been enhanced, they are also a dispersed group. They are scattered not only because, by and large, they prefer seclusion to sociability, but also because many of their social equals and most of their social superiors have left the town altogether. The class on whom Middlesbrough is financially dependent, the owners and managers of its industries, are absentees.

A town which lacks cohesion so markedly is urgently in need of a centre to pull all its component parts together. Industry used to be the focus and the very *raison d'être* of Middlesbrough. But industry has become huge and economically unstable, depersonalised and dispersed. Nowadays it is not run by paternalistic employers who live on the spot and know their workmen, but by remote grandees from an outer world.

Moreover, work has ceased to be the sole driving force of the town. Its people now have time to rest; indeed, they have been forced to be idle during long periods of depression. Their pursuits have become more varied, for Middlesbrough is increasingly developing its function as a service centre for the Tees-side and Cleveland area.

So the sovereignty of industry has been challenged. It still dominates Middlesbrough, but it is no longer the magnet which draws the whole town together. There is no such magnet at present. For although the importance of other institutions, administration, trade and services, has recently grown, they do not yet have sufficient cohesive power.

In terms of its social relationships, Middlesbrough now lacks a focus. But in terms of physical movement it has, of course, a central area. It is in the heart of the old town, amid all the rather tattered rows of workers' cottages of the late 19th century. Here, just across the railway, round and about the northern end of "Main Street", Linthorpe Road, are the station, the bus terminus, the town hall and the chief shopping and service centres.

Because of its institutional equipment, this area is still the chief meeting place of Middlesbrough. But it is no longer its centre of gravity. All the northern residential districts are at its doorstep, but the people from the southern suburbs and housing estates can reach it only by a comparatively long journey. As a result, central institutions, major shops and services, are slowly shifting further southwards, thus diminishing the importance of the central area.

Indeed, this very "centre" is becoming diffused. Being now, in fact, at the periphery of the town, it cannot claim its former status or fulfil its present functions adequately. It does not provide sufficient room for the new, more spacious and more complex institutions required. Most important, because of its position, it is unable to do what is most necessary, that is, to restore the balance of the town.

Yet lack of balance is the keynote of Middlesbrough's problems. It is not a town the structure of which shows severe gaps and major dislocations. It suffers from comparatively minor ailments only, all of which are the typical legacy of its period of growth. It suffers from social and geographical segmentation and from an unequal distribution of amenities throughout the town. The old quarter now needs reconditioning because it was neglected whilst the suburbs sprawled southward.

It is predominantly a town of wage-earners and it lacks its full complement of social classes. Instead it is split into a variety of small social groups, the division between which is maintained by minor social differences and geographical separation.

But although there is diffusion, there is not sufficient diversity. The scope of activities which can be carried out within, or around, the town is still rather limited. There is a lack of diversity in industry. Opportunities to express and develop social and cultural interests are scarce. Middlesbrough is still rather monotonous.

Altogether, there is a lack of balance between work and leisure. All these incongruities exist because the town has not yet caught up with its own growth.

Middlesbrough now needs to be pulled together. The isolated parts of the town will have to be joined to the remainder. Circulation between the different areas will have to be eased so as to facilitate relationships between them. The reconstruction of the blighted wards will provide the opportunity to restore the geographical and social balance of the town; to equalise the distribution of amenities and to obliterate the division between the north and the south. The centre, the chief meeting place of Middlesbrough, will either have to be shifted altogether or decidedly accentuated. The range of its institutions will have to be expanded. The town needs a definite nucleus; its component parts need to be rounded off and given equal status. Middlesbrough will reach maturity only when the complementary processes of centralisation and localisation have been considered and are controlled.

II

THE DEMARCATION OF NEIGHBOURHOODS

1. Definitions of Neighbourhood

The Function of a Neighbourhood Survey

The general overhaul of Middlesbrough's structure, and the reconditioning of particular blighted areas necessitates some reshuffling and further shifting of its population. Some 7,400 houses in the extreme northern belt of the town are obsolete; population density in the whole northern area will have to be substantially reduced; and it is estimated that in addition to the households thus displaced about 5,000 new households will require new dwellings on, so far, undeveloped sites.[2] Such redistribution can be carried out in an orderly and painless fashion only if the habits of the people and the pattern of neighbourhoods are taken into account. Moreover, the process of fusing all the component parts of the town into a coherent whole requires a thorough knowledge of their individual characteristics.

Consequently, the planning of Middlesbrough as a social entity had to be preceded by a survey of its neighbourhoods. They had to be demarcated from each other. Their living conditions had to be investigated as well as the adequacy of the institutional equipment of, and the degree of social integration within, each of them. The consideration of these aspects is relevant in view of the planner's reluctance to disturb stable and closely knit neighbourhoods and of his desire to create new alignments. These aspects also influence his policy of grouping homes and siting institutions.

The Neighbourhood Unit

The concept of the neighbourhood unit, which is generally regarded as one of the most progressive and important recent contributions to town-planning, implies considerable localisation. It assumes the tendency for, and the desirability of, social integration on the level of the small territorial group. Each neighbourhood unit is supposed to be equipped with a number of institutions for the use of its own residents. An admixture of social groups within its boundaries is usually considered desirable. The validity of these assumptions and the suitablility of these suggestions have to be checked. They cannot be applied unless the elements of, and the conditions for creating, neighbourhood cohesion have been investigated.

While attempting to do this, we are halted at the outset by the vagueness of the neighbourhood unit concept. Its practical purpose is easily understood. The structure of a town is a function of its component parts and thus the cell principle is essential both in planning and administration. It also provides for the convenient siting of amenities and institutions, particularly of those which should be within a short distance from homes. Thus one of the deplorable defects of inter-war housing, the shapelessness of new estates and the paucity of their institutional equipment, can be eliminated. In terms of convenience, the concept of the neighbourhood unit presents no difficulty and is indeed a step forward.

Its romantic intentions are more doubtful. It is not clear either why the resuscitation of village life within urban communities should be regarded as being so delightful and so progressive nor how it is to be accomplished. We cannot assume, of course, that people will become "neighbourly" merely because they live in a neighbourhood unit. But, if this were achieved, what precisely would be its symptoms? In other words, how are "neighbourliness" and "neighbourhood" defined?

In the absence of a universally recognised definition, the task of discovering neighbourhoods and delineating their boundaries is not straightforward. But the very vagueness of the concept makes it even more important to do so since we shall never be able to establish "neighbourhoods" if we do not know whether and where, and under what conditions, they already exist.

Definitions of Neighbourhood

Consequently, it is first of all necessary to interpret the popular and rather vague usage of the word "neighbourhood" and to give it a precise definition. The word is often used to imply merely "a distinct territorial group, distinct by virtue of the specific physical characteristics of the area and the specific social characteristics of its inhabitants". Alternatively, the word refers to a distinct territorial group which also possesses the attributes of "neighbourliness". According to this second meaning of the word, it has to be defined as "a territorial group the members of which meet on a common ground within their own area for primary social activities and for organised and spontaneous social contacts".[3]

"Neighbourhood", in terms of the second definition, is at first sight identical with "community". But the territorial aspect of community is missing from some interpretations of the word, and, whenever it is implied, the area covered is supposed to be larger than that of the neighbourhood so that face-to-face contacts are, of necessity, less a feature of communities than of neighbourhoods. The community is characterised chiefly by common ideas, the neighbourhood by common social contacts within a limited geographical setting. Consequently, a community may be defined as "a territorial group of people with a common mode of living, striving for common objectives". A "neighbourhood", in the second sense of the word, is not yet, but may well become a part of a "community".

Distinct Territorial Groups

The two definitions of "neighbourhood" indicate what evidence is needed to establish the existence of either type. Neighbourhoods, according to the first interpretation of the word, i.e. distinct territorial groups, stand out quite plainly from a series of maps showing the distribution of various physical and social indices. Houses of the same age and type tend to cluster together, so do rateable values of the same rank and particular social, occupational and religious groups of the population. Geographical boundaries, railways, roads, open spaces and undeveloped sites, contribute to this differentiation. The pattern revealed by any one of these factors is often repeated by one or several of the others. In other words, the distributions of the different indices tend to be correlated. Where houses are old, rateable values are comparatively low, and these houses are inhabited by people with low incomes. Consequently, the superimposition of these different factors shows the pattern of distinct territorial groups in the town.

Integrated Neighbourhoods

It is more difficult to find neighbourhoods which are not only distinct territorial groups but the inhabitants of each of which are also in close social contact with each other. It is difficult, not merely because the additional indices needed are less readily available, but chiefly because such neighbourhoods rarely exist.

The chief additional indices required are those which reflect the concentration of primary social activities and social contacts within the area of a distinct territorial group. If the institutions for which there is universal and continuous rather than occasional demand, for instance, schools, shops, welfare centres and clubs, and which are situated within that area, are chiefly used by its inhabitants, one aspect of concentration, the absence of inflow into the area, is indicated.[4] Furthermore, if the people in that district rarely visit such institutions in other districts, the complementary aspect of concentration, the absence of outflow, is indicated also. The fact that the use of institutions is concentrated among a particular territorial group further implies that the spheres of influence of different types of institutions are roughly coincident.

The existence and degree of concentration or dispersal of the essential and organised social activities is shown by the catchment area maps of the relevant institutions. The incidence and the geographical spread of spontaneous social contacts are not so easily discovered or presented. It can be ascertained only through an intensive study into the extent of relationships between neighbours, acquaintances and friends in particular areas. How are such informal associations brought about, what principles determine their selection, what form do they take? Such a study is as relevant for the differentiation between neighbourhoods as the survey of institutional catchment areas. But it is of less immediate importance to the planner who has to make concrete proposals within a short space of time. He is primarily interested to see the existing group pattern of the town; the location of institutions in relation to each other and in relation to homes; and the catchment areas of institutions. For the present purpose we had, therefore, to rely largely on a detailed survey of essential and organised activities. But it has been supplemented by observations of the more subtle aspects of social life.

II. The Discovery of Neighbourhoods

(A) THE DEMARCATION OF DISTINCT TERRITORIAL GROUPS

The first step, consistent with the two definitions of "neighbourhood", was the discovery of distinct territorial groups. A series of maps showing the distribution of environmental conditions and indices of social differentiation was consulted.

MAPS CONSULTED FOR THE DEMARCATION OF TERRITORIAL GROUPS

Indices	Extent and Date of Information
I. Major Indices	
1. Rateable Value	Complete Enumeration 1944
2. Age of Buildings	" " "

Indices	Extent and Date of Information
3. Type of Housing, e.g. classified by ownership and housing density . . .	Complete Enumeration 1944
4. Number of Habitable Rooms per Dwelling	" " "
5. Net Population Density . . .	National Registration, 1939
6. Distribution of the R.C. School Population	Complete Enumeration for June 1944
7. Births and Infant Deaths . . .	Complete Enumeration for the first four months of 1943 and 1944
8. Head Infestations of School Children .	Complete Enumeration, Summer term, 1943
2. Supplementary Indices	
9. Occupations of Chief Wage Earners .	Sample: 1 in 25·8; June-July 1944
10. Absences from School	All Court and Committee cases during the first four months of 1944
11. Distribution of Poverty Shops: Pawnshops, Junkshops, Fried Fish Shops .	Complete Enumeration for June 1944
12. Distribution of Working Mothers whose Children Attend War-time Nurseries .	Complete Enumeration for July 1944

Most of the factors were chosen because of their general relevance for neighbourhood differentiation and because they can be clearly presented on maps. Others related to the specific group structure of the town. Roman Catholics, for instance, form a considerable proportion of the Middlesbrough population and they tend to live together. The majority also belong to a definite social group, they live in the poorest areas of the town. The Church of England community, on the other hand, is rather scattered so that a companion map of the C. of E. school population shows no definite grouping and was not used for this purpose.

Major Indices

Each of the first five maps showed a clear pattern of geographical differentiation and so did the maps of the R.C. school population, of births and infant deaths and of head infestations. In other words, there are definite clusters in terms of each of these individual indices. The boundaries between different areas are indicated by the break between, for instance, one level of rateable values and the next level. Thus, by and large, an area is demarcated because it is homogeneous in terms of one factor. But, sometimes an area stands out because it contains, for example, an admixture of rateable values.

When the patterns derived from the different maps were superimposed on each other and thus compared, they were found to be largely coincident. The neighbourhood structure of the town, in terms of distinct territorial groups, was clearly visible for the first time.

Geographical Divisions

In part, this congruence of patterns is derived from, and accentuated by, the fact that Middlesbrough is broken up by a number of geographical divisions. Two of its parts, St. Hilda's ward and North Ormesby, are cut off from the remainder of the town; two others, the small settlement of Cargo Fleet and the Brambles Farm housing estate, are entirely isolated. Consequently, on every one of the maps referred to, these areas stand out clearly. Linthorpe Road, Middlesbrough's "Main Street", is also a dividing line and yet another one runs through Albert Park. The two remaining municipal estates, Whinney Banks and Marton Grove, on either edge of the southern suburbs, are also distinct geographical entities.

Correlation of Neighbourhood Indices

But the different patterns correspond, even apart from geographical demarcations, because the conditions they reflect are closely interrelated. Old and shabby houses are of low rateable value, have comparatively few rooms and are in areas of high population density. And these houses are, of course, occupied by poor people, many of whom are Roman Catholics, whose parents migrated to Middlesbrough during the great iron rush and during the steel rush. The well-to-do people, at the other end of the social ladder, live in substantial new houses which possess all the resultant positive characteristics. The intermediate stages are also represented in distinct districts most of which are fairly homogeneous in character. The remaining districts which contain an admixture of types of houses and of people are demarcated because of their very heterogeneity.

Supplementary Indices

The first tentative neighbourhood structure which emerged from the comparison of the major indices had to be checked against a number of additional maps. None of these showed quite so detailed a differentiation as the previous maps but since they brought out broad divisions within the town, they were useful for cross-reference. The map presenting the distribution of occupations of chief wage earners throughout Middlesbrough revealed such broad divisions.[5] The map showing the distribution of the most serious cases of school absences confirmed the demarcation of certain problem areas. The map of pawnshops, junk shops, and fried-fish shops helped in drawing a definite "poverty line". It showed, firstly, the location of acute poverty in the extreme northern areas where all three types of "poverty shops" are concentrated. It showed, secondly, the line beyond which, towards the south, there are no poverty shops of any kind. The last map on which the addresses of working mothers whose children attend wartime day-nurseries are indicated, emphasised again the division between the working-class and the middle-class areas of the town.

These contributory indices helped to fix the boundaries of distinct territorial groups more firmly. After they had been drawn, they were checked once more against each of the individual indices. The result was our first map of "neighbourhoods", i.e. of distinct territorial groups.[6]

Adjustment by Enumeration Districts

For the purpose of tabulating the quantitative distribution of different indices for each of the neighbourhoods, an adjustment was required. Such material could be handled only if it is known how many people a neighbourhood contains. But the smallest unit for which published official population statistics are available is the ward, which is clearly too large for our purpose. We had to compile our material for small cells of the town from which larger units which, in view of the information collected, were later found to be significant, could be built up. An arbitrary grid would not answer the purpose; we had to deal with standard cells for which basic information was available. Therefore, it appeared to be the most practical solution to divide the town into the 133 enumeration districts of the 1939 National Registration, and to group all materials accordingly. Each of the districts contains on an average in Middlesbrough about 1,000 people.[7]

Details concerning the population of each of the "neighbourhoods" can then be derived from their component enumeration districts as long as the boundaries of the former coincide with those of the latter. In a few instances, a slight revision of neighbourhood boundaries was, therefore, necessary. The homogeneity of some of the neighbourhoods is thereby unavoidably impaired. But, by and large, the neighbourhood structure, as derived from the major indices, is not significantly altered in our second map which shows the adjustment for enumeration districts.[8] This map has, therefore, been used throughout for the detailed study of distinct territorial groups, of which there are altogether 26 in Middlesbrough.

B. NEIGHBOURHOODS IN TERMS OF SOCIAL ACTIVITIES

Having discovered neighbourhoods which correspond to our first definition, it was necessary to find out whether any of these distinct territorial groups also possess the attributes of "neighbourliness", corresponding to our second definition. The chief test applied was the extent of the concentration of social activities within each of them.

Institutional Catchment Areas

A series of maps showing the catchment areas of different institutions had previously been prepared. All those referring to primary social activities were now consulted.

MAPS CONSULTED FOR THE DEMARCATION OF NEIGHBOURHOODS IN TERMS OF SOCIAL ACTIVITIES

Indices	Extent and Date of Information
1. Catchment Areas of All Elementary and Secondary Schools	School Census, June 1944.
2. Catchment Areas of Youth and Adult Clubs	Club Census, June 1944.
3. Catchment Areas of Post Offices	Sample of 25·8 per cent. of the Middlesbrough population.
4. Catchment Areas of Shops for : (*a*) Sugar registrations (*b*) Greengroceries	Sample of 25·8 per cent. of the Middlesbrough population.[9]

These catchment area maps can provide the answers to three questions. Firstly, are the catchment areas of the different institutions largely coincident? Secondly, does the pattern of these catchment areas correspond to that of the distinct territorial groups as previously delineated? Thirdly, are social activities concentrated within the areas of distinct territorial groups?

If the first question were answered affirmatively, that is, if the catchment areas of different institutions, in fact, tended to correspond, the second question might be answered affirmatively also. And if that were so, if the catchment areas of institutions and neighbourhood boundaries were congruent, the third question would certainly be answered positively. The concentration of the relevant social activities within neighbourhoods would then be clearly indicated. Distinct territorial groups would also be neighbourhoods according to the second definition.

Negative Results

However, the analysis of catchment areas showed that only a few territorial groups possessed these additional attributes. The answers to all three questions were largely negative.

To settle the first and the second question, generalised outlines of the catchment areas of the different institutions were traced and then superimposed on each other. But it was not possible to do this for all the relevant institutions. The spheres of influence of, for instance, the different social youth clubs interlock to such an extent that no generalised outlines could be drawn.

The remaining catchment areas, when shown on a map, were found to be so widely divergent that, with the exception of a few districts, there was certainly no indication that either the catchment areas of the different institutions correspond or that these coincide with the boundaries of distinct territorial groups. The only territorial groups which stand out clearly on this map are five which are more or less isolated. Three other territorial groups are also fairly distinct. The boundaries of all the other eighteen territorial groups are completely blurred behind the screen of criss-cross catchment area lines.

Dispersal of Social Activities

An additional, more detailed, map was prepared for each territorial group in order to check the conclusions derived from the general map, and to establish the extent of the concentration of social activities within each of them. All the relevant institutions situated in a particular neighbourhood were indicated together with their catchment areas. These maps showed clearly the extent of inflow for organised and essential social activities into the area. Through cross-reference, the outflow from the area could also be ascertained. Thus the concentration of social activities within each territorial group could be measured. By and large, the evidence of the previous, more general, catchment area map was confirmed. On the whole, social activities are dispersed, they are not carried out within the boundaries of distinct territorial groups.

III

DESCRIPTION AND GRADING OF NEIGHBOURHOODS

1. Method of Grading Neighbourhoods

The map of neighbourhoods, i.e. of distinct territorial groups, is based on the specific environmental and social features of each of them. But it is, of course, not sufficient to know that such distinct territorial groups exist. Their particular attributes have to be described; the extent of the social differences between them has to be assessed. We want to know which neighbourhoods have satisfactory and which have unsatisfactory environmental conditions; which contain chiefly poor and which contain chiefly prosperous households; which are adequately and which are inadequately equipped with social institutions. Some neighbourhoods will clearly be in need of reconditioning and remodelling and will thus be subjected to disturbances and population shifts. Therefore, it is most important to be able to anticipate, and thereby to soften, the impact of such upheavals. Stable, closely knit neighbourhoods would clearly suffer more during this process than those which are only loosely held together. Hence the degree of social integration of each of them has to be indicated. The conditions which are associated with social integration have to be examined.

Relevant Aspects

Neighbourhoods were graded according to four aspects:

(1) Living Conditions;
(2) Institutional Equipment;
(3) Neighbourhood Integration, i.e. concentration of social activities within the neighbourhood;
(4) Geographical Demarcation.

Indices

Multiple indices were constructed for each of the first three aspects. These indices were derived from the quantitative distribution of all those factors for which neighbourhood statistics were available, using the relevant figures for the whole of Middlesbrough as the base. This applies to all the factors used in the multiple indices of living conditions and institutional equipment.

Classification

Other factors relating to geographical characteristics were more easily assessed when presented in map form. The grading of neighbourhoods in terms of these factors was obtained through classification, not quantification and is, therefore, less precise. This applies to one of the factors used to assess neighbourhood integration, i.e., inflow into the neighbourhood. The classification was based on the map showing the catchment areas of each of the relevant institutions in a particular neighbourhood. From this map we can see whether the people using a particular institution come primarily from within or without the neighbourhood and how widely they are dispersed. It would be preferable, in future similar enquiries, to obtain the same picture in the form of a table rather than of a map.[10]

The rating of neighbourhoods in terms of the last aspect, geographical demarcation, was also, and will always have to be, based on the classification of the geographical pattern.

Rating

When the indices for each of the four aspects had been obtained, a uniform notation was applied to each of them, in order to facilitate comparisons between the different aspects and also between the different neighbourhoods. The same rating, from one to six, was used for the indices of living conditions, of institutional equipment and of neighbourhood integration. The rating of one to four was used for the classification of neighbourhoods in terms of geographical demarcation. "One" indicates the lowest and most negative rank in each distribution; "six", or "four" respectively, indicates the highest and most positive rank. A common yardstick for the measurement of variations in terms of the different aspects was thus obtained.

2. The Index of Living Conditions

Factors Considered

The multiple index of living conditions was derived from the following six factors:

Net population density;
Number of houses per acre;
Percentage of houses with rateable value of less than £11;
Percentage of non-owner-occupiers;

Percentage of chief wage earners with incomes of less than £5 per week.[11]

Number of poverty shops per 1,000 people, i.e. junk shops, pawnshops, fried fish shops.

The first three of these factors are indices of environment; the following three factors are indices of social rank. By and large, of course, the level of environment corresponds to the level of incomes and occupations. Poor people live in poor houses, prosperous people live in substantial houses. The close relationship between environment and social status was clearly visible when we compared the relevant indices for each neighbourhood.[12]

Only one group of neighbourhoods is exceptional in this respect, the new housing estates. It is only in their case that environmental and social characteristics are not consistent, on the contrary, they differ sharply from each other. The people from the poor northern neighbourhoods who moved to the new estates did not thereby increase their incomes, nor did they change their occupations, but they now live in new and fairly satisfactory houses. Hence, whilst by and large, the index of living conditions is also an index of social rank, it does not serve this dual purpose in the case of the new housing estates.

Table 1 shows the grading of all neighbourhoods in terms of living conditions. Both the index numbers and the resultant final rating, from one to six, are shown. The poorest neighbourhoods are at the beginning of the list; those which are most prosperous are at the end. In considering this rank order, it should be remembered that all the "A" neighbourhoods are in the north, all the "B" neighbourhoods are in the south. Albert Park is in the centre of the dividing line which runs from east to west.

Rank Order

The pattern of socio-geographical differentiation is now clearly visible. The poorest neighbourhoods, where living conditions are worst, are all at the extreme northern edge of the town. Only slightly less poor are the neighbourhoods of the next residential belt, in and around the old centre of the town which is still its centre of communications. The intermediate residential belt, north-east, north-west and south of Albert Park, contains all the neighbourhoods of intermediate environmental and social rank, that is, those with a rating of three or four. Further to the south are all the prosperous neighbourhoods, those in groups five and six.

NEIGHBOURHOODS : TABLE 1

RANK ORDER OF NEIGHBOURHOODS ACCORDING TO INDEX OF LIVING CONDITIONS

Neighbourhoods		Index of Living Conditions	
No.	Name	Index Number No.	Rating Group
A 2	Newport	168	1
A 7	Shopping Centre	165	1
A 16	Cargo Fleet	159	1
A 1	St. Hilda's	150	1
A 12i	Vulcan	147	1
A 6	Cleveland	141	2
A 14	North Ormesby	138	2
A 8	Acklam	135	2
A 9	Waterloo Road	124	2
A 10, 11, 12	Civic Centre	121	2
A 5	Parliament Road	109	3
A 3	North Ayresome	101	3
B 8, 9	Lower Marton Grove	81	4
A 17, 18	Brambles Farm	80	4
B 6	Linthorpe Village	75	4
B 5	Ayresome Park	73	4
B 10	Upper Marton Grove	69	4
A 4	West Lane	64	4
B 1	Whinney Banks	61	4
A 13	The Longlands	50	4
A 15	Pallister Park	37	5
B 2	West Acklam	36	5
B 3	West Linthorpe	34	5
B 7	South Linthorpe	27	6
B 11	East Grove Hill	21	6
B 4	Mid-Linthorpe	17	6
	All Middlesbrough :	100	3

The New Estates

The housing estates, Lower and Upper Marton Grove, Brambles Farm, Whinney Banks and West Lane, have intermediate rank, as a result of their comparatively favourable environmental conditions. But in terms of social status their rank is much lower. Although they are geographically part of 20th century Middlesbrough, their income level is that of the 19th century part of the town. But in all other neighbourhood groups, variations in income levels are consistent with variations in environment.

INCOME LEVELS OF NEIGHBOURHOOD GROUPS

Neighbourhood Groups According to Index of Living Conditions Group	Proportion of Chief Wage Earners with Incomes under £5 per week in each group %
1	91·0
2	87·0
Housing Estates[13] . .	87·0
3	84·0
4, excl. Housing Estates .	60·0
5	43·0
6	35·0
All Middlesbrough . .	78·0

Social Homogeneity

The new estates are distinguished from the other neighbourhoods in the intermediate groups in yet another way. The people who live on Brambles Farm all belong to the same social group; their houses are very much alike; and even family sizes are fairly uniform. The same is true for Whinney Banks and for each of the sections of Marton Grove. Although these neighbourhoods differ slightly from each other, there is hardly any variety within each of them.

The other neighbourhoods around Albert Park are far less homogeneous in character. In fact, they are the only parts of the town within which there is some mixture both of living conditions and of social groups.

Contrasts

The sharp contrast between the different groups of neighbourhoods is accentuated by the lack of variety within most of them. Poverty and prosperity have their entirely separate quarters. Nine-tenth of all chief wage earners at the northern edge have an income of less than £5 per week; at the southern end, two-thirds earn more than £5 weekly. In the old town there are hardly any owner-occupiers; in the outer suburban ring, almost every householder is an owner-occupier. The poorest neighbourhood has a net population density of 138 people per acre; the most prosperous neighbourhood, one of 19 persons per acre. Almost every house in Newport has a rateable value of less than £11; not a single house in Mid-Linthorpe is at so low a level. And neither Newport nor Mid-Linthorpe are merely isolated extreme cases, they represent the broader, entirely opposite groups to which each of them belongs. Hence the picture of Middlesbrough's social structure has hardly any mixed tints. Black, grey and white are its only essential colours.

3. The Institutional Equipment of Neighbourhoods

The picture of Middlesbrough's institutional equipment also reveals sharp divisions as the map of Neighbourhood Services shows at first sight. A more equal distribution of services and amenities is clearly required, not only from the point of view of convenience, but also because it might possibly help to knit territorial groups more closely together. If important social institutions are missing, the social activities of a neighbourhood can hardly be concentrated within its own boundaries.

Relevant Aspects

To test the implications of the existence or absence of the necessary services, the institutional equipment of each neighbourhood had first to be considered. Two aspects are relevant: the number and also the variety of institutions. The latter, that is the range of institutions, is more important than mere quantity. A neighbourhood which possesses a number of churches, or even shops, but hardly anything else, is less adequately equipped than another which has one of each kind of neighbourhood institutions, although it has one of each kind only.

Neighbourhood Institutions

But which are "neighbourhood institutions"? All those which should be within daily reach or which provide for the most essential social activities have been included in this category.[14] These are, in addition to foodshops:

Elementary Schools.
Post-offices.
Surgeries.
Churches.
Clubs.
Public Houses.

Industry is excluded from this list since nowadays the place of work is no longer a part of the urban neighbourhood. The separation of industry from homes is often unavoidable and is usually regarded as desirable although there is little doubt that neighbourhood integration has been weakened as a result.

The Index of Institutional Equipment

The index of institutional equipment was, therefore, based on two factors:

(*a*) The number of neighbourhood institutions per 1,000 people of the relevant age-groups in each neighbourhood.[15]

(*b*) The range of neighbourhood institutions in each neighbourhood. Since "six" is the number of institutions listed, apart from shops,[16] this figure indicates the widest possible range.

Neighbourhoods with the highest resultant index numbers, therefore, have comparatively the best institutional equipment in the town.

Reversal of Inequalities

If we now consider the average institutional index for each of the six groups of neighbourhoods in the rank order of living conditions, we see a complete reversal of inequalities. The poorest neighbourhoods are comparatively most adequately equipped. The most prosperous neighbourhoods have the smallest number and the least variety of institutions.

NEIGHBOURHOODS : TABLE 2

INSTITUTIONAL EQUIPMENT OF NEIGHBOURHOOD GROUPS

Index of Living Conditions Compared with Index of Institutional Equipment

Neighbourhood Group According to Index of Living Conditions	Index of Institutional Equipment Index Number
1	3,000
2	1,870
3	650
4	485
5	370
6	340

NEIGHBOURHOODS : TABLE 3

RANK ORDER OF NEIGHBOURHOODS ACCORDING TO INDEX OF INSTITUTIONAL EQUIPMENT*

Neighbourhoods		Total Population in Each	Index of Institutional Equipment	
No.	Name	No.	Index Number No.	Rating Group
B 7	South Linthorpe	1,376	45	1
A 4	West Lane	1,026	56	1
B 2	West Acklam	2,190	164	1
A 15	Pallister Park	1,035	230	2
B 8, 9	Lower Marton Grove	6,388	240	2
A 13	The Longlands	3,222	292	2
A 3	North Ayresome	3,780	302	2
B 11	East Grove Hill	2,222	328	2
A 17, 18	Brambles Farm	5,098	356	2
B 1	Whinney Banks	7,079	372	2
B 3	West Linthorpe	4,258	692	3
B 4	Mid Linthorpe	2,408	768	3
B 5	Ayresome Park	5,142	856	3
A 8	Acklam	7,620	952	3
B 10	Upper Marton Grove	3,949	965	3
A 5	Parliament Road	6,451	1,014	3
A 9	Waterloo Road	6,241	1,200	3
A 2	Newport	13,103	1,392	4
A 6	Cleveland	5,723	1,435	4
A 12i	Vulcan	4,821	1,625	4
B 6	Linthorpe Village	2,535	1,656	4
A 16	Cargo Fleet	1,188	2,250	5
A 14	North Ormesby	10,083	2,274	5
A 10, 11, 12	Civic Centre	8,010	3,582	6
A 7	Shopping Centre	5,695	4,494	6
A 1	St. Hilda's	5,399	7,470	6
All Middlesbrough		126,042	1,800	4

* The index number for the whole of Middlesbrough is derived from the following factors :

A	Average number of schools, post-offices, churches, surgeries, clubs per 1,000 of the relevant age groups, i.e.	100
B	Number of pubs per 1,000, aged 20 and over, i.e.	100
C	Number of foodshops per 1,000 total population, i.e.	100
D	Range of Institutions, i.e.	6
Final index number (A+B+C) D, i.e.		1,800

The Middlesbrough population figures, as shown on this table, are derived from the National Registration, 1939. Population in institutions, and of some outlying small groups of houses not belonging to particular neighbourhoods, are excluded.

Paucity of institutions has been the price paid for the southward migration. The people in the south have left slums and decay behind them, but they have also left the social amenities of the north. Those who remained amid a poor environment have been rewarded accordingly. For they have not only retained easy access to the major shopping and civic centre of the town, but the depletion of the northern population has also left them with a correspondingly greater number of institutions per person.

The Rank Order of Institutional Equipment

The position is summarised once more on Table 3 which shows neighbourhoods not grouped according to their social rank order but according to the rank order of their comparative institutional equipment.

All the neighbourhoods with the lowest rating, one or two, which is indicative of entirely inadequate institutional equipment, are at the periphery or at the outskirts of the town. All have only been fairly recently developed. The only one of the neighbourhoods on the new estates which is not among them is Upper Marton Grove, the oldest and the best designed part of the new estates. But even this neighbourhood has only achieved a slightly higher rating.

The intermediate group, with a rating of three, is also geographically intermediate. Its shape is that of a broad belt of neighbourhoods north and south of Albert Park. The only geographically adjacent neighbourhood which has a higher rating is B 6, Linthorpe Village. Here is the present centre of gravity of the town and a number of institutions have, therefore, shifted southward into this neighbourhood. Here is also an important shopping centre.

Only the poorest and oldest neighbourhoods in the extreme north are comparatively well equipped with institutions. Even the small settlement of Cargo Fleet has a high rank since it has one of each of the essential schools, post-offices, churches, and clubs. There is a public house and there are also several shops. Only a surgery is missing. North Ormesby, which used to be a separate township, has retained all its old urban equipment. Best provided are, of course, the neighbourhoods of the present shopping and civic centres and St. Hilda's, the oldest, and for a long time the most vital, part of the town. Being so near to the waterfront and adjacent to the Ironmasters' district, St. Hilda's has not yet been completely deprived of its previous importance. Many of its institutions have survived and it has still, for instance, a prodigious number of churches, of clubs and, most of all, of public houses.

Of course, the neighbourhoods of the civic centre, of the shopping centre, and to a lesser extent, St. Hilda's and some of the others in the north, share their institutions with the rest of the town. They are well equipped not as the result of a deliberate allocation of neighbourhood services, but because they are long established and still in the mainstream of Middlesbrough's communications.

The Quality of Institutional Equipment

In considering their position, it must also be remembered that the rank order of institutional equipment is not based on an accepted standard, but that it is only derived from a comparison between the different neighbourhoods of Middlesbrough. Therefore, even the neighbourhoods which are most adequately equipped, in relation to the remainder, might be found to be ill-provided if measured by another yardstick. The variations within Middlesbrough, however, are relevant for our purpose. In order to assess the influence of living conditions and of institutional equipment on neighbourhood integration, the town's own standards have to be applied.

Moreover, this index compares only the quantity and variety of institutions, but not their quality. Neighbourhoods which are fortunate because they have most of the essential services may not necessarily have the best of each of these. A study of individual institutions, particularly of schools, shows that this is, in fact, the case. The old northern schools, in the neighbourhoods of institutional prosperity, are inferior in quality to those in the outer ring.[17] But for the purpose of comparing the institutional equipment of the different neighbourhoods, the accessibility of the whole range of neighbourhood services is primarily relevant, rather than the individual value of each of them.

Variations in the Population Size of Neighbourhoods

The institutional equipment of neighbourhoods is also in part dependent on their population size. With the exception of the housing estates, all the neighbourhoods which suffer from a paucity of institutions are too small to be able to support a wider range. In the case of the housing estates, lack of foresight is primarily responsible for the singular lack of essential services.

Linthorpe Village and Cargo Fleet are the only neighbourhoods which are small and yet comparatively well equipped. In each case, there are rather exceptional reasons for this combination of circumstances. Linthorpe Village is in an especially favourable location and its institutions are used by the other southern neighbourhoods as well. Cargo Fleet is long established and so isolated that it can not entirely depend on services elsewhere.

On the other hand, some of the northern neighbourhoods, though still large, have gained in institutional status through a gradual loss of population. The people who have remained behind now have a correspondingly greater share of the existing amenities.

The variations in the population size of the different neighbourhoods are quite remarkable.

Only nine of the twenty-six neighbourhoods have a population of more than 4,000 and less than 7,000, which is roughly the number usually stipulated for a neighbourhood unit. A further three have population totals between 7,000 and 10,000. Only two, Newport and North Ormesby, exceed that figure. The remainder, i.e. twelve neighbourhoods, are definitely too small to stand on their own. These considerable divergencies in the size of territorial groups are, of course, to be expected, since they have been formed spontaneously and irregularly, but not through the process of planning. If neighbourhoods are to be more equal in terms of their institutional equipment, they will have to be less varied in size.

4. The Concentration of Social Activities

Are any of the Middlesbrough neighbourhoods, in fact, "neighbourly"? In other words, which of the distinct territorial groups are also neighbourhoods in terms of our second definition? We can discover them only if we test the degree of concentration of social activities within each neighbourhood.

The Index of Neighbourhood Integration

Such concentration exists if the people who live within the boundaries of a particular territorial group use their own neighbourhood institutions and, furthermore, if these institutions are used almost exclusively by them. Hence in establishing the relevant classification, both the incidence of coming into, and of going out from, the neighbourhood was taken into account. The rating for inflow was derived from the individual neighbourhood catchment area maps as previously described. The rating for outflow was also obtained from these catchment area maps through cross-reference which showed:

(*a*) the number of outside institutions visited by people from a particular neighbourhood;
(*b*) the number of outside neighbourhoods to which they went for this purpose.[18]

The comparative degree of social integration for each neighbourhood is shown on Table 4.

Neighbourhoods of the rank of six show a definite concentration of social activities, so do those of the rank of five, although to a lesser extent. Neighbourhoods of the rank of four disperse for some activities, yet not over a wide area, and concentrate for others. The same mixture is found in neighbourhoods of the rank of three but

NEIGHBOURHOODS : TABLE 4

RANK ORDER OF NEIGHBOURHOODS ACCORDING TO INDEX OF NEIGHBOURHOOD INTEGRATION

Neighbourhoods		Index of Neighbourhood Integration	
No.	Name	Index Number No.	Rating Group
A 1	St. Hilda's	12	6
A 16	Cargo Fleet	12	6
A 17, 18	Brambles Farm	12	6
B 8, 9	Lower Marton Grove	35	5
A 14	North Ormesby	50	5
A 9	Waterloo Road	72	4
A 2	Newport	75	4
A 5	Parliament Road	75	4
A 3	North Ayresome	75	4
A 15	Pallister Park	75	4
A 7	Shopping Centre	82·5	4
A 12i	Vulcan	87·5	4
B 1	Whinney Banks	90·0	4
B 10	Upper Marton Grove	97·5	4
B 11	East Grove Hill	97·5	4
A 6	Cleveland	120·0	3
A 8	Acklam	127·5	3
A 4	West Lane	128·0	3
B 6	Linthorpe Village	130·0	3
B 5	Ayresome Park	140·0	3
B 7	South Linthorpe	165·0	2
B 3	West Linthorpe	175·0	2
A 10, 11, 12	Civic Centre	187·5	1
B 2	West Acklam	195·0	1
A 13	The Longlands	200·0	1
B 4	Mid Linthorpe	210·0	1

the range of dispersal is wider. Dispersal is definitely prevalent in group 2, and there is total dispersal in group 1.

Considerable concentration of social activities exists only in five of the twenty-six neighbourhoods in the town. All the remainder are merely distinct territorial groups, without the additional attributes of social integration which have been considered.

It is not surprising that St. Hilda's heads the list. Although it is one of the poorest, we should have expected it to be also one of the most closely knit neighbourhoods in the town, because of its history and its geographical location. But why has Mid-Linthorpe, the most prosperous neighbourhood, the lowest rank for integration? Why are its social activities entirely dispersed?

Inflow and Outflow

The comparative extent of both inflow and outflow tells part of the story. Although a good many people come into St. Hilda's for their social activities, the St. Hilda's people hardly go outside their own area. Although Cargo Fleet is small and isolated, it has five of six essential neighbourhood institutions and its inhabitants go hardly ever further afield than North Ormesby. Brambles Farm is too isolated for its few institutions to be visited by outsiders, and for the most essential activities which cannot be carried out on the estate itself, its tenants visit only a few of the north-eastern neighbourhoods. The position of Lower Marton Grove is very similar. Its activities are comparatively concentrated, although the tenants leave the area for a number of activities, chiefly because the institutions within this part of the estate cater chiefly for the inhabitants. The major part of North Ormesby, which is also isolated, again receives few visitors from outside since its institutions fulfil a strictly local function.

So the respective weight of inflow and outflow varies with the different neighbourhoods in groups six and five. In none of these are both inflow and outflow nil; thus absolute concentration of social activities never exists. But the concentration implied by one aspect is always sufficiently great to offset some dispersal, as indicated by the other aspect. Therefore, although even these neighbourhoods are not self-contained, their social activities are still far more concentrated than those of any of the others.

But whilst none of the neighbourhoods are self-contained, the social activities of many of them are entirely dispersed. Thus, the lower the position of a territorial group in the rank order of integration, the greater, and the more equally matched, is the incidence of both coming into and going out from the neighbourhood.

Why should the activities of some neighbourhoods be so dispersed while in others they are comparatively concentrated? Which particular characteristics produce this differentiation? At first sight it looks as though geographical isolation is chiefly responsible for integration. All the isolated neighbourhoods in the town have obtained the most positive rank in this respect: St. Hilda's, Cargo Fleet, Brambles Farm and North Ormesby. The fifth neighbourhood which has achieved equal rank for the concentration of social activities is Lower Marton Grove, which is also geographically quite distinct, right at the southern fringe of the town. Moreover, there is considerable social distance between its tenants and their suburban neighbours, and also, though to a lesser extent, between Lower and Upper Marton Grove, which is, on the whole, of a slightly higher social status.

Have these particular neighbourhoods any other characteristics in common?

5. Factors which Contribute to Neighbourhood Integration

Summary of Neighbourhood Indices

To answer this question, the three neighbourhood indices which have been obtained are set out on Table 5. A fourth one has been added, an index of geographical demarcation. Definitely isolated neighbourhoods have been classified as "one"; those which are geographically clearly distinct as "two"; those which are less distinct as "three"; and those which merge completely into others as "four".

For each of the other three indices the previous rating from "one" to "six" is shown to facilitate the comparison between them.

In reading this table, it should be remembered that "one" is always the most negative rank. For the index of neighbourhood integration, it implies least integration, i.e. dispersal of social activities. In the rating for geographical demarcation, it stands for isolation. In the index of living conditions, "one" denotes extreme poverty. For the index of institutional equipment, it implies an acute lack of institutions.

Neighbourhoods are grouped in this table according to the rank order of integration. We can now see that those in groups 6 and 5,

NEIGHBOURHOODS: TABLE 5
COMPARISON OF NEIGHBOURHOOD INDICES

Neighbourhoods		Rating for Indices of:				Total Population In Each
Grouped According to Index of Neighbourhood Integration		Neighbourhood Integration	Geographical Demarcation	Living Conditions	Institutional Equipment	
Number	Name					
A 1	St. Hilda's	6	1	1	6	5,399
A 16	Cargo Fleet	6	1	1	5	1,188
A 17, 18	Brambles Farm	6	1	4	2	5,098
B 8, 9	Lower Marton Grove	5	2	4	2	6,388
A 14	North Ormesby	5	1	2	5	10,083
A 9	Waterloo Road	4	3	2	3	6,241
A 2	Newport	4	3	1	4	13,103
A 5	Parliament Road	4	3	3	3	6,451
A 3	North Ayresome	4	3	3	2	3,780
A 15	Pallister Park	4	1	5	2	1,035
A 7	Shopping Centre	4	3	1	6	5,695
A 12i	Vulcan	4	3	1	4	4,821
B 1	Whinney Banks	4	2	4	2	7,079
B 10	Upper Marton Grove	4	2	4	3	3,949
B 11	East Grove Hill	4	3	6	2	2,222
A 6	Cleveland	3	4	2	4	5,723
A 8	Acklam	3	3	2	3	7,620
A 4	West Lane	3	2	4	1	1,026
B 6	Linthorpe Village	3	3	4	4	2,535
B 5	Ayresome Park	3	3	4	3	5,142
B 7	South Linthorpe	2	3	6	1	1,376
B 3	West Linthorpe	2	3	5	3	4,258
A 10, 11, 12	Civic Centre	1	3	2	6	8,010
B 2	West Acklam	1	3	5	1	2,190
A 13	The Longlands	1	3	4	2	3,222
B 4	Mid Linthorpe	1	4	6	3	2,408

the most "neighbourly" territorial groups, have two characteristics in common, and both are negative characteristics.

Geographical Isolation and Poverty

Four of these five neighbourhoods are geographically isolated, the fifth is geographically clearly distinct. All are poor, since even the new housing estates, Brambles Farm and Lower Marton Grove, are of low status although their physical setting is comparatively favourable. Moreover, they are also all socially homogeneous, which is a feature which most planners regards as undesirable in neighbourhood design.

Institutional Equipment

It appears, therefore, that the positive aspect of neighbourhood integration is associated with a combination of negative characteristics. Further scrutiny of the table confirms this impression. For the five neighbourhoods in question have varied ranks for institutional equipment. Three of them, St. Hilda's, Cargo Fleet and North Ormesby have comparatively adequate institutional equipment. But there is a marked paucity of institutions on the new estates, Brambles Farm and Lower Marton Grove. Thus the adequacy of institutional equipment appears to be less decisive a factor than one might assume. Even where institutions are lacking, there may only be a comparatively small degree of dispersal. Few people would come into the neighbourhood and those who live there may have few interests and use only the inevitable schools and shops. Or else, they may attach themselves to one adjacent group only and use their institutions exclusively. The social activities of such a neighbourhood would, therefore, be concentrated, although not necessarily entirely within its own boundaries.

Characteristics Associated with Neighbourhood Integration

But what of the neighbourhoods at the other end of the scale which are marked out because of the complete dispersal of their social activities? It is remarkable that they have hardly any characteristics in common. Thus it does not appear as though the presence of any particular characteristics creates dispersal, but as though dispersal is the very norm. It is only broken when a particular combination of negative characteristics occurs: the co-existence of geographical isolation, of poverty, and of social homogeneity. Not any one of these characteristics but their very combination is probably the decisive factor.

But as poverty implies social homogeneity, and is often allied with geographical isolation, a more extensive inquiry might show that poverty contributes most to social integration. It may prove to be significant, therefore, that only two of the twelve neighbourhoods in group 4, all of which are at the verge of social integration, are prosperous.

The size of neighbourhoods matters less than we might assume. For both the most and the least integrated neighbourhoods have very varied population totals.

6. The Implications of the Neighbourhood Pattern

Population Shifts

The aspects which matter most for immediate practical application stand out very clearly. The concentration of social activities within a neighbourhood implies that its inhabitants are closely tied to their own part. Thus the immediate social consequences of uprooting such neighbourhoods would be severe. Its impact would be most painful for the people in the neighbourhoods of groups 6 and 5, as indicated on Table 5. Since some of these neighbourhoods are scheduled for clearance and reconstruction, the process should be undertaken with great care. Population shifts would even disturb the neighbourhoods in group 4 which are still comparatively stable. If upheavals are necessary, the people from any one of these territorial groups should be shifted simultaneously and swiftly. Their new environment should contain some of the positive features of their old neighbourhood: a fairly close grouping of people and familiar institutions.

Planning Principles

However, the implications of this survey of neighbourhoods for the more general discussion of planning principles are more controversial. Neighbourhood integration appears to be the exception and to be associated with a combination of negative factors at present, at least in Middlesbrough, and there is no reason to assume that it is so in Middlesbrough alone. Therefore, how can it be recreated? It now exists in the setting of poverty and geographical isolation. Can it now grow as the result of alternative conditions?

Only the experiment of planning can provide the answer to this question. Until now, distinct territorial groups have been formed haphazardly, not according to a pattern designed to meet people's needs. Consequently, neighbourhood institutions are unequally distributed and each has usually been sited, and is functioning, without reference to any of the others. Thus we find only rarely that institutions are closely grouped in relation to the district which they serve. They are usually scattered and, therefore, their spheres of influence do not coincide. When a more convenient allocation of services and amenities has been achieved, integrated neighbourhoods may no longer be exceptional.

But it is unlikely that even then neighbourhoods would be self-contained. Institutions can never, and should never, be completely standardised. Thus proximity cannot possibly ever be the only consideration which affects people's choice of schools, shops and clubs.[19] And the importance of proximity is bound to vary with different age and social groups, even in the most carefully planned neighbourhood unit.

Mothers, children and old people, who are all rather tied to their homes, are most dependent on facilities within easy reach. Others have to rely more on institutions which are near to their place of work than on those which are near to their homes. By and large, poor people have less choice than well-to-do people. For freedom of movement is derived from the possession of both time and money; and it is utilised because of the consquent development of varied interests and tastes.

Hence, the choice of the institutions we frequent is not subject to distance alone, but to a variety of additional considerations and characteristics. We all want to be able to pick and choose. There is a tendency to go for the more specialised activities to the centre of the town, to the area which has most of everything.

Neighbourhood Groups

All this, which is evident from the maps of institutional catchment areas, implies that the design of residential areas should be flexible. Convenient access to institutions is essential, but standards of convenience vary for different groups and for different types of services. There will inevitably be a good deal of criss-cross movement and residential cells should, therefore, be closely related to each other. The pattern of urban areas should express and facilitate the coherence of groups of neighbourhoods; it should not be split up by a number of small subdivisions.

The Integration of Middlesbrough

The primary need in Middlesbrough is the integration of the

town, as a whole, rather than that of individual territorial groups. The cleavages between major areas have to be obliterated. They need not lose their individual identities if their living conditions are more equal and they are thereby more closely bound together. Having got to know each of them, the planner can prepare their readjustment.

PART II

HEALTH SERVICES

I

MIDDLESBROUGH'S HEALTH PROBLEMS

1. The Rapid Growth of The Town

Many of the most acute health problems in Middlesbrough have arisen as the result of the extremely rapid growth of the town. In the course of the nineteenth century, the population of the Township, the Borough, and finally of the County Borough, rose from 25 to 91,302 between 1801 and 1901.

The phenomenal increase in population was brought about by an influx of workers to serve, first the coal export trade, then the iron industry (after 1850), and finally the steel industry (after 1885). The vast majority were navvies and unskilled labourers, emigrants not only from the agricultural districts of England, for example Norfolk, but also from Ireland and from Poland and the Baltic States. In addition to this remarkable immigration, the rate of natural increase was high, and the increase in population was thus accelerated.[1]

Housing Conditions in the 19th Century

The working population was employed almost entirely in the iron and steel industry, and housed as near as possible to their places of work. The provision of houses for the large immigrant population is described by Lady Bell. "There springs into existence a community the members of which must live near their work. They must therefore have houses built as quickly as possible; the houses must be cheap, must be as big as the workman wants, and no bigger; and as they are built, there arise, hastily erected, instantly occupied, the rows and rows of little brown streets, of the aspect that in some place or another is familiar to all of us. A town arising in this way cannot wait to consider anything else than time and space: and none of either must be wasted on what is merely agreeable to the eye, or even on what is merely sanitary. It is, unhappily, for the most part a side issue for the workman whether he and his family are going to live under healthy conditions. The main object of his life is to be at work; that is the one absolute necessity".[2]

A "Thoroughly Bad" Site

The lack of sanitary equipment and the poor condition of the houses built in the nineteenth century were even worse than this description suggests. To begin with, the site on which the houses were erected was, in the words of the first Medical Officer for Health, "thoroughly bad". "Few worse sites upon which to found a large and increasing town could have been found".[3] Most of the working class houses were erected upon "the Marshes" which extended from the northern side of St. Hilda's ward, across the railway and into Cannon and Newport wards. These were subject to periodic floods, and were difficult to drain because they were so low-lying. Damp rot, therefore, hastened the deterioration of the poorly constructed dwellings.

Sanitation

The difficulties connected with the drainage of this site were largely responsible for the delay in installing adequate sanitary equipment. The only sanitary conveniences in existence when the houses were built were privy middens. Water was supplied by a tap which served a considerable number of houses.

In 1869, 94·0 per cent. of the then existing houses were served by privy middens only, and it was not until 1914 that the last of these was abolished. In the meantime, a large number of houses were equipped with pan closets. These were emptied into carts, and the contents either transfered to barges and deposited in the North Sea, or sold to local farmers for manure. In 1912, after a considerable number of the pan closets had been converted to water closets, there were still 15,000 pan closets in use. At that time, there were approximately 23,000 houses in the town.

Infectious Diseases

The existence of privy middens, the cleaning out of pan closets and the carting of "night soil" through the streets increased the danger of infectious diseases. In 1854 Edward Pease noted in his diary that "the cholera yet continues in Middlesbrough". In 1897–1898 there was a very serious smallpox epidemic when 1,411 cases of smallpox occurred and there were 198 deaths. One peculiar disease was very prevalent in Middlesbrough, it got the name of "Middlesbrough Pneumonia" because it resembled that disease, but it was also infectious. Enteric fever was common too. The exceptionally high death rate from infectious diseases in the early years of the twentieth century was attributed in part to the very primitive sanitary arrangements. The incidence of such diseases as enteric fever seemed to be directly related to the lack of proper sanitation.[4]

The conversion of all pan closets to water closets was not completed until 1925. As a result, the incidence of infectious diseases has decreased considerably, though it is still high.

Overcrowding

Apart from the bad sanitation of the hastily constructed houses, overcrowding in the poor and densely built-up areas was responsible for a good deal of ill-health. In St. Hilda's ward, the death rate was consistently far higher than in the rest of the town. This was attributed to high housing densities and to overcrowding, for which this ward was particularly notorious. "In 1901–1905, the high death rates occurred in blocks of houses which were situated in yards or were back-to-back, in other words, houses which did not have a free circulation of fresh air, either around or through them. These houses are built in such proximity to each other that the population of a small area is often very great".[5]

Most of the houses for the working classes were of the small four-roomed type, and they were often inhabited by large families. Lodgers were frequently taken in. According to Lady Bell, lodgers were to be found in about one-third of all working class houses.[6] As there were usually only two bedrooms, adequate sleeping accommodation was rarely available. In the M.O.H. Annual Reports in the early years of this century, frequent reference is made to the use of "bed places" for sleeping. These, according to the 1907 Report, "are usually small closets or recesses under the stairs and have originally been intended for pantries and closets. They are not more than a few cubic feet in area, many have no light except when the door is open, and many have no ventilation".

Smoke Pollution

The working conditions did not compensate in any way for the poor home environment. It has been stated that "for the majority of iron workers, the main equipment needed is health and strength".[7] But the dusty, smoky and heated atmosphere in the works was not conducive to good health, and practically nothing was done by employers to improve working conditions.

As a result of the dust and smoke polluted atmosphere, pulmonary diseases were prevalent, and rheumatism was common also. As most of the workers lived in St. Hilda's, Cannon, Newport, Vulcan and Exchange wards, they did not only breathe in a polluted atmosphere during their hours of work, but also when they were at home. What Lady Bell has called the "odours and vapours" from the works, penetrated into the homes of the workers, made it difficult for them to keep their houses clean, and continued to have a deleterious effect on the health of the workers and their families.[8]

Since the early years of this century, the application of successive Factory Acts has helped to decrease smoke pollution. Since many works in the district were closed after the first world war, there are now fewer sources of smoke and grit. But a smoke pall still hangs over the northern part of Middlesbrough, shutting off the sunlight and depositing soot and grime on household goods and furniture.

2. POVERTY AND BLIGHT

Slum Clearance

Whilst the town expanded further in the first two decades of this century, until it reached a population of over 131,000 in 1921, the poorest wards decayed rapidly and their congestion was hardly relieved. The Medical Officer of Health suggested in 1902 that "to improve the health of this district (St. Hilda's), the speediest method would be some scheme of rehousing a large proportion of its population". And yet, it was not until 1934 that any extensive slum clearance scheme took place in that ward, and this was the first considerable effort of this kind in Middlesbrough. Less than 90 houses had been demolished altogether by the Corporation between 1920 and 1934. In the following five years, before the outbreak of the war, about a further 700 houses in the old northern wards were pulled down.[9] First, some of the closely packed back-to-back houses, later most of the houses fronting on to small terraced courts, were taken down. But slum clearance has been piecemeal. Many of the cleared sites have remained vacant, and thus the derelict appearance of the northern neighbourhoods is accentuated.

Population Shifts

The recent movement of population from the old northern wards to the outskirts has, however, been more considerable than is indicated by the figures of slum-clearance. As the more prosperous people have moved further and further outwards, and as many of them have left the town altogether, a slow but general shift from north to south has taken place. Many of the old residential dwellings in the northern areas are now used as commercial premises or as lodging houses. Under war-time conditions, a great number of the already empty houses have been allowed to fall completely into disrepair. In other cases, bomb blast has hastened the process of decay. When we nowadays walk through the northern neighbourhoods on either side of the railway, it is difficult to guess whether blitz or blight is responsible for the miserable appearance of the skeleton houses. But we learn that neglect has been the chief cause of destruction.

Rehousing

The development of low density housing in the outskirts, which began in the 1920's and was accelerated in the 1930's, has assisted the shift from the northern areas. About a third of all the houses built since 1914 were erected by the Corporation who took the initiative in rehousing in the 1920's. In the subsequent years, their efforts have been matched, and even exceeded, by private enterprise.[10]

But the local authority have been responsible for meeting the most urgent needs. They have transferred families from the poorest and most blighted wards to the new housing estates which now have 12·0 per cent. of all Middlesbrough houses and about 18·0 per cent. of the total Middlesbrough population.[11]

Problems of the New Estates

By 1939, over 4,000 households, most of whom had previously been living in overcrowded and insanitary conditions, had been moved to the new estates in the southern and eastern parts of the town. The structure of their new houses was incomparably better than that of the small, old houses they had left, and they were living in a more healthy and less polluted atmosphere. They now had gardens and lived within easy reach of the open country. With all these advantages over their former housing conditions, it might have been expected that the health of the settlers would immediately improve, and that diseases connected with their former environment would no longer be prevalent. Yet so great an immediate improvement did not occur.

Most of the tenants settling on the estates in the 1930's were selected because their housing conditions in the northern parts of the town were outstandingly poor. Overcrowded families living in very insanitary circumstances were given priority. Their health had already suffered considerably from the deficiencies of their former environment and they could not, therefore, recuperate very quickly.

Furthermore, many of these families could not easily shake off the habits engendered by their former environment. Hardly any houses in the northern neighbourhoods have baths, and many have only cold water laid on. Soot and dirt continually cover clothes and furniture. Unless the housewife is very strong and very house-proud, she is defeated by these difficulties and gives up the struggle for cleanliness. Dirt diseases, such as scabies, impetigo and vermin infestation occur, and the chance of infection is increased. And even though furniture is disinfested when the family moves to the new estate, dirt diseases may continue. Families who settle permanently on the new estate usually adjust their habits. They discover how much easier it is now to keep clean and there is a marked improvement in their appearance and in the condition of their houses. If the health and housing authorities would help the tenants in the first period of settlement, the process of assimilation could certainly be accelerated.[12]

But the chief cause of continued ill-health on the new estates, as reflected, for instance, by high infant mortality rates, is the poverty of the people. The removal to the new home has not solved but often rather accentuated the problems of an inadequate family income. Some outlay is required for the setting up in the new house, particularly if it is larger than the previous one. The housewife may find that her expenditure on essential requirements is increased, especially if she makes an effort to adjust her habits to the new environment. But the greatest increase in the cost of living is probably due to the cost of transport: to work, to the shops, and, in the early years on the estates, to school. This expenditure is unavoidable, especially since so few neighbourhood amenities are provided on the estates, and since places of work are at some distance. The economic position of the immigrants might, therefore, even deteriorate after they have settled on the new estates. For all these reasons, improvements in health are only slow.

Present Conditions in the Old Northern Area

The people who remained behind in the old northern wards still have to fight against both poverty and blight. Half of all the houses in Middlesbrough are still without baths, but the relevant proportions are far higher in the northern neighbourhoods. In Newport, for instance, only 4 per cent., in Cannon only 10 per cent., and in St. Hilda's only 15 per cent. of the houses have baths while the relevant proportion in Linthorpe is 91·0 per cent.[13]

Every house in the town is now provided with a separate water-closet, but at least half of these are still outside in yards or gardens. About 2,000 old dwellings in the north still have no indoor water taps, and in St. Hilda's there are even now groups of houses sharing a common tap.

Almost a fifth of all the houses in present-day Middlesbrough are at a density of over 50 houses per acre, but again most of these dwellings are in the northern neighbourhoods. Hence, two-thirds of the houses in Newport ward, more than half of all the houses in Cannon ward, and an only slightly lower proportion in St. Hilda's, are grouped at so high a density. Population density follows the same pattern.

Almost all the houses which have these striking deficiencies are over 70 years old. Hence blight is concentrated in the northern neighbourhoods which have all but 7·0 per cent. of the old houses of which there are still about 10,000 altogether, that is, almost a third of the total present number in Middlesbrough. Hardly any new building has taken place in St. Hilda's and Cannon wards since 1877. Less than a tenth of their present dwellings were built after that date, in the last decades of the 19th century. By comparison, almost all the houses in the southern area are of fairly recent origin.

Derelict houses are characterised by the co-existence of several adverse factors. A sixth of all the houses in Middlesbrough to-day are over 70 years old, are at a density of over 50 houses per acre, and are also without baths. Only a few of these are in the south. But every second house in the neighbourhoods on either side of the railway is of that type.

The Background of Middlesbrough's Health Problems

This is the background against which Middlesbrough's health services have to be viewed. A substantial town has grown in the course of a century, chiefly for the purpose of producing iron and steel. Crowds of immigrants were hastily and miserably housed near their places of work. Most of these homes, in which there has been so much poverty and illness in the past, still remain. They are still inhabited by people with low incomes who have known long periods of unemployment in the 1920's and 1930's. Smoke pollution and the violent changes of temperature to which the labourers at the steel works are exposed, cause the specific danger of pulmonary diseases. A minority of people from the blighted wards have been moved to the new estates, but their economic problems have not thereby been solved. Hence the improvement in their environment has not yet produced a corresponding improvement in their physical condition. The only neighbourhoods in which there are no specific health problems are those few in the south which do not suffer either from poverty or blight.

3. Vital Statistics

Comparison with other Towns

Middlesbrough's vital statistics reflect its specific health problems. Like most areas which are characterised by poverty, the town has had consistently a high birth rate and a high infant mortality rate. In the quinquennium 1935–1939, Middlesbrough had the fourth highest crude birth rate of all the county boroughs of England and Wales, i.e. 19·3 live births per 1,000 people. Only Bootle, Liverpool and Sunderland had higher rates.[14]

In the same five-year period, Middlesbrough had the second highest infant mortality rate of all county boroughs, that is, 79·4 infant deaths per 1,000 live births. Only in Wigan was the position still worse.[15]

Maternal mortality, too, has been comparatively high in

Maternal Mortality 1937–1943

Year	Maternal Death Rate* for Middlesbrough Deaths per 1,000 total births	Maternal Death Rate for England and Wales Deaths per 1,000 total births
1937	4·59	3·11
1938	4·18	2·97
1939	4·43	2·82
1940	3·24	2·16
1941	1·85	2·23
1942	2·25	2·01
1943	2·67	2·29

*Information obtained from the Annual Reports of the Middlesbrough Medical Officer of Health.

Middlesbrough's Vital Statistics, 1898 to 1943.

(See Graph 10 in pocket at end of book).

Information obtained from the Annual Reports of the Middlesbrough Medical Officer of Health.

Middlesbrough. Although the relevant rate is still higher than that for England and Wales, it has considerably declined since the war, and more so locally than nationally. However, such a comparison is not entirely reliable as a detailed study by age of mothers and by order of births could not be made.

Intra-Town Comparison

Within Middlesbrough itself, there are considerable differences between the birth and infant mortality rates of different areas of the town. But these have to be considered against the background of differences in age structure.

The only recent figures of age structure available are those of the National Registration of September 1939. Evacuation and call-up had already affected the town at that time and we have, therefore, as far as possible, made the necessary corrections.[16] Although these figures are not entirely reliable, they can be taken to reflect major differences.

The Major Areas of Middlesbrough

For the purpose of this comparison, it is convenient to distinguish between four major areas of the town only.[17]

They are:

Area I, the poorest and most blighted part in the extreme north, which is adjacent to the industrial zone on the bank of the Tees.

Area II, the new housing estates, which are akin to the northern wards in terms of social status, though not of environment.

Area III, the geographically and socially intermediate wards. This area is not as homogeneous as either the first or the second. There is no real social barrier between areas I and III, in fact, they shade into each other.

Area IV, comparatively the most prosperous districts in which practically all the inter-war speculative and private house building took place.

Age-Structure

The housing estates, area II, have by far the largest proportion of children under 16 years of age; well over a third of their total population are in this age-group. A more detailed comparison of age-structure showed, moreover, that it is chiefly the 6–16 year age-group which is comparatively so strong on the new estates. The specific age-structure of these new estates is, of course, due to the selection of tenants. The majority of dwellings have four or more rooms, and hence large families with young children, and particularly those who were previously overcrowded were chosen. Comparatively few new babies arrive after these families have settled in their new homes.

More than a quarter of the population in area I, the poor northern wards, are children under 16, as compared with a fifth in the intermediate area III, and only a sixth in the comparatively prosperous area IV.

HEALTH SERVICES: TABLE 1

AGE-STRUCTURE OF THE MAJOR AREAS OF MIDDLESBROUGH: NATIONAL REGISTRATION 1939

Area	Population				Total
	Under 16 years %	16–25 years %	26–45 years %	46 years and over %	%
I. Poor Northern Wards	26·0	18·0	28·0	28·0	100·0
II. Housing Estates .	37·0	16·0	29·0	18·0	100·0
III. Intermediate Wards	20·0	17·0	31·0	32·0	100·0
IV. Prosperous Southern Wards . .	16·0	15·0	34·0	35·0	100·0
All Middlesbrough .	24·0	17·0	30·0	29·0	100·0

The proportion of old people, and particularly of those over 65 years of age, also varies considerably in the different areas. It is generally highest in areas III and IV but the proportion of old people in some of the poor wards in area I is also considerable. More than 8·0 per cent. of the total population in St. Hilda's is over 65 years of age, as compared with only just over 3·0 per cent. on the new estates.

As Table 2 shows, the poor wards and the housing estates are particularly in need of health services for mothers and children. Over two-thirds of the Middlesbrough child population live there, although these areas contain only just over half of the total Middlesbrough population.

Infant Mortality Rates

The specific need of the poor areas is emphasised even more by the variations in infant mortality rates which reflect the acute differences of social status and environmental conditions between

HEALTH SERVICES: TABLE 2

PROPORTION OF TOTAL NUMBER OF MIDDLESBROUGH PERSONS IN PARTICULAR AGE GROUPS LIVING IN EACH AREA

NATIONAL REGISTRATION 1939

Area	Children under 16 years of age %	Old People over 65 years of age %	Total Population %
I. Poor Northern Wards .	41·0	38·0	38·0
II. Housing Estates . .	27·0	9·0	18·0
III. Intermediate Wards . .	18·0	26·0	22·0
IV. Prosperous Southern Wards	14·0	27·0	22·0
All Middlesbrough .	100·0	100·0	100·0

the different parts of Middlesbrough. The average annual infant mortality rate for the quinquennium, 1939–1943, was far higher in the poor northern wards than in any other area of the town.[18] Even on the new estates, where environment is far better, the infant mortality rate is still high, although a definite decline is visible. It remains to be seen whether in time this improvement will become as marked as the progress in the educational standards of the children on the new estates.[19]

ANNUAL AVERAGE INFANT MORTALITY RATE FOR THE QUINQUENNIAL PERIOD 1939–1943

Area	Infant Deaths Per 1,000 Live Births
I. Poor Northern Wards	92·0
II. Housing Estates	73·0
III. Intermediate Wards	55·0
IV. Prosperous Southern Wards . .	54·0
All Middlesbrough	74·0

Fertility Rates

As we were not able to obtain reliable annual estimates of the total population in each area during the same five-year period, comparable birth rates could not be computed. It is, however, worth while to consider the birth and fertility rates for 1939, which can be based on the population figures of the National Registration of that year. Although these are not as reliable as the quinquennial averages, they are again indicative of the major variations within Middlesbrough.[20] As the areas differ in age-structure, the fertility rate, i.e. the number of births per 1,000 women of the child bearing age-groups, is, of course, a more sensitive index than the crude birth rate.

BIRTH AND FERTILITY RATES FOR 1939

Areas	Birth Rate No. of Live Births per 1,000 People	Fertility Rate No. of Live Births per 1,000 Women aged 16 to 45
I. Poor Northern Wards	25·0	108·0
II. Housing Estates	12·5	53·0
III. Intermediate Wards	19·0	76·0
IV. Prosperous Southern Wards	14·0	52·0
All Middlesbrough	19·0	78·0

On the whole, the fertility rate declines steeply as we move from the poor to the prosperous areas. However, the rate for the housing estates is an exception, chiefly because of the particular circumstances of tenant selection. Most families already have several children and tend, therefore, to be complete when they move to the new estates.

Thus, the major difference is between the fertility rates of the old and of the new parts of the town. Comparatively far more babies are born in the blighted north than in the new south and yet the chances of survival in the first year of life are much smaller in that area.

II

HEALTH SERVICES FOR DIFFERENT AGE-GROUPS

I. MATERNITY AND INFANT WELFARE SERVICES

Middlesbrough's vital statistics imply that the town has to pay particular attention to the provision of adequate maternity and child welfare services. A special study of these services and of their use was, therefore, undertaken, for the purpose of which details of all births during the first four months of 1944 were obtained.[21]

The Sample

During that period, a total of 970 confinements were notified in Middlesbrough.[22] Among these, there were 41 still-births; a further 52 children died before they were three months old. As the health visitors do not usually follow up these cases, it has not been possible to secure much information concerning them. The records analysed relate, therefore, chiefly to the 887 infants who were born during this period and who survived the first three months of life.

Almost a third of all these were first births, but the relevant proportion was lower in the poor northern wards and on the housing estates than in the remainder of the town.

Nearly half of the infants in the sample were born into families where the weekly wage packet was the chief source of income, and over a quarter were born into families where the Forces' allowance was the main income. Only a tenth had fathers who were non-manual workers and most of these were in area IV.[23]

In most of these families, the expenditure on the expectant mother and the new-born child would have to be restricted. The extent to which maternity services were freely available was. therefore of considerable importance.

Ante-Natal Services

There are various types of ante-natal care available for the expectant mother. Since extra rations and clothing coupons are granted to women declared by an authorised person to be pregnant, most expectant mothers are anxious to secure these benefits at an early stage in pregnancy. A few, mainly those in the higher income groups, apply to their own family doctors, and are examined by them at regular intervals during pregnancy. Over half of all the mothers in the sample, those who were subsequently confined at home and delivered by a midwife, visited the midwife early in pregnancy and were examined only by her. If no obvious complications occur during pregnancy, it appears that the midwife will not visit the case again until the time of confinement, but if the mother is concerned about her own health, she may call in the midwife before then. In that case the midwife will usually recommend her to see her own doctor or to visit an ante-natal clinic.

Fortnightly ante-natal sessions are held in the premises of four of the infant welfare centres in the northern part of the town. But the chief ante-natal clinic is at the Municipal Maternity Hospital. It is open four mornings a week and is staffed by the medical officer and the midwives of the hospital. Mothers who intend to be confined at the hospital come to this clinic to book their confinements, and are encouraged to attend regularly during pregnancy. Other expectant mothers who need medical attention or supervision are sent to this clinic by their doctors or the midwives. Advice and treatment at all municipal ante-natal clinics are free. About 35·0 per cent. of the mothers in the sample are known to have made use of them. Another 3·0 per cent. are known to have consulted their own doctors.

Care during Confinement

Just over one-half of all the mothers were delivered at home and attended by midwives only.[24] There are twenty-six qualified midwives working "on the district" in Middlesbrough and nineteen of these are in the municipal midwives service. The municipal midwives each work in one district of the town and they attend, on the average, about six cases a month. When labour begins, a mother sends for the midwife, with whom she has booked, who then stays with her until the child is delivered. After that, for the first few days, the midwife will attend the case twice daily, then once a day until the fourteenth day after birth, when the mother is in most cases considered strong enough to look after the child herself. If complications arise during labour, and the municipal midwife considers that medical assistance is required, she is able to get the mother admitted as an emergency case to the Municipal Maternity Hospital, or else she may call in a doctor. If infection occurs during confinement, such as puerperal fever, a municipal midwife is no longer permitted to attend the case and the mother is either removed to the Isolation Hospital, or else nursed in her own home by a district nurse. The usual charge for the services of a municipal midwife in Middlesbrough is £1. 15s. 0d. If the family is unable to pay this fee, however, the sum to be paid is assessed according to income.

The care of the rest of the family, while the mother is confined, creates many domestic difficulties. There are only seven home helps in Middlesbrough and they work under the direction of the municipal midwives. Their function is to carry out the domestic duties of the household while the mother is confined. Applications for home helps come mainly from the more prosperous wards and the service, which was only started in 1943, is not widely used.

Mothers who have booked to have their confinements at the Municipal Maternity Hospital, are taken there by ambulance when labour begins. The hospital is in a converted house to which several additions have been made. There are fifty-eight beds, forty-nine of these being available for lying-in, and the remainder for isolation and ante-natal treatment. During the war, the demand for accommodation increased considerably. This is partly reflected in the increase in the proportion of all confinements which took place in institutions (mainly the hospital), i.e. 30·0 per cent. in 1939, compared with 36·0 per cent in 1943. It is likely that this increase would have been greater if more hospital accommodation had been available. But under present circumstances, admission had to be restricted. Since January 1944, the hospital authorities have had to refuse admission to all but complicated confinement cases from the area outside Middlesbrough. They also now have to discharge mothers who have had normal confinements on the ninth or tenth day after the birth.

It appears that the hospital, which was established in 1920, was originally intended to take only complicated and emergency confinements. Even in 1943, a quarter of all the cases admitted were emergencies. The second priority is given to mothers for their first confinements. Almost half of all maternity hospital cases in the sample are first confinements, although these represent only 32·0 per cent. of the total confinements in the town.

The cost of confinement at the maternity hospital varies according to income. However, emergency cases are admitted without any stipulation as to ability to pay. If the husband is an insured worker, the mother is entitled to £2 maternity benefit, and she receives an additional benefit of the same amount if she herself has been working.

For a few of the mothers in the most prosperous parts of the town, it is economically possible to be confined at a nursing home. Only one small nursing home functions in Middlesbrough itself, but there are also two others, at Stockton and Nunthorpe, which are used by Middlesbrough mothers.

Infant Welfare and Post-Natal Services

The supervision of the health and care of infants is less spasmodic and haphazard than the ante-natal care of expectant mothers. Of all the children born during the first four months of 1944, 94·0 per cent. had been visited by the health visitors when they were about a fortnight old. There are ten health visitors, each working in one district of the town. Approximately, 1,200 children under five years of age are in the care of each health visitor, who pays three-monthly visits to children until they are twelve months old, and less frequent visits subsequently, until they are five years old.

The health visitors have to make about thirty visits daily in order to adhere to their schedule.[25] In addition, they have many other duties, such as giving advice at infant welfare centres and paying special visits to homes where illness or other difficulties have occurred. All this means that their routine visits are bound to be brief though they are able to inform the mothers of the various services available to them and to their children, and especially to encourage them to use the infant welfare centres.

Over 60·0 per cent. of all cases in the sample, and about the same proportion from each area, visited one of the seven infant welfare centres, which are distributed throughout the town. The one exception is the Brambles Farm estate, the only district which does not have a centre within easy reach. The nearest one is three-quarters of a mile away and the majority of Brambles Farm mothers do not, therefore, make use of it.

Five of the centres are open one afternoon a week; the remaining two have two sessions per week. The centres are staffed by health visitors and clerks from the maternity and child welfare department. A medical officer is in attendance to inspect the children and to advise the mothers. Baby foods and vitamins are sold at the centres.

None of the centres are housed in premises built especially for the purpose. Church or public halls are used for four of them. The mothers usually assemble and undress their children in the main hall, where the babies are also weighed and the advice of the health visitor is obtained. Those who wish to see the doctor are taken to one of the smaller rooms. These halls are dark, gloomy and often draughty, in spite of coal fires or central heating, and there are no covered sheds in which to park prams. They are certainly not well suited for use as infant welfare centres. The other three centres are in former residential houses. These are used as infant welfare centres only and are more convenient than the public halls, having less gloomy rooms and more adequate sanitary facilities. Only one large room, however, is used for waiting, undressing the children, weighing them, talking to the health visitors and purchasing baby foods. This room is usually very crowded, and the older children who accompany their mothers are unable to play in so confined a space. On the whole, all the premises in which the centres meet are inconvenient and unattractive.

The main post-natal service for mothers is a weekly clinic held at the maternity hospital. It is chiefly used by mothers who had been confined in the hospital but other women are also recommended to go there by their doctors, the midwives or the health visitors.

Factors which Influence the Use of Maternity Services

On a first analysis of the survey results, it appears as though order of birth is the most important factor influencing the use of maternity services. Mothers in their first pregnancies receive ante-natal care and have institutional confinements proportionately far more frequently than the remainder, and they also use infant welfare centres to a slightly greater extent.

However, on closer inspection it is clear that birth order, though important, affects the use of maternity services indirectly rather than directly. Regardless of birth order, mothers who have been confined at the hospital also receive ante-natal care and use infant welfare centres to a far greater extent than those who have been confined at home and attended by midwives. The educational influence of the hospital is, in fact, the dominant factor. Its importance is merely obscured at first since hospital confinements are more frequent among mothers in their first pregnancies than among the remainder. Only 17·0 per cent. of all mothers confined at home received ante-natal care, as compared with 94·0 per cent. of those who were confined in the hospital or in nursing homes, and the relevant proportion was substantially the same for first, second and subsequent pregnancies.

Of course, the relationship between hospital confinement and ante-natal care is bound to be close, as the hospital authorities make a point of asking the mother to attend the ante-natal clinic. Midwives do not appear to do so.[26]

It is far more remarkable that the influence of the hospital

HEALTH SERVICES: TABLE 3

USE OF MATERNITY AND INFANT WELFARE SERVICES

Middlesbrough Confinements, January 1—April 30, 1944

Type of Service	Proportion of all Mothers using each kind of Service %	Proportion of Mothers having First Confinements who use each kind of Service %
ANTE-NATAL CARE		
Mother received ante-natal care .	38·0	60·0
Mother did *not* receive ante-natal care	42·0	27·0
Mother's ante-natal record unknown*	20·0	13·0
Total Per Cent. .	100·0	100·0
CARE DURING CONFINEMENT		
Domiciliary, attended by midwife only	53·5	31·0
Domiciliary, attended by doctor .	8·5	9·5
Institutional, at Municipal Maternity Hospital	33·0	51·5
Institutional, in nursing home .	4·0	7·0
Type of confinement unknown .	1·0	1·0
Total Per Cent. .	100·0	100·0
CARE AFTER BIRTH		
Mother using infant welfare centre	61·0	67·0
Mother *not* using infant welfare centre	39·0	33·0
Total Per Cent. .	100·0	100·0
Total Number .	877	277

* In analysing the cases whose ante-natal record is unknown by type of confinement and number of previous pregnancies, it was possible to deduce that only 35·0 per cent. of these had in fact received ante-natal care. The total number of mothers in the sample who had received ante-natal care would, therefore, be increased by only 7·0 per cent.:

i.e.: Mothers who had received ante-natal care . 45·0 per cent.
Mothers who had *not* received ante-natal care . 55·0 per cent.

For mothers who had had their first confinements, the comparable estimate is as follows:

Had received ante-natal care . . . . 67·0 per cent.
Had *not* received ante-natal care . . . 33·0 per cent.

extends to attendance at infant welfare centres as well. Mothers who have been confined at the hospital and have, therefore, usually received ante-natal care, also use infant welfare centres far more frequently than the remainder, and this is again true irrespective of birth order.

In fact, a cumulative process is at work. The mother is always encouraged by the hospital authorities to attend the ante-natal clinic, then at the ante-natal clinic, regardless of whether she has been sent there by the hospital, by her doctor or, far more rarely, by the midwife, she is encouraged to use the infant welfare centre. Birth order is important, chiefly because it is taken into account in the selection for hospital confinement. But the educational influence exercised through the institutional maternity services appears to be the chief factor in promoting the all-round use of them.

The Influence of Social Status

The use of maternity services also varies with social status. The proportion of institutional confinements, both for first and subsequent births, is greater in the well-to-do than in the poorer parts of the town. Thus, well-to-do mothers are more likely to benefit from the hospital influence than poor mothers. Conversely, midwives working largely in the poorer districts of the town, have a harder task in educating the mothers whom they attend and who find it difficult to spare the time and energy to visit clinics. Thus, just in the poor districts where specialist services are most needed, their influence is more limited than in the more prosperous parts of the town.

However, it does not necessarily follow that the striking difference between the ante- and post-natal histories of mothers who have been confined at home and of those who have been confined in hospital, can be chiefly attributed to variations in social status. The present evidence is not conclusive.[27] But it shows that although institutional confinements are proportionately most frequent in the prosperous area, still only just over one-third of all mothers who had been confined in hospital come from area IV. Hence it appears as though the educational influence of the hospital is indeed an independent factor of considerable importance. It is probably reinforced by the fact that a higher proportion of mothers confined in hospital are able and willing to use the available services than mothers who have been confined at home and attended by midwives.[28]

The Limited Use of Maternity Services

There is clearly a need for studying the causes which now limit the use of maternity services and for eliminating the restricting influence wherever possible. Limitation of use is the most striking result of this enquiry. More than half of all mothers in the sample did not receive ante-natal care; and the same proportion were confined at home and attended by a midwife; two-fifths did not attend infant welfare centres at all during the first three months after the birth of their babies.[29] Both ante-natal and infant welfare services should be used by every mother, before and after each confinement. But only every fourth mother in Middlesbrough had contacted both types of services; and as many as a fifth of the group used neither.

The Present Position

Most of the usual maternity services are available in Middlesbrough but they will have to be expanded considerably to make it possible for more mothers to use them. Shortage of space and of staff are the most obvious deficiencies at present. The demand for beds in the maternity hospital has compelled the authorities to shorten the normal length of stay and to refuse admission to normal cases from the area outside Middlesbrough. The infant welfare centres, now attended on the average by about 50 mothers in each session, are often crowded. All of them are in inadequate premises. Mothers and children have to wait for as much as one hour before the baby can be weighed by the health visitor in charge or before the doctor can be seen.

Apart from the fact that the number of beds in the maternity hospital is limited, many mothers are prevented from being confined there because of their domestic ties. Those in the poorer parts of the town are usually unwilling, or financially unable, to use the home helps' service, and in any case only a few home helps are now available in Middlesbrough.

Only a small number of home confinement cases are attended by a doctor, and those attended by a midwife often receive only rather perfunctory ante-natal care; the babies are taken less to infant welfare centres than those born in other circumstances. It is true that emergency and complicated confinement cases are transferred to the maternity hospital when possible, but more adequate ante-natal care in the first place may prevent serious complications arising, and may reduce the disproportionately large number of still-births and of deaths in the first few months of life in the poor areas of the town.

Proposals

The most urgent requirement in the immediate future is, therefore, to give greater attention to the ante-natal care of mothers who are confined at home, and to the care of their new-born children. The midwives who attend these cases should encourage the mothers to make much more use of ante-natal clinics and welfare centres.

As soon as building policies permit, the accommodation in the maternity hospital should be increased, and more mothers from the poorer parts of the town should be encouraged to have their confinements there.

However, a considerable increase in the number of institutional confinements will not be achieved unless the rest of the family can be adequately looked after while the mother is in hospital. In some cases, it may be best to have temporary residential homes for the older children, but it is likely that an extension of the home helps service would be a more satisfactory arrangement. The charge for such a service must be kept very low so that the families who need it most can make use of it.

The staff of the various maternity services should also be increased. It has been estimated, for example, that at least fifteen health visitors, instead of the present number of ten, are needed to deal with the current work.

Makeshift premises should be discarded. A plan for Middlesbrough should include the provision of ante-natal clinics and infant welfare centres, designed to serve their purpose, and evenly distributed throughout the town, in the old as well as in the new areas.

2. Wartime Institutions for Young Children

As the employment of women increased considerably during the war, specific institutions for the day-time care of young children had to be established. At first, the children were usually left under the supervision of a neighbour or a grandmother but it was soon evident that some supervision of these *ad hoc* arrangements was required.

Day-Guardians Scheme

For this purpose, the day-guardians scheme was instituted by the maternity and child welfare department, in collaboration with the local office of the Ministry of Labour.[30] When the mother herself has found another woman, either a relative or a friend, to look after her child while she is at work, she notifies the child welfare department. A health visitor is then sent to interview the proposed "guardian" who is registered in her new capacity if she is considered to be suitable. In addition to any wages paid to her by the mother, she receives four shillings per week from the Ministry of Labour. The payment of this nominal sum makes it possible for the child welfare department to supervise the care of the child, to insist on attendance at an infant welfare centre, and to make sure that the child is provided with baby foods and vitamins.

In March 1944, there were 156 of these registered "guardians" looking after 183 children. Most of them live in the poor northern wards of the town. The scheme has never worked very well and can only be regarded as an emergency arrangement. As the accommodation in war-time day nurseries has been expanded in 1944, very few new day-guardians are now being registered.

War-Time Day-Nurseries

There are now, in the summer of 1944, five war-time day-nurseries, two of which were established in 1942, while the others were only recently opened. Four of the nurseries are in special temporary premises. Accommodation is provided for 278 children and there are five children to each member of the staff.[31]

The shortage of trained staff has been one of the obstacles to expansion. Each nursery has a nucleus of trained workers, a matron, deputy matron, one or two nursery nurses, a warden or teacher and a cook. To assist these workers, there are also a number of untrained and part-time helpers. The babies are separated from the children over two and have different rooms to play in.

There is still an acute shortage of nursery places in the poor northern wards of the town, which are served by two nurseries only, one in Cleveland Ward and one in North Ormesby. A third nursery is just north of the Park, one is adjacent to Whinney Banks estate, and one is on Marton Grove.

As the nurseries are so widely apart, the catchment area of each of them is considerable. Mothers have to bring their children to any nursery at which a place is available, regardless of distance. Only children of mothers in full-time employment are eligible and hence the nurseries are attended by boys and girls from all parts of the town, with the exception of the prosperous southern neighbourhoods.[32]

As in all other parts of the country, the day-nurseries are greatly appreciated by working mothers and the children are well looked after. The Matron of one of the northern nurseries stated that the mothers knew very little about child care and were extremely grateful for advice. The contrast between the children in that nursery and those of the same age who were seen in the streets was certainly remarkable. Those in the nursery were bright looking, clean and usually rather well dressed. Those in the streets were covered with dirt and ragged.

The day-nursery is certainly now regarded as a permanent institution. Facilities should be expanded so that children of mothers who are not working can be admitted as well. At present, the greatest need for more nursery accommodation is in the northern area of the town.

3. The Lack of Health Services for Adolescents and Adults

In Middlesbrough, as in other parts of the country, very few health services are provided for people from the age when they leave school until such time as they contract so serious a disease that they are entirely incapacitated and need prolonged institutional treatment. The chief institutions available are the compulsory National Health Insurance scheme for all employees, and any private insurance schemes or doctors' clubs to which people may voluntarily contribute.

Adolescents

Adolescents and housewives are the two groups which suffer particularly from the lack of facilities for diagnosis and early treatment. When the young people have left school, where their health had been supervised by the school medical service,[33] they are not immediately eligible for health insurance benefits. Only the claims of those who have paid contributions for six months are met.

Housewives

Housewives, who are not working, are not at present included in the insurance scheme. They very rarely pay sufficient attention to their own health and no official encouragement is given for them to do so, except in the specific case of pregnancy.

Wage Earners

Although the men who work in the iron and steel industry are exposed to considerable dangers and may contract serious respiratory diseases, only the minimum of first aid posts and medical equipment demanded by the Factory Acts are provided at the works. In order to continue in the heavy labouring jobs, the men must keep themselves very fit, and the duty of keeping them adequately clothed and fed falls largely on their wives. A great part of the family income may be spent on the chief-wage-earner for whom the housewife often sacrifices many things, such as food, clothing and, above all, some leisure, all of which are needed to maintain her own health.

4. The Care of Old People

Apart from the universal problems connected with the care of old people, Middlesbrough has a special difficulty.

Middlesbrough's Special Problem

During the first world war, many single men came to work in the steel firms in Middlesbrough. After the war, and particularly after the great depression began in 1929, many of these immigrants became unemployed. A considerable number of them stayed on in the town, living in the common lodging-houses in St. Hilda's ward. Although the employment position gradually improved during the 1930's, a large number of these men were regarded as too old when younger men were also available, and they never returned to work. Many of them are now over 65 years of age and are, therefore, in receipt of pensions. Most of these old single men still live on their own in poor lodgings in the northern wards.[34]

Under a special section of the Middlesbrough Corporation Act of 1933, the Medical Officer of Health can get a court order to remove infirm or neglected old people to an institution. This clause was not very extensively used in 1943, when there were only two removals by court order, but it enables the public health authority to handle the worst cases of destitution and neglect among old people.

Institutions for Old People

Old people who are destitute are transferred to Holgate Institution, the former "workhouse". The premises, built in 1874, are rather bleak and unsuited for their purpose, according to modern standards. There is accommodation for some 170 old people, the majority of whom are men, and also for a few mental defectives.

Even now, the old people are very reluctant to enter the "workhouse" and they find it rather difficult to adapt themselves to their new surroundings.

The Municipal Infirmary, although in the same building as the Holgate Institution, is regarded much more favourably. It was recently opened to accommodate old people who are chronically ill and who cannot be looked after at home. There are some 80 places which are always occupied and there is a considerable waiting list. Admission is not dependent on poverty and hence the stigma of the workhouse is not attached to this institution.

In addition, there is one small private charitable institution for old people of the Roman Catholic faith, Nazareth House, which is primarily an orphanage for girls. Its inmates come from the whole area of the Roman Catholic diocese of Middlesbrough which extends far beyond the county borough boundary.

Middlesbrough's particular problem of the care of old single men is likely to become less extensive in time, as the immigration of steel workers has not continued on the same scale as before 1918. But the general need for the institutional care of old people still remains. As long as the aged poor are treated as a separate group, the old workhouse tradition will not be forgotten.

III

THERAPEUTIC SERVICES

1. Hospitals

Middlesbrough has a fair range of hospital accommodation, which is, however, split up in small units and rather inconveniently distributed. All but two of the buildings were established in the late 19th century and are now out of date.

Buildings

Two of the three voluntary hospitals, which were built in the 1870's and 1880's respectively, have as far as possible been kept in good repair and further wings have been added. But the structure and lay-out of the buildings is no longer adequate and their sites are too small to allow further expansion. The municipal hospitals, with the exception of the Maternity Hospital, also need reconditioning if not complete rebuilding.[35] But their location is, on the whole, better than that of the two old voluntary hospitals. Two of the municipal hospitals are on the same fairly extensive site which could be used to build a new large institution.

Area Served by Municipal Hospitals

The administration of Middlesbrough's municipal hospitals has been complicated by the fact that a considerable proportion of the hospital services of the town have been inherited from the old Poor Law Union. The Municipal General Hospital, the Municipal Infirmary and St. Luke's Mental Hospital were all Poor Law institutions, and served, not only Middlesbrough, but the whole of the Cleveland district, which covered approximately the area on the northern side of the Cleveland Hills and south of the Tees. When these hospitals were taken over by the public health department, as a result of the Local Government Act of 1929, special consideration was given to the people living within the former Cleveland Poor Law Union. Cases from this area who are admitted to the Municipal General Hospital or the Municipal Infirmary do not pay the full cost of their treatment, but are charged at a reduced figure.[36]

The Isolation Hospital was never a Poor Law institution and has, therefore, a more limited responsibility. But since the Tees-

HEALTH SERVICES: TABLE 4

HOSPITALS IN MIDDLESBROUGH*

	Name of Hospital	Approximate Date of Establishment	Administering Authority	Scope of Hospital	No. of Beds	Outpatients' Department
1.	Municipal General Hospital	1870's	Hospitals' Committee of the Corporation	Medical Surgical Tubercular Children	69 76 46 82 } 273	Yes
2.	St. Luke's Mental Hospital	1870's	Mental Welfare Committee of the Corporation	Mental	Not known	No
3.	Municipal Infirmary	1874	Hospitals' Committee of the Corporation	Chronic Sick	80	No
4.	West Lane Isolation Hospital	1890's	Hospitals' Committee of the Corporation	Infectious Diseases Tubercular	203 30 } 233	No
5.	Municipal Maternity Hospital	1920	Hospitals' Committee of the Corporation	Maternity	50	Yes
6.	North Riding Infirmary	1870's	Voluntary Hospital Committee	Medical Surgical	140	Yes
7.	North Ormesby Hospital	1880's	Voluntary Hospital Committee	Medical Surgical	192	Yes
8.	Carter Bequest Hospital	1926	Committee of Trustees	Medical Surgical Children	52	No

* The information shown on this table was compiled in 1937. However, all the hospitals are still functioning for the same purposes and to approximately the same extent in 1944, with the exception of the Municipal Maternity Hospital where the number of beds has been increased to 58.

side area is not well served with hospitals for infectious diseases, two of the adjacent local authorities have made arrangements with Middlesbrough for cases of infectious diseases occurring in their areas to be admitted to the Isolation Hospital. Seamen who suffer from such diseases are treated there also.[37]

Hence patients come to Middlesbrough municipal hospitals from the greater part of the North Riding of Yorkshire. A few come from County Durham, north of the Tees. These are chiefly from the places just across the river from Middlesbrough. In two weeks, selected at random, in December 1943 and June 1944, 17·0 per cent. and 11·0 per cent. respectively of the patients came from outside the county borough boundary.

Area Served by Voluntary Hospitals

The three voluntary hospitals in Middlesbrough also serve a wide area, without financial discrimination between those who live in the town and those who come from outside. The North Riding Infirmary and the North Ormesby Hospital both work contributory schemes; and the great majority of firms in the area operate the scheme of one or the other of these two hospitals. Their employees who contribute are entitled to free treatment. Patients are interchanged between these two hospitals which appear to co-operate closely with each other. They also share one full-time residential medical officer.

The firms who operate the contributory schemes are situated in Middlesbrough and the other steel towns to the east of Middlesbrough, in the iron mining villages in the Cleveland Hills, and also on the north bank of the Tees, at Billingham, Norton, Stockton and Haverton Hill.[38] In each of the two sample weeks, in December 1943 and June 1944, about 60·0 per cent. of the patients who were admitted to these two voluntary hospitals came from outside Middlesbrough.

The Carter Bequest Hospital is a small and rather select institution, financed by endowment and by fees. It is used to a considerable extent by doctors for their private patients, many of whom do not live in the town.

Integration of Hospital Services

A start has been made in the integration of hospital services in Middlesbrough. In 1936, the Hospitals Advisory Joint Committee was set up and there is already a good deal of co-operation between the municipal and voluntary institutions. As the former provide more varied services than the voluntary hospitals, they also admit patients who have contributed to the schemes of the voluntary hospitals and treatment is given to them at a reduced charge.

Out-of-Town Treatment of Middlesbrough Patients

Arrangements with other local authorities also make it possible for Middlesbrough patients to be sent elsewhere for specialised treatment. Newcastle hospitals receive most of the Middlesbrough patients who do not have to pay the full cost of treatment but are charged according to their means.

A number of residential special schools and of public assistance institutions outside the town take children and adults from Middlesbrough who are mentally defective.

Patients in the early stages of pulmonary tuberculosis are sent to the Poole Sanatorium, near Nunthorpe, which is administered jointly by several municipal authorities in Yorkshire and County Durham. There are 300 beds at the Sanatorium, 75 of which were available to Middlesbrough cases before the war. The number has recently been reduced and there is now no accommodation for children; but in peace-time fifteen beds were provided for them.

There is also a hospital owned by the Middlesbrough Corporation at Hemlington, a village just to the south of the borough boundary. Originally this hospital was intended for smallpox cases; more recently, before the present war, it was used as a children's convalescent home. It is now an emergency war-time hospital, chiefly for patients in the Forces, with 480 beds and up-to-date equipment. This hospital will revert to the use of Middlesbrough patients after the war.

The Scope of Middlesbrough's Hospitals

The Middlesbrough hospitals provide institutional care for maternity cases and for patients suffering from most of the usual illnesses. Four of the municipal hospitals do specialist work, and there are three general hospitals, the largest of which is run by the Corporation, the two others by voluntary committees. In addition, there is a small voluntary hospital which fulfils the function of a nursing home. As the incidence of tuberculosis is rather high in Middlesbrough, treatment is given at two of the municipal hospitals and, in addition, also at the Poole Sanatorium outside the Borough.

Outpatients' Departments

The three general hospitals all have outpatients' departments.

The Municipal General Hospital has a weekly dental clinic, a fortnightly ear, nose and throat clinic and a fortnightly ophthalmic clinic, as well as a regular minor ailment clinic. Specialists attend the clinics and treat cases in the hospital. They also see outpatients recommended to them by the district medical officers and the private medical practitioners in the town.

A particularly large number of outpatients come to one of the voluntary hospitals in the poorest part of the town, near the Ironmasters' District. There appears to be a great demand in this area for the treatment of minor ailments.

Future Plans

Until the system and scope of the new National Health Service is decided, it is not possible to make definite plans for the development of Middlesbrough's hospital services. Their size will depend on the area and population which they will have to serve. But in any case, if the policy of compulsory health insurance and free treatment for all is accepted, a great expansion in the provision of diagnostic and therapeutic services will be required.

As Middlesbrough is the only county borough in the lower Tees Valley, and has already a fairly comprehensive hospital service, it is possible that hospital services for the surrounding area, including lower Tees-side, and a considerable part of North Yorkshire and South Durham, might become centralised here.

Centralisation of hospital services is certainly needed. It would eliminate the need for complicated arrangements between different local authorities about the admission of their patients. It would make it possible for all patients to receive the same kind of treatment, at the same cost, irrespective of detailed administrative boundaries. Moreover, amalgamation of hospital services in fewer and larger units would be more economical and efficient.

It has, therefore, been suggested that two large hospital groups should be established for Middlesbrough, one on the site of the present Municipal General Hospital and of the Infirmary, and one on the site of the present Hemlington Hospital, outside the borough boundary. The first would be convenient for emergency and short term cases; the second, which is in the countryside, has the environment which is essential for long term cases and for convalescents. A new location, preferably on the outskirts of the town, for an enlarged maternity home will also have to be found.

2. Clinics and Dispensaries

Interchange of Medical Staff

A number of special municipal clinics also provide diagnostic and therapeutic services. They have recently been assisted in their work by the medical staff of the municipal hospitals. This arrangement has made it possible for the Medical Officer of Health to distribute the limited number of doctors in the municipal service to best advantage and to carry out specific war-time functions, such as the supervision of evacuation and diphtheria immunisation.

Clinics

A special treatment clinic for venereal diseases was established in the 1930's and is open every day. An almoner and a special health visitor were appointed in 1943 to trace cases and to encourage attendance at the clinic.

A tuberculosis dispensary was opened in 1913 and has been functioning since that time. Tubercular cases and contacts are daily examined and treated and, if necessary, arrangements are made for transfer to institutions. The nurses who are attached to the clinic also visit patients in their homes. A scheme for rehousing families in which there are tubercular cases has been in operation since 1931.

As the incidence of skin diseases is considerable in Middlesbrough, a new scabies clinic was recently established to replace the old cleansing centre in St. Hilda's ward.. A special health visitor is in charge. All the members of a family in which scabies have occurred are treated at this clinic.

Dispensaries

The dispensaries, which are run by the district medical officers, are not a part of the general services provided by the public health department, but they are special institutions for the poor. The district medical officers themselves are appointed and supervised by the social welfare committee. There are two of them, one working east and one west of Linthorpe Road. They act as general practitioners for people on relief; they visit their patients and hold surgeries every morning and afternoon.

When free medical treatment is available for all, a special medical service for the poor will no longer be required. But the experience of the district medical officers will certainly be useful in the establishment of "grouped practices" and health centres in the poorest parts of the town.

3. Nurses and Doctors

District Nursing Association

The Queen's District Nursing Association in Middlesbrough was set up about fifty years ago to care for the "necessitous sick poor", in their own homes. The Association, which is run by a voluntary committee, was originally financed by donations. But in 1941, a contributory scheme was organised, whereby people can pay a penny per week, through their firm, through organisations to which they belong, or to individual collectors. No further charge is made when they are sick and require the services of a district nurse.

The Association co-operates closely with the public health department from which they also receive grants.

There are now thirteen qualified district nurses, each working in a particular area of Middlesbrough. They are only allowed to care for sick people at the request of a doctor and they are called on both by doctors in private practice and by those in the municipal service. They work an eight-hour day, and do general nursing only. Cases of infectious diseases are looked after by special municipal nurses and normal confinements are attended by midwives only.

Since an increase in the number of district nurses is anticipated, the question whether they should all be accommodated in one central institution or in smaller subsidiary homes in various parts of the town is being discussed. The existing hostel for nurses could be expanded, and it is convenient from the point of view of organisation and training if all the nurses are housed in the same building. On the other hand, it is an advantage if the nurses live nearer to the districts in which they operate, many of which are, in any case, in considerable need of health services. There are now no doctors' surgeries on or near any of the new estates, and the immediate provision of neighbourhood health services is essential.

Distribution of Surgeries

There is a shortage of surgeries of general practitioners in the town, and this shortage is particularly acute in the poorest districts. For instance, there is not a single surgery in Cannon ward, and the position on the new housing estates is even more serious. But in the centre of the town, there is a concentration of surgeries in several streets.

The unequal distribution of general practitioners affects the poor areas most. In spite of the panel system for insured workers, poor people are reluctant to call in a doctor unless there is a serious illness. When the surgery is at some distance from their homes, minor ailments tend to be neglected. Therefore, many of the poor people in the wards near the railway do not get adequate medical attention at the present time.

Private Addresses of Doctors

The surgeries of the general practitioners are not usually situated in their private houses. A few doctors live in the area north of the Park, but the great majority either live in the most prosperous neighbourhood, Mid-Linthorpe, or outside the Borough. Although they may visit the homes of the poorer people, they do not live in the same areas or use the same social institutions. Both the geographical and social distance between doctors and patients is considerable.

IV

COMMUNAL FEEDING

The close relation between malnutrition and poor health is by now taken for granted. During the war, we have all become "nutrition-conscious". Special institutions have been established, which are all likely to remain, though perhaps in an altered form: industrial canteens, British Restaurants and school meals. At these institutions, considerable attention is paid to balance of diet. This is of particular importance to Middlesbrough people who are used to a rather soft and starchy diet. The calcium content of the water is low. A very limited variety of vegetables is sold and there are few market gardens in the surrounding area.

Industrial Canteens

Middlesbrough now has nineteen industrial canteens, which are distributed in the steel works and foundries, on the docks and railways, in the chemical works, and even among some of the smaller service industries. However, the use of canteens is still rather limited. It appears that only about 5·0 per cent. of the total insured population have daily meals at a canteen.[39] Considering the attempts that have been made during the war to instal canteens for all industrial workers, this figure is extremely low.

Packed Meals Service

As many industrial workers in Middlesbrough do not, in fact, have access to a canteen, and are accustomed to eating their meals "on the job", an alternative provision has been arranged for them, which is known as the "Packed Meals Service."

This service was instituted by the food office in Middlesbrough in 1942. Workers in heavy industries, who do not have access to a canteen during their "meal breaks", can apply to their managers or foremen for a certificate stating that they are eligible for the service. They present the certificate at the food office, where they are given additional meat coupons of the value of an extra two shillings worth of meat per week, above the usual civilian ration. They or their wives can then purchase this extra ration at one of the three "Packed Meal Centres", which are organised for this purpose by the staff of the British Restaurants. The extra meat is made up by the housewife into sandwiches which the worker can eat "on the job".

Approximately 8·0 per cent. of the insured population in Middlesbrough use these facilities, about one-quarter of them being women employed in the chemical industry, on the railway and in the steel works.

The service has plainly met a very urgent need, but it cannot be regarded as more than an emergency scheme. The practice of eating meals in the grimy and smoky atmosphere in which many of the employees work cannot be conducive to health. Adequate and accessible canteen facilities should be provided for a far greater proportion of the industrial workers.

British Restaurants

Middlesbrough's five British Restaurants are all situated in the northern part of the town. The largest is in the central commercial area and is chiefly visited by office workers and shop assistants. The others are used by the families who live in the surrounding districts and also by industrial workers.

Commercial Restaurants, Hotels and Cafés

The commercial restaurants and cafés in Middlesbrough are able to provide a considerably larger number of meals than either the British Restaurants or the industrial canteens. During a sample week in June 1944, almost 29,000 meals were served at commercial restaurants, as compared with 11,000 in British Restaurants and 15,000 in industrial canteens.[40] But the commercial catering establishments, with the exception of a few small snack bars, are hardly used by industrial workers; they are chiefly frequented by Middlesbrough's middle class. Most of the restaurants and cafés are concentrated in the central shopping area; there are none in the north-eastern and southern part of the town. But for a few fish and chip shops, there is no provision for communal feeding on the new housing estates.

Lack of Communal Catering Facilities

Communal feeding is still in its very early stages in Middlesbrough. Apart from the school meals service, provisions for eating meals outside the home are still scarce for all sections of the population, except the black-coated workers. The new housing estates suffer most from the lack of communal catering facilities. This deficiency should be remedied in future housing development.

V

CONCLUSIONS

Middlesbrough's Needs

Conditions in Middlesbrough illustrate the national need for a universal health service which should be preventive as well as curative and which should cover all groups in the population. But Middlesbrough's needs are particularly acute, as a result of its history, and because of its physical, social and industrial structure. The environment in the northern 19th century area of the town, widespread poverty, and conditions of work in industry, all lower the general standard of health. High birth rates and high infant mortality rates make it necessary to pay special attention to the provision of health services for mothers, infants and children.

Deficiencies of Health Services

As everywhere, easy access to medical attention, particularly for dormant and minor ailments, is still the privilege of those who can afford to pay for it. Adolescents and housewives are not looked after; the care of old people is rudimentary and it leads to segregation. Above all, the chief object of the existing services is still the cure of illness rather than the maintenance of good health.

Nutrition

Standards of nutrition also appear to be low. Moreover, communal catering facilities are limited and there are none at all in the neighbourhoods of recent housing development.

Proposals

A number of proposals, which can only be elaborated when new legislation has been enacted, are implicit in the description of present conditions. The use of maternity and infant welfare services is still far too limited; more staff and premises are needed at every stage of the work. All old people who are not adequately cared for in their homes should be looked after, and not only those who are destitute or infirm. Accommodation suitable for them should be provided in every neighbourhood. Middlesbrough's hospital services are dispersed and most of the buildings are obsolete. The establishment of grouped hospitals is recommended. Many of the functions of the present out-patients departments might be taken over by health centres, the creation of which would make it possible to supervise the health of all age-groups and to integrate all those services which are frequently needed and which should, therefore, be conveniently located. One principal health centre and several subsidiaries, distributed throughout the town, would meet this need. They should contain grouped surgeries, dental clinics, dispensaries, and possibly also the special clinics for maternity and child welfare work and for the school medical service.

The people of Middlesbrough need all these specific services, but they are even more in need of a general improvement of their living and working conditions. The application of town planning principles, the clearance of obsolete and insanitary houses, the proper distribution of open spaces, and the modernisation of plant, will be the most effective contribution towards the raising of health standards.

PART III

EDUCATION SERVICES

I

THE SCOPE OF THE SURVEY

The Education Act of 1944

During the summer of 1944, when the Middlesbrough Survey and Plan was being prepared, the Education Act of 1944 was the most concrete and advanced of all post-war planning measures. Educational reconstruction had a definite legislative framework in terms of which local needs could be interpreted and related to other aspects of the plan. Since its objectives and scope were defined, the outline of the survey of the relevant services was clearly indicated.

To ensure equality of educational opportunity is no longer a planner's dream, it is now the duty of every local education authority. The survey, therefore, had to show how this duty could best be carried out. The nature and extent of existing inequalities had to be explored.

Before education services can be redistributed and expanded, as stipulated by the Act, it is necessary to find out which of the present schools and ancillary services no longer function adequately. The physical structure and equipment of school buildings, access to playing fields, swimming baths and school clinics, are all relevant aspects. The present range of secondary and further education has to be studied most carefully since it is in this sphere that the Act requires greatest expansion in order to ensure diversity as well as equality of opportunity.

In the past, school building in Middlesbrough has lagged behind the building of new housing estates. For several years, after families had settled on the new estates, even the infants and juniors have had to attend schools two miles away from their homes, in the northern area of the town. In future, the siting of old and new education services must be related to the geographical distribution of the school population. This implies also that some of the northern schools may become redundant when further population shifts take place.

Education in Relation to Other Services

Moreover, in the siting of all neighbourhood services, their interrelationship has to be considered. If the nursery and infant school is adjacent to the local shopping centre, the mother does not have to make two separate journeys to take her children to school and to do her daily shopping. If the local authority is to carry out adequately its function of providing free medical treatment for its pupils, as laid down in the Act, school clinics should be equally accessible for children from all parts of the town.

In some neighbourhoods, the use of school premises and playing fields by the adult population might also be possible. It has often been argued that adults dislike the memory of their school days so much that they can only be persuaded with difficulty to use school buildings for their own recreation. This argument surely implies that if the conditions of school life are improved, the idea of an extended use of school buildings need not be discarded.

However, detailed recommendation on the siting and use of schools and ancillary services, in relation to other institutions, will depend on observations of the present part played by schools in the social life of their neighbourhoods. It might well be unrealistic to adopt a standard lay-out, featuring the school as the focus of each neighbourhood.

The Social Pattern of the Town

All these aspects of education services are directly relevant to the implementation of the Act. But, in addition, a study of the school population can also contribute more widely to the formulation of a town-plan. It can help to establish the picture of the social pattern of the town and it may also reveal deficiencies in institutional equipment.

Maps of school catchment areas show the distribution of specific social groups. The catchment areas of the Roman Catholic schools, for instance, indicate the size and location of the Roman Catholic community in Middlesbrough. They show that it is concentrated in specific districts. Information on the health, cleanliness and attendance records of the school children in different parts of the town often reflects differences in home conditions. The heavy incidence of dirt diseases in certain districts points to, and confirms, the fact, which has been ascertained independently, that domestic washing facilities are inadequate, and that in the past the local authority has not paid sufficient attention to this problem. The frequency of "avoidable" school absences, particularly among senior girls, is due to the fact that their mothers are overworked and require more convenient homes and neighbourhood facilities. In fact, the detailed information collected by the local education authority shows that the redistribution and expansion of education services will have to be a part of Middlesbrough's general plan for reconstruction.

II

THE DEVELOPMENT OF MIDDLESBROUGH'S EDUCATION SERVICES

1. Outline of Development

The development of Middlesbrough's education services has followed closely that of the rest of the country in the last 75 years. But since the town is young, and its population is largely working-class, containing a high proportion of young children,[1] its education problems have been especially acute. Education has been largely the responsibility of the local authority, yet since, on the whole, rateable values in the town are low, per capita receipts from rates are also low. In 1938–39, they were between £3 to £3 5s. Only Darlington and West Hartlepool of all the county boroughs in England and Wales had lower rate receipts.[2] The income of the local education authority from rates has, therefore, never been high, and since the establishment of the school board in 1870 up to the present day, the problem has always been how to provide adequate education facilities for a proportionately large number of children at the lowest possible cost. In recent years, central government grants have slightly mitigated this difficulty, but the problem still remains.

Schools before 1870

Before the school boards were established in 1870, the only schools were those maintained by voluntary bodies, usually of a religious character. The first school in Middlesbrough was erected in 1843, by the British and Foreign Schools Society, when the population of the town was about 6,000. This school had accommodation for 120 boys and 100 girls. It is still in use as a domestic science centre for elementary school girls. The Church of England and the Nonconformists started building schools in Middlesbrough in 1860. Some of the founders and industrialists of the town were anxious that working class children should receive at least a rudimentary education. For example, Thomas Richardson, one of the original owners of the Middlesbrough Estate, suggested that "it might be given out that neither boys nor girls will meet with employment that cannot read nor write".[3] A part of his income was left in trust to promote public education, and the proceeds were later taken over by the school board. But in spite of the work done by the voluntary agencies, it has been estimated that there was a deficiency of 3,000 places in Middlesbrough Schools in 1870, and this figure probably refers to school accommodation for children under ten years only.[4]

The School Board

To meet these difficulties, a school board was established in each locality under the Education Act of 1870 to provide and administer schools where voluntary agencies had not been able to make adequate provision. In Middlesbrough, as elsewhere, the religious bodies were strongly represented on the school board, although the voluntary schools continued to function separately. By 1902 the school board had provided places for 12,229 children, but there was still a recognised deficiency of 853 places. Having established the schools, the second function of the school board was to enforce attendance. A series of Acts of Parliament were passed from 1876 to 1900, first prohibiting the employment of children under the age of ten years (1876), then making attendance at school compulsory until children reached the age of twelve (1899), and further giving school boards permissive powers to raise the compulsory school age to fourteen years (1900). To administer these Acts, the school board employed several school attendance officers or school wardens, as they were then called, and a marked increase in the number of children attending schools, far above the increase in population, was observed

After 1891, the financial aspects of the enforcement of school attendance began to lose some of their importance. School fees were no longer compulsory and the system of payment by results was discarded. The school attendance officers then took on other duties. Hence towards the end of its existence, the school board began to interest itself in the problem of defective children under the relevant Act of 1899, a problem which became obvious when compulsory school attendance was introduced. But the major advances in child welfare were only made after the establishment of the local education authority in 1902.

The Local Education Authority

The local education authority inherited the functions of the old school board. The task of providing elementary education became more exacting as the town grew in numbers and area. Further duties were laid on the local education authority by the

Education Act of 1902. Voluntary schools were supervised more closely since financial assistance for maintenance and teachers' salaries was given to them. The local education authority was also given powers to provide higher education for the children in its area.

But it was not until the Education Act of 1918 was passed that the compulsory school-leaving age was raised to fourteen years. At the same time the employment of school children was strictly controlled, the local education authority being given powers to licence and, if necessary, to prohibit the employment of all children of school age. The placing of children in full-time employment after they leave school was the subject of permissive legislation in 1910, and the Juvenile Employment Bureaux were established by all local education authorities in 1924.

The scope of child welfare was extended gradually. The school medical service was instituted in 1907. Various Acts dealt with the education of dull and mentally defective children for whom special schools were created. In 1933, the care and protection of derelict children and some administrative functions concerning juvenile delinquents were passed to the local education authority from the Poor Law Guardians.

The local education authority of to-day is not merely providing school accommodation and enforcing school attendance. Its task during the last 40 years has been to raise educational standards, to improve school amenities and to increase the scope of child welfare services. If children are ill, mentally defective, undernourished and neglected, they cannot take advantage of the education services provided. The local education authority has to make arrangements for their treatment and care.

2. Elementary Schools[5]

All but the earliest phase of the building of elementary schools is still represented in Middlesbrough to-day. Two schools opened before 1860 no longer exist. But most of the schools built after that year are still in use.

Church of England Schools

The Church of England schools are now the oldest in the town. In the 1860's they formed a triangle covering the greater part of the then built-up area. To-day, their neighbourhoods are densely

DATES OF OPENING OF PRESENT ELEMENTARY SCHOOLS

Date of Opening	Name of School	Extension of School	Denomination	Remarks
1863	St. John's	—	C. of E.	—
1868	St. Paul's	—	C. of E.	Bombed in 1941; now sharing premises with Newport Road School
1869	St. Hilda's	—	C. of E.	—
1869	Southend	—	—	Taken over by the School Board from the British and Foreign School Society
1871	Linthorpe	1912	—	—
1873	St. Mary's	—	R.C.	—
1873	St. Patrick's	1906 and 1912	R.C.	—
1874	Denmark Street	—	—	—
1876	Lower East Street	—	—	—
1876	Derwent Street, North Ormesby	—	—	Taken over from North Riding of Yorkshire, 1913
1878	Smeaton Street, North Ormesby	—	—	Taken over from North Riding of Yorkshire, 1913
1885	St. Alphonsus, North Ormesby	1896	R.C.	Taken over from North Riding of Yorkshire, 1913
1885	Newport Road	1906	—	—
1892	Victoria Road	—	—	—
1898	Marton Road	—	—	—
1902	Ayresome	1907	—	—
1906	St. Philomena's	—	R.C.	—
1906	Marsh Road	—	—	—
1909	Lawson	1913	—	Taken over from North Riding of Yorkshire, 1913
1913	Archibald	—	—	—
1927	St. Richard's	—	R.C.	—
1927	Marton Grove	—	—	—
1928	St. Joseph's	—	R.C.	—
1934	Beechwood	—	—	—
1935	Brambles	—	—	—
1935	St. Francis	—	R.C.	—
1938	Whinney Banks	—	—	—
1938	Fleetham Street	—	—	—

covered by houses; apart from bombed and cleared sites, there are no open spaces nearby.

Catholic Schools

Unlike the Church of England, the Roman Catholics, who started building schools in the 1870's, did not cease to do so when the town expanded. The oldest Catholic schools are in the areas of the poor unskilled labourers where a high proportion of the Catholic population still live. But since members of the Catholic community also participated in the general shift southwards, new Catholic schools were established later, first one, in 1906, in Ayresome ward; subsequently in the inter-war years, two further schools on the new housing estates and one in the northern area, the opening of which facilitated the reorganisation of the old Catholic schools in that part of the town. The seven Catholic schools now in existence have altogether 4,000 children on their roll, that is, a fifth of the total elementary school population of Middlesbrough in 1944.

Buildings Erected by the School Board

While the Roman Catholics were building schools in the 1870's, the school board was trying to fill in the gaps left by the voluntary agencies. Five of the present elementary schools in the town were built by the school boards of Middlesbrough and of the North Riding of Yorkshire during that decade.[6] The first of these was established in Linthorpe Village, as it was then called.

When the worst of the industrial depression of the late 70's and early 80's had passed, the school board once again started to build schools, this time chiefly in districts where no voluntary agency was operating. The town was expanding rapidly southward, and since school attendance up to the age of 10 years had been made compulsory by the Mundella Act of 1880, schools had to be provided in areas of new settlement.

Building Activities of the Local Education Authority

In the meantime, school accommodation in the older areas had become inadequate for the increasing child population and it was, therefore, the task of the Middlesbrough local education authority, in the first twelve years of its existence, from 1902–1914, to remedy these deficiencies. Space standards introduced by the newly established Board of Education, also made it necessary to extend existing school premises. Two new schools were built during this period in the old north-western area of the town and one at its north-eastern tip, in Cargo Fleet.

But in the most recent phase of school-building, during the inter-war years, the local education authority was once more primarily concerned with the southern areas of recent housing development. Four of the five schools opened by them during that period are on the new Corporation housing estates.[7] Unfortunately, however, the building of houses and of schools was not synchronised. It was not until families were settled on the estates and their children were forced to travel anything up to two miles to school, that the building of a school was considered. For instance, in 1933 there were about 600 children of compulsory school age living on Whinney Banks Estate, most of whom had to attend schools in the northern part of the town. There and on Brambles Farm, emergency classes had to be organised in temporary huts. When the Unemployment Assistance Board was established in 1935, applications for further allowances were made by the unemployed men living on the estates because their children had to travel by bus to schools in the centre of the town.[8] Whinney Banks school came into use in 1938, when many families had been living on the estate for eight years. The children of Marton Grove waited six years for the first local authority school and an additional seven years for the second school.[9] The first settlement on the Brambles Farm estate was in 1930, the school was opened in 1935. Even now this school caters for children under 11 years only, those who are older leave the estate daily to attend school in Cargo Fleet.

The Old and the New Schools

When the schools on the new estates were finally opened, the children attending them were delighted, and even those who were left behind in the old parts of the town gained some advantages. "The man who built this school had good ideas", wrote one of the pupils from Brambles school in an essay on the school and the estate. And although she made some sound suggestions for further improvements, she added: "I think that the rest of the school is perfect". Compared with one of the buildings dating from the 1870's, Brambles school, opened in 1935, is indeed perfect. It represents the great advance which has taken place since that time, not only in the physical standards of school buildings and playspace, but also in educational technique. Modern schools have an incomparably wider range of activities than those built 70 years ago when the three R's were the main, if not the only, items on the curriculum. With the successive raising of the compulsory school-leaving age, there has been a tendency, especially in the inter-war years, to separate, where possible, the different age-groups and also to separate senior boys and girls. In a few cases, special classes have been instituted for children under five years and also for retarded children. But in most of the older schools, the limitations set by obsolete premises have made such differentiation impossible.

Yet even some of these schools in the areas of slum clearance have benefited from the emigration of many of their previous pupils to the new housing estates. They now have fairly adequate classroom space for the children who remained behind. One school, for example, opened in 1876, now accommodates only a senior mixed department with about 100 pupils. According to pre- 1918 standards, this school had places for 410 children. However, in all other respects, these old schools are definitely out of date. Their physical structure is obsolete; ancillary facilities and playgrounds are totally inadequate.

There are, therefore, only a few "perfect" schools in Middlesbrough to-day, and these are in the southern area of recent development. Seven of the present number of twenty-eight elementary schools were opened before 1875; seven between 1875 and 1900 (one of these buildings is now shared by two schools); five between 1900 and 1913 and eight since 1927. None of the most ancient buildings, dating from the 1860's, and only three of those built in the latter part of the 19th century, have been extended since that period. Almost half of the elementary school population attend schools opened before 1900; less than a third are in buildings opened since 1927. Hence, the immediate task of reconstruction, resulting from physical obsolescence alone, is considerable.

3. Higher and Technical Education

The Earliest Sponsors of Higher Education[10]

The local industrialists were the earliest sponsors of higher education in Middlesbrough. The iron and steel industry needed clerical workers and technicians of a higher level of education than the early elementary schools could give to their pupils. Hence in 1877 the industrialists financed the first institutions for higher education in Middlesbrough: first, the Upper Boys' School for vocational training, which no longer exists; and secondly, the High School, which is still functioning and which originally was also attended by boys only. A separate department for girls was added later.

Funds for several scholarships were provided by the local industrialists and, in addition, the High School trustees received a grant from the central government in 1889 towards the financing of fifteen scholarships for local boys from families with an annual income of less than £200. The school board contributed three

DATES OF OPENING OF SCHOOLS AND COLLEGES FOR HIGHER AND TECHNICAL EDUCATION

Date of Opening	Name of School or College	Denomination	Remarks
1877	High School . . .	—	Originally for boys only. Girls admitted later
1904	St. Mary's College for Boys (Direct Grant Secondary School)	R.C.	
1906	St. Mary's Convent for Girls (Direct Grant Secondary School)	R.C.	
1907	Hugh Bell Selective Central School	—	The premises of this school were built in 1892 and before 1907 used as an elementary school
1911	Kirby Girls' Secondary School	—	—
1919	Junior Technical School .	—	Housed in the premises of the Hugh Bell Central School
1929	Constantine College . .	—	—
1935	Acklam Hall Secondary School	—	Housed in a converted 18th century country house

further scholarships of £16 annual value, tenable for five years.

But in spite of financial help from both public and private sources, the High School trustees found themselves unable to bear the cost of maintaining the school, which was, therefore, handed over to the local authority in 1896. A new governing body was set up, eight of the fifteen members of which were nominated by the council.

The Local Education Authority

When the local education authority took office in 1902, it was estimated that only 2·0 per cent. of the total Middlesbrough school population over 11 years of age received higher education. In 1944, the comparable proportion is 30·0 per cent. Gradually during the last 42 years, the extension of the relevant services was accomplished.

First, in 1907, the local education authority established the Hugh Bell Selective Central School in the premises of a former elementary school. This was followed in 1911 by the opening of the Kirby Girls' Secondary School in Linthorpe. There was no equivalent boys' school in the southern part of the town until a family mansion, Acklam Hall, was purchased by the local education authority and converted into a boys' secondary school in 1935.[11]

Roman Catholic Secondary Schools

In the meantime, two Roman Catholic secondary schools, one for boys and one for girls, had also been established.[12] These are "direct grant" schools which have only a small number of "special" places. Their pupils come from a wide area, including most of Cleveland and South Durham. These schools do not take all children from the Catholic elementary schools who pass the scholarship examination; quite a number attend instead the secondary schools run by the local education authority.

Technical Education

The local education authority has not concerned itself so much with the provision of technical education, as with general higher education. The initiative in providing technical education has more or less stayed in the hands of local industrialists and business men, with some financial assistance from public funds. Soon after the High School was founded by a group of industrialists in 1877, a controversy was started as to whether the curriculum should be more technical and vocational or rather more general. In 1882, Sir Bernhard Samuelson started the "Technical College Movement" to promote the scheme of a Technical College for Tees-side. In the following years various projects for technical classes for apprentices and others were instituted, but the local authority did not make full use of its powers under the Technical Instruction Act of 1889.

In 1909, High School courses were made more vocational, such subjects as machine construction and metallurgy being added to the curriculum. H.M. Inspectors reported, however, that the equipment was poor and accommodation inadequate.

In 1916, the old project of a Technical College for Tees-side was revived. The Cleveland Institute of Engineers collected subscriptions for it, one of which, the contribution of the shipowner, Sir Joseph Constantine, was so substantial that the College, finally completed in 1929, was named after him.

In the meantime the local education authority had established a Junior Technical School which is housed in the premises of the Hugh Bell Central School. Entrance, which is for boys only, is by means of a scholarship examination at the age of twelve. The object of this school is to prepare students for the Technical College, and since Constantine College has been opened, the Junior Technical School has regularly used its equipment, particularly the laboratories and workshops.

The scope of technical education in Middlesbrough is still rather narrow, particularly in view of the town's industrial activities. Moreover, technical education is not directly linked with industrial and technical research, for Constantine College is a training institution only, it is not a research body. The nearest universities or university colleges are Durham, Leeds and Hull.

The New "Secondary" Education

Under the Education Act of 1944 both the terms "secondary" and "technical" education will acquire a new meaning and the relevant facilities will have to be greatly expanded. It is hoped that, according to the Act, every child from eleven to sixteen years will receive full-time secondary education at a grammar, technical or modern school, which should all be of equal status. It will, therefore, not be sufficient merely to enlarge the present institutions for higher education. It is chiefly necessary to raise the standard of the pre-1944 senior elementary schools to the secondary school level.

4. Adult Education

The Three R's

The earliest attempts to introduce adult education in Middlesbrough were also undertaken by the local industrialists. During the 1880's the High School was used for evening classes, teaching simple technical subjects. An evening school for boys and men was instituted in 1885 in Southend School, the subjects being the "three R's".

In the following years, the local authority started several other centres of the same type. By 1902 all the evening classes had a total of 790 students. In those days the shift system in the works was an obstacle to regular attendance. No recreational subjects were taught, and equipment was inadequate.

Improvements

After 1902, the local education authority took steps to improve facilities for adult education. Fees for elementary subjects were abolished entirely, and the curriculum was made more attractive by the addition of some recreational subjects. Accommodation and equipment, however, were not greatly changed though more of the elementary schools were opened for evening classes.

Facilities in 1944

In 1944, women living on the Marton Grove and Whinney Banks housing estates are able to attend evening classes at the elementary schools in their neighbourhoods. The chief centres for adult education in the northern part of the town are the Hugh Bell Central School and the Constantine Technical College where most of the usual subjects for evening classes are taught. All classes which need special equipment take place at the College. Only two other schools in the central area are also used for evening instruction at the present time.

In the winter session 1943–4, classes were arranged by the local authority for young people from fourteen to sixteen years, and for adult women. Most of these classes were either technical or vocational in character; very few courses in cultural subjects were organised.

Voluntary societies have attempted to fill this gap in adult education services. The Workers Educational Association, which started classes in Middlesbrough before World War I, has tried to provide classes on cultural subjects; philosophy, history and various aspects of economic, political and social life are being discussed. The Townswomen's and Co-operative Women's Guilds have organised similar courses with a view to educating women in citizenship. The Little Theatre regularly performs plays in public, and also runs a weekly play-reading circle for its members. The voluntary societies, however, can touch only a very small proportion of the population. Hence an attempt on the part of the local education authority to broaden the curricula of its courses might meet with considerable response.

5. School Playing Fields

In the days of the school board and even of the local education authority before 1918, the inclusion of organised games in the school curriculum was not considered very seriously. In 1870, the town covered a small area, and although it was hemmed in on the west and north by the river, the ironworks and the railway, no houses were more than half a mile from the fields to the south of the town. But as housing sprawled southwards, the children from the mean and cramped streets near the railway and Newport Road were cut off from the fields.

Development of Space Standards

The problems of outdoor recreation for children in large and densely populated towns was recognised in the Education Act of 1918 and in subsequent legislation. In trying to keep pace with this legislation, the great difficulty confronting the Middlesbrough education authority in the 1920's was the location of playing fields in relation to the schools using them. No vacant sites were available near the centre of the town, and small children could not be expected to walk anything up to the maximum distance of two miles before they started to play games.

Although a playground with swings was provided in Albert Park, the chief playing space for Middlesbrough's children was the street, and the occasional open spaces of waste ground, such as the Newport "Recreation Ground", an asphalted area near the railway in Cannon and Newport wards.

In school hours the elementary school children had only the crowded school playgrounds for their games. The High School and Kirby Secondary School were equipped with fields, but little was done for the elementary school children in the 1920's. The local education authority made very little immediate use of its powers, conferred by an Act of 1921, to provide playing fields for "voluntary" as well as "provided" schools. Even when building Marton Grove School in 1927, adjacent playing fields were not included in the lay-out, although open space was available and the Marton Grove Estate had not grown to its present size.

The lack of play-space is reflected in the report of the school enquiry and child welfare section for 1933 which, in dealing with juvenile delinquency, states that "two-thirds of the offences were committed by children under fourteen years of age. The largest group of charges concerned breaches of the Highways Acts, for example, playing football in the streets".

Advance in the 1930's

But in the 1930's new provisions for outdoor recreation were made. Three schools built by the local education authority during these years, Brambles, Beechwood and Whinney Banks on the new estates, were all supplied with adjacent playing fields of considerable acreage. An attempt was also made to get every senior elementary school child and as many juniors as possible on to a playing field for 40 minutes a week. Open air classes were started as an experiment in 1939 for the children of St. Hilda's ward who suffer most from the lack of play-space. Once a week, children from

St. Hilda's and Lower East Street schools were taken, transport free, to North Ormesby field. There they stayed the whole day, having lessons and playing games.

Apart from the use of playing fields in school hours, the teachers organise after-school games, and a school sports association has been formed for this purpose. Inter-school matches are arranged. Each school has its annual sports and then there is a Grand Competition once a year. Such occasions, and the physical training demonstrations by school children, take place at the Cleveland Park Greyhound Stadium, the most suitable place in Middlesbrough for mass sports.

The Present Scarcity of Open Spaces

However, the provision of playing fields for school children has only just begun in Middlesbrough. There are still no open spaces in the densely built-up northern area where the majority of children live. Wartime conditions have further reduced the available space: one field, previously used by the High School, has been entirely taken over by the military authorities; others have been partly ploughed up.

There are only six playing fields, providing two acres of space for 1,000 pupils, for the entire elementary school population. Two of these fields are theoretically shared by all the northern elementary schools and by the Central School. But as the communal fields are at some distance from the school buildings, and as space is limited, four of the elementary schools in this area use no playing field at all, while only a small proportion of the pupils from the other seventeen northern schools play organised games during school hours.

The elementary school children at the outskirts have far more convenient access to playing fields, but even they have by no means sufficient space for sports in terms of present standards. Four of the seven schools in this area have adjacent playing fields, one of which is also used by the special schools, but two Catholic schools on the new estates do not use playing fields at all.

Pupils receiving higher education are comparatively most fortunate; they have five playing fields, including one which is temporarily requisitioned during war-time. They share these fields with the Technical School and College. But only 12·4 acres per 1,000 pupils are available.

The present allocation of playing field space is temporarily even more restricted than is shown on the table below, on which the pre-war acreage is recorded. The number of acres per 1,000 pupils available is computed on the basis of the total school population. However, since playing space is so restricted and inconveniently distributed, in fact, only about a third of all elementary school children make use of any playing fields.

EDUCATION : TABLE 1

NUMBER AND ACREAGE OF SCHOOL PLAYING FIELDS

Type of School	No. of Fields	Total Acreage	School Population*	No. of Acres per 1,000 pupils
A Elementary Schools †				
1) Northern Area .	2	17·25	14,849	1·16
2) Outer Ring .	4	25·00	5,721	4·35
Total . . .	6	42·25	20,570	2·05
B Higher Education .	5	50·60	4,065	12·40
Grand Total . .	11	92·85	24,635	3·75

* This includes the following number of pupils in each category who use the relevant fields :

Elementary Schools, northern area : 609 pupils of the Central School.
Elementary Schools, outer ring : 190 pupils of the Special Schools.
Higher Education : 207 pupils of the Preparatory School.
244 pupils of the Technical School.
1,600 students of Constantine College.

† The northern area consists of districts I to VI, shown on Table 3 ; the outer ring, of districts VII to X, as shown on that Table.

According to the minimum standards, formulated in accordance with the 1944 Education Act, the new primary schools, which will be attended by juniors only, should have ten acres of playing fields per 1,000 pupils, as compared with the present provision in Middlesbrough of two acres per 1,000 for the existing elementary school population which includes both juniors and seniors. The new secondary schools, which will absorb all the present senior elementary pupils, should have 28 acres per 1,000 pupils, as compared with the existing 12·4 acres per 1,000 in the present, much more restricted, secondary schools. Therefore, if we take the redistribution of pupils into the new primary and secondary schools into account, we find that more than four times the present acreage of playing field space is now required, even before the school leaving age has been raised.[13]

III

THE GROWTH OF CHILD WELFARE SERVICES

I. SPECIAL SCHOOLS AND CLASSES

Physically and Mentally Defective Children

The need for child welfare services was first recognised by the school boards when it became clear that an unexpectedly large proportion of the school population were not able to absorb even the most rudimentary lessons because of some physical or mental defect. Special provisions for the education of blind and deaf children up to the age of sixteen years were made in an Act passed in 1893. Permissive legislation in 1899 gave school boards powers to ascertain the number of mentally defective and epileptic children who could not benefit from the usual type of elementary education. The provision of suitable education for these children was made obligatory in 1914.

Special Schools

In Middlesbrough, a Special School, at present accommodating 147 dull and mentally defective children, was established, and a Deaf School, now attended by 31 children, was instituted in the premises of the Hugh Bell Central School.[14]

Children who are certified as mentally deficient enter the Special School at the age of seven, and they are compelled to stay there until the age of sixteen. The school premises are old and inadequate and have recently been condemned. There is not sufficient accommodation for the number of children who are certified as mentally deficient. Facilities for vocational training are lacking as well. An effort is made, however, to give the children as much physical exercise as possible.

Special Classes

The interruption of schooling during the war has further accentuated the problem of dull and backward children. In many of the older schools, there is only one class for each age-group and, as a result, the backward children do not get the attention they require, and the bright girls and boys cannot proceed as quickly as they would otherwise. On the other hand, in most of the more modern schools, there are as many as three classes for each age-group, and some of these schools have also organised special classes for retarded children. This practice should be copied in other schools and sufficient accommodation provided for this purpose.

2. The School Medical Service

Its Functions

When special provisions had been made, more or less adequately, for the education of children suffering from major defects, the much wider problem still remained of discovering minor ailments before they could become serious. The school medical service was, therefore, set up to keep a check on, and to improve, the general health of the school population. Its main function in the past was diagnostic rather than therapeutic. All school children had to be examined three times in the course of their school careers. But treatment has also been given increasingly to cases of minor ailments. The therapeutic side of the school medical service will have to be extended considerably under the 1944 Education Act, according to which the local education authority has to provide free medical treatment for all pupils attending its schools and county colleges.

Staff

In Middlesbrough, the school medical service started in 1908 with a staff of one doctor and one school nurse. In 1944, there are three full-time assistant school medical officers and six nurses, besides several part-time A.R.P. nurses and specialists.[15]

The Medical Officer of Health is also the head of the School Medical Service.[16] During the war, the medical staff has been considerably reduced. It is only now, in 1944, being increased again.

Routine Examinations

Because of shortage of staff, the routine medical examination of school children was curtailed. Elementary school children were only examined on entering and on leaving school; the intermediate inspection had to be left out. But in some respects the work of the school medical staff has increased during the war; for example, they now undertake diphtheria immunisation.[17]

Clinics

The premises originally used by the school medical service

were in an ordinary dwelling house in the northern area. To-day, there are four school clinics: the central clinic, a well-equipped modern building next to the education office, north of Albert Park; two clinics in school premises on the new housing estates; and a fourth, recently opened in a chapel in Cannon Street, one of the old northern mean streets.

Children living in Ayresome, Ormesby, and the northern part of Grove Hill Ward, have to go a considerable distance to reach a clinic. Many of them, therefore, never attend at all. For example, before the Cannon Street clinic was opened, comparatively few children came to the central clinic from Cannon and Newport Wards where the home environment is the poorest in the town. The distance, of approximately a mile, was too great and there were several heavy traffic routes to cross. However, when the new clinic in Cannon Street was opened early in 1944, a great many children came, and this clinic is now very popular.

Treatment

Ailments and diseases treated during 1943 at the school clinics included skin diseases, teeth, eye, ear and throat troubles, speech and orthopaedic defects, anaemia and general debility:[18] A rheumatic clinic used to be held, but had to be discontinued because of shortage of staff.

Child Guidance

Recently, a Child Guidance clinic was opened in Middlesbrough, primarily for children who suffer from minor nervous troubles. However, inadequate premises and the war-time shortage of staff have so far seriously limited its work. There are at the moment no facilities for psychiatric treatment. The educational psychologist, who now attends merely for one and a half days per week, and who is the only officer in attendance, can do little more than to advise parents.

Future Scope

Since, in future, free treatment as well as diagnosis will have to be provided by the school medical service, a considerable increase in the medical and nursing staff will be necessary. Adequate premises, suitably located, so that all school children have convenient access to clinics, will have to be established. It is possible, of course, that the work of the school medical service may be linked to that of new health centres, distributed throughout the town.

3. School Meals and Milk

Provisions Before the War

In 1906, powers were given to local education authorities to provide meals for children "unable by reason of lack of food to take full advantage of the education provided for them".[19] Until 1939 only children from the lowest income groups were entitled to receive free meals. Since, therefore, the stigma of charity was attached to this essential service, many parents refused to accept the offer of free meals for their children. In 1933, about one-third of the 1,715 children recommended for the first time for free meals did not have them for this reason. An additional group of children was not considered to be sufficiently poor to receive free meals. Consequently, only one half of the children found to be in need of extra nutrition in 1933, were in fact provided with free meals. As conditions of employment improved, fewer free meals were provided; in 1935, for example, only 277 children were newly recommended: forty-two of these were disqualified on grounds of income, and only about half of the remainder accepted the offer of free meals.

Numbers Receiving Meals and Milk Now

During the war, about one-third of the elementary school population and slightly more, i.e. two-fifths, of the secondary school children had school meals, either paid for or free. About three-quarters of the elementary school population had milk at school. When parents are unable to pay for school meals and milk, their children can obtain them free on the basis of the school attendance officer's reports on family income. Since food rationing has been introduced, and more mothers go out to work, there is less reluctance to accept free meals, although a modified form of a means test is still applied. Hence, at the present time, the proportion of children having meals at school does not vary significantly between the poor and the more prosperous parts of the town. A number of temporary kitchens have been erected in school playgrounds, and the children have their dinner in their school building.

In future, the provision of school meals is likely to be altered and extended. Proposals have been made to supplement family allowances by providing meals and milk free of charge for all school children. Irrespective of these proposals, the Middlesbrough education authority are planning to supply meals for 75·0 per cent. of all school children in the near future. Hence it will not only be necessary to build more school kitchens, but each school will also have to be equipped with an adequate dining-room.

4. Nursery Schools and Classes

Since a considerable number of mothers have taken up work during the war, daytime institutional care of children under compulsory school age had to be provided by both the health and education departments. The war-time nurseries are administered by the health department, but the education department has also tried to meet the problem by organising nursery classes in some of the elementary schools for children of four to five years. The schools on the new housing estates have nursery classes and so have several schools in the centre of the town. In a number of cases, it was not possible to accommodate these classes in the school buildings, and temporary huts were erected in the school playgrounds. Because of the shortage of staff, the local education authority have appointed a number of fourteen-year-old girls who have just left school as helpers, both for the children under five and also for some of the infant departments.

The erection of huts in school playgrounds to house nursery classes cannot be more than an emergency measure. The establishment of more permanent premises and of training facilities for teachers and helpers is essential, especially as the provision of nursery schools and classes is promised in the Education Act of 1944.

5. The Care of Delinquent, Neglected and Derelict Children

Powers of Local Education Authority

Since the Children and Young Persons Act of 1933, the supervision of delinquent children has been partially in the hands of the local education authority who now administer the Remand Home and do most of the preliminary work connected with the committal of children to approved schools. At the same time, the care of derelict and neglected children was transferred from the poor law guardians to the local education authority, who also received powers to arrange for the adoption of children.[20] It is now the responsibility of the child welfare department to find suitable persons to adopt, or to act as foster-parents to, neglected or derelict children who are not accommodated in the Children's Home.

Residential Care of Children

There are four institutions, either public or private, for the residential care of children who cannot live with their parents:

RESIDENTIAL INSTITUTIONS FOR THE CARE OF CHILDREN IN 1944

Name of Institution	Administering Authority	No. of Children who can be accommodated	Ages of Children	Sex of Children
1 Broomlands Home	Local Education Authority	72	3–15 years	B & G
2 Holgate Institution	Social Welfare Committee	20	6 months to 3 years	B & G
3 Nazareth House	R. C. Church	150	2–18 years	G
4 Holy Rood Home	C. of E.	21	0–15 years	B & G
Total . .		263		

Broomlands Home and Holgate Institution were formerly the Poor Law institutions for the Cleveland Poor Law Union. They still take cases from the Cleveland District outside Middlesbrough.

Broomlands, the Children's Home, is now under the administration of the local education authority. It is run on the cottage home principle, with six small houses, each accommodating twelve children who are looked after by a "foster-mother". The home is filled to capacity. Apart from the garden and asphalt yards surrounding these houses, there are no facilities for recreation, no workshops, playing fields and no hall where the children could meet together. A building, formerly used as a children's hospital, stands in the grounds, but is now requisitioned. After the war, it could be converted into workshops and playrooms for the children.

The home is hardly large enough for the number of children needing accommodation. Moreover, since the premises are inadequate at the present time, it is impossible to separate children according to the type of care they require. Children whose parents have been sent to prison for neglecting them are in the same "house" with others who are only temporary inmates while their mothers are in hospital.

The part of Holgate institution which is now used to accommodate young children is rather badly equipped. There are two fairly large wards with cots in them, and there is also a garden which gets very little sun. Alternative premises are being prepared.

The former casuals ward, a small house in the grounds of the Institution, which is more pleasant and convenient than the old premises, is being reconditioned.

Nazareth House, a large mansion, is a Roman Catholic orphanage for girls, run by a sisterhood of nuns. Girls come to the home from all parts of the Roman Catholic diocese, which covers a wide region, including Hull. Some girls are placed in the home by the local authority. Classes are held on the premises.

The Holy Rood Home in Marton Road is run by a sisterhood of Anglo-Catholic nuns, who were formerly in charge of North Ormesby Hospital. As the local authority contributes a considerable proportion of the income of the home, and also places children there, the maternity and child welfare department have powers of inspection.

The institutional care of children who cannot live at home with their parents should receive further attention in the future. The stigma of poor relief and charity lies heavily on the existing homes. It is not only the poorest and most neglected children who may need residential accommodation, although they should, of course, have priority. If illness, death or other disturbing events occur, it may often be preferable for children to be temporarily separated from their families. But this cannot be done successfully unless different methods of care are applied to children who come from different types of homes.

6. Child and Juvenile Employment

Child Employment

The Education Act of 1918 gave local education authorities the power to control the employment of children under fourteen years of age. Paid child employment had to be licensed and a strict control of hours of work was enforced. The supervision of child employment was undertaken by the school attendance officers. The standard age at which a child might be employed was raised from twelve to thirteen years through a local bye-law in 1937.

The Juvenile Employment Bureau

The Juvenile Employment Bureau in Middlesbrough is housed in the education department, although it operates under the Ministry of Labour. Every term, head teachers send in reports on all school leavers and make recommendations for their future careers.

7. School Attendance Officers

Their Functions

In connection with all these services to promote the health and welfare of children and young persons, the functions of the school attendance officers have been greatly expanded. They act as interpreters between the education office and the parents. Nowadays, they are no longer merely concerned with enforcing school attendance. It is also their duty to investigate the need for, and to inform parents about, particular child welfare services.

Hence, in Middlesbrough, the proportion of visits made by school attendance officers for other reasons than school attendance increased from 1·0 per cent. in 1930 to 12·0 per cent. of all visits in 1938. These other reasons for visits are the registration of deaf and defective children, the employment of young persons, and the provision of free meals. In addition, investigations into the case histories of all children summoned to appear before a court are undertaken by the school attendance officers, who are also required to accompany children to approved and residential special schools. Since the war their job has become even more exacting. The dispersal of families and the general increase in child welfare services, such as school meals, have burdened them with new duties. At the same time, there has been only an insignificant increase in staff, from six officers in 1934 to eight in 1944, and the level of qualifications required has not been raised either. As a result, it has been exceedingly difficult for them to carry out all these varied functions efficiently during the war.

The "School Bobby"

It is not surprising, therefore, that the name of "School Bobby" is still applied to the school attendance officers, and that in the poorer districts of the town their visits are not always welcomed. To some extent this may bc due to the fact that no special qualifications are required for this post. In consequence, the men who take up this important office are not always capable of handling the rather intimate family problems with which they are confronted every day.

8. The Need for Premises and Staff

The objectives and provisions of child welfare are likely to expand. It is, therefore, important that these services are not restricted for want of suitable premises and that they are, furthermore, properly interpreted to the parents. In a town like Middlesbrough, which has a high proportion of children who come from poor homes, a particular effort should be made to overcome the parents' suspicion and ignorance of public services. Otherwise, the provisions for child welfare will lose much of their value and may not touch the very households which need them most.

IV

THE SCHOOL ENVIRONMENT IN DIFFERENT DISTRICTS OF THE TOWN

1. Elementary Schools

The School Population

In 1944, the elementary schools in Middlesbrough provide education for all but a very small number of children between the ages of five and eleven years[21] and for two-thirds of the pupils over eleven years of age who attend schools administered by the local education authority. The remainder of this age-group receive higher education in secondary, central and technical schools. The total number of children receiving elementary education is just under 20,000.[22] Pupils are distributed over 28 schools which have altogether 68 separate departments.

The Average Standard of School Environment

The average equipment of elementary schools in Middlesbrough is certainly inadequate for present-day needs. There is, on an average, less than one hall for each department and there is only one additional room, including play-rooms, practical rooms and gymnasia, for three departments. Education is still rather undifferentiated. Furthermore, two-thirds of the elementary population do not attend a playing field at all.

The average level of school environment in Middlesbrough is so low because the majority of schools are completely out-of-date. They have not even reached this level, which has only lately been raised by the building of some of the new schools in the inter-war period. But since most of these new schools are in the outer residential ring, only the children in that part of the town have, as yet, profited from the introduction of modern standards.

As a result, the variations in the school environment of the different districts of Middlesbrough are striking. They are visible even at first sight. The modern schools on the outskirts are spacious, light and airy,[23] while the older schools are on narrow sites, and are dark, often poorly ventilated, grimy and bleak. For instance, in one of these schools, classrooms are lit by skylights only; in others, windows are about six feet from the floor. Eight schools have no halls at all, and it is not always possible for even one department to assemble together in one room. In some cases, where halls exist, other accommodation is so cramped that one part of the hall is being used as a class-room, while tables are being laid for dinner at the other end. Sanitary and washing arrangements are primitive in several of these schools; only cold water is laid on. Their playgrounds are small asphalted yards, on which air raid shelters have been erected. The nearest communal playing fields are at a distance of $\frac{3}{4}$ of a mile to $1\frac{3}{4}$ miles from the school buildings and are, therefore, often not used at all.

In fact, these old schools have the worst of everything: old structures which are often in poor repair, a serious lack of equipment, a small site area, and they do not even have easy access to other ancillary facilities and playing fields in the town. Moreover, they are all concentrated in the poorer areas of Middlesbrough, where houses are dense and often blighted, where the air is smoke polluted and where there are not even any trees or green patches to relieve the picture of urban squalor. Not only the school environment, but also the home environment, of the children attending these schools is the poorest in the town.

Index of School Environment

From initial visits to schools and observations in their neighbourhoods, it is thus evident that the standard of school environment in the different districts of Middlesbrough is related to the level of home environment. Since hardly any new school building has taken place in the old northern districts, the worst schools are there, and we find that schools standards improve gradually as we move from the parts which are intermediate, both in terms of age and geographical location, to the outer residential ring which has only recently been opened up.

In order to check these observations and to obtain a more precise reading of the variations in school environment, four indices were used and applied to each school. They are:

(*a*) The average number of classes per age-group.[24]
(*b*) The number of halls per department.
(*c*) The number of additional rooms, including gymnasia, play-rooms, practical rooms, laboratories, per department.
(*d*) The proportion of the total number of pupils on roll who attend a playing field.

The standard of each school, in terms of these four aspects, was contrasted with the average standard of all Middlesbrough schools. The addition of the four resulting index numbers provided the general index of school environment for individual schools. In the same way, when all schools in a given district were considered together, the district index of school environment was obtained.

In order to facilitate the reading of these index numbers, they were divided into five categories, ranging from "one", denoting the worst schools, to "five", denoting the best schools.

Schools or areas ranking as "one" or "two" are below the average standard of educational facilities in Middlesbrough. In fact, the rank of "one" indicates that schools are out of date to such an extent that they cannot possibly be reconstructed. The rank of "three" is equivalent to the average for Middlesbrough which, however, must be regarded as rather low, in terms of recent requirements. Only the rank of "five", well above the average for Middlesbrough, indicates that school facilities are definitely up to date.

Variations in School Environment

Table 2 is a summary of the results obtained through the application of the indices of school environment.[25] The majority of schools are either completely out-of-date so that they cannot be reconstructed, or definitely sub-standard. Just under half of the total elementary school population attend these schools. Only just over a quarter of all the pupils have a school environment which can be regarded as being up-to-date.

EDUCATION : TABLE 2—VARIATIONS IN SCHOOL ENVIRONMENT : NUMBER OF ELEMENTARY SCHOOLS AND PROPORTION OF PUPILS IN EACH CATEGORY

Index of School Environment		Number of Schools in Each Category	Proportion of School Population in Each Category
Rating	Classification	Number	%
1	Completely out-of-date	8	22·0
2	Sub-standard	9	22·5
3	Partly sub-standard	5	28·5
4	Fairly up-to-date	4	15·5
5	Completely up-to-date	2	11·5
	Total	28	100·0

District Variations

Moreover, the children attending the worst schools are con-

EDUCATION : TABLE 3

SCHOOL ENVIRONMENT AND DISTRIBUTION OF THE ELEMENTARY SCHOOL POPULATION IN DIFFERENT DISTRICTS OF MIDDLESBROUGH

District		Number of Elementary Schools	Dates of Opening of School Buildings	Index of School Environment		Proportion of Total Elementary School Population
			(Dates of extensions are shown in brackets)	Area Average :		
No.	Name	No.		Index No.	Rating	%
I	St. Hilda's	3	1869 ; 1873 ; 1876	43·0	1	5·4
II	Cannon and Newport	4	1869 ; 1873 ; (1906 and 1916) ; 1874 ; 1906	47·5	1	14·1
III	Vulcan and Exchange	2	1863 ; 1898	87·0	2	9·9
IV	North Ormesby and Cargo Fleet	4	1876 ; 1878 ; 1885 (1896) ; 1909	62·0	2	12·2
V	Cleveland, Acklam, Ayresome*	6	1885 (1906) ; 1902 (1907) ; 1906 ; 1913 ; 1938	77·0	2	25·6
VI	North of Albert Park	2	1892 ; 1927	107·0	3	5·0
VII	Marton Grove Housing Estate	3	1927 ; 1928 ; 1934	125·0	4	11·5
VIII	Brambles Farm Housing Estate	1	1935	160·0	4	3·9
IX	Whinney Banks Housing Estate	2	1935 ; 1938	365·0	5	9·4
X	Linthorpe	1	1871 (1912)	172·5	4	3·0
	ALL MIDDLESBROUGH	28	—	100·0	3	100·0

* One of the schools in this area, Newport Road, now shares its premises with St. Paul's School, C. o E. Hence there are only five school buildings but six elementary schools in this area.

centrated in the most blighted wards, whilst the pupils of the new "perfect" schools live at the southern fringe of the town and on the new housing estates. In fact, as Tables 3 and 4 show, our initial observations are confirmed: the variations in school environment are associated with the variations in the general environmental conditions of the different districts of Middlesbrough.

Table 3 presents the index of school environment for each district, while Table 4 gives the actual figures on which the index is based.

Each of the ten districts shown on these tables is delimited not by ward boundaries but by school catchment areas, although the names of wards are used in several cases for convenience. Since school catchment areas do not coincide either with wards or neighbourhoods, specific school districts had to be used for the purpose of assessing the variations in school environment. Within most of these districts there is a considerable degree of social homogeneity.

EDUCATION : TABLE 4

DETAILS OF SCHOOL ENVIRONMENT IN DIFFERENT DISTRICTS OF MIDDLESBROUGH

District	No. of Classes per Age-Group No.	No. of Halls per Department No.	No. of Additional Rooms per Department No.	Proportion of Pupils Attending Playing Field %
I	1·20	0·14	0·14	8·00
II	1·20	0·40	0·00	14·60
III	1·10	0·80	0·30	13·60
IV	1·60	0·25	0·00	34·00
V	1·20	1·00	0·06	17·60
VI	1·25	0·75	0·50	18·40
VII	1·90	1·00	0·14	55·00
VIII	2·75	1·00	0·00	100·00
IX	2·00	1·00	2·80	79·00
X	2·25	1·50	0·00	100·00
All Middlesbrough:	1·50	0·70	0·31	34·00

The Ten Districts

To interpret these tables, some details about each of the ten districts should be recalled. They can be identified most easily by reference to the four major areas of Middlesbrough which have been previously described.[26]

Districts I to IV are roughly coincident with Middlesbrough's major area I, the poor northern wards.

Districts V and VI are largely equivalent to the major area III, the geographically and socially intermediate wards.

The new housing estates, districts VII to IX, form the major area II.

District X, Linthorpe, is slightly smaller than the major area IV, the prosperous southern wards.

The social and environmental characteristics of each of these four district groups correspond to those of the major areas, although the boundaries of both types of sub-divisions are not entirely coincident.

Playing Fields

The pattern of socio-geographical differentiation in Middlesbrough, broadly represented by these ten districts, is not blurred but rather accentuated by the corresponding variations in school environment.

For instance, all the children who had moved from the slum clearance area, St. Hilda's, to the Brambles Farm estate now use playing fields, while only 8·0 per cent. of those who remained behind do so. Less than 15·0 per cent. of the pupils from the blighted area II, Cannon and Newport, use a playing field, as compared with 100·0 per cent. of those in the select southern part of Linthorpe.

The major reason for this discrepancy is that all the school playing fields are at the outskirts of the town. Hence only the newer elementary schools in those areas have adjacent fields, and thus their infants and juniors as well as their seniors have the opportunity of using them.[27] In principle, infants aged five to seven years do not use a playing field, unless there is one adjacent to the school; juniors go once a week for forty minutes, but only if their schools are within walking distance of the field; while, in theory, all seniors use a playing field once a week for forty minutes, regardless of distance. This principle implies that none of the infants and hardly any of the juniors in the densely built-up areas have the chance to attend one of the two communal fields. Indeed, as these are already used to full capacity, there is hardly any space left for juniors, and even the ruling that all seniors must go cannot be adhered to.[28]

The teachers are trying to give their pupils more opportunities for recreation by arranging games and matches after school hours. But the inequality between the school environment of the densely built and of the newly developed districts is too great to be bridged merely by such voluntary efforts.

Swimming Baths

The provision and distribution of other ancillary facilities is also deficient. There is only one swimming bath in the town, in the heart of the old northern area, although it is a part of the curriculum that children in the oldest age group of the junior departments should attend a swimming bath, at least once a week for twenty minutes. Since space is inadequate, each child is allowed only a short period of swimming during school hours. Moreover, two-thirds of all pupils, those from districts V and VI to X, have to travel a distance from three-quarters of a mile to two miles to the swimming bath.[29]

Domestic Science and Handicraft Centres

The teaching of handicrafts and domestic science is included only in the curriculum of the senior departments. The boys attend one of the four centres for handicrafts, the girls one of the five centres for domestic science. All the former are in the larger and newer schools, on the southern side of the town, so that the boys in the North are in this respect also at a considerable disadvantage. Domestic science, however, is also being taught in St. Hilda's ward, in the hundred year old building of the first elementary school in Middlesbrough, which is now being used for this purpose, as well as in two other of the northern and in two of the more modern schools. Children attend these centres for an entire morning or afternoon per week. The distance is considerable for many of them, both the senior boys and girls from North Ormesby, for instance, have to travel 1¾ miles to their classes. Neither before the war nor now has free transport been provided for them.

Planning Proposals

Even before the survey results were available, it was recognised that the schools in the poorest and most blighted areas are completely unfit for further use. In fact, the preliminary proposals of the Director of Education are confirmed, by and large, by the ranking of the individual schools derived from the index of school environment. According to the final proposals, which are based on this survey, and which are stated in the Middlesbrough Plan,[30] ten schools in the northern districts I to VI should be closed, and in all but one case their present sites should be abandoned. Only two of the ten remaining school buildings in that part of the town are not in immediate need of thorough reconstruction or extension. Playing field acreage will have to be increased throughout the town. Even most of the schools on the outskirts, in districts VII to X, are considered to require extensions, chiefly for recreation and for the establishment of nursery classes. The building of new primary schools, and the transfer of present senior departments to new secondary schools will facilitate the reorganisation of Middlesbrough's education services.

2. POVERTY PROBLEMS

The improvement of the school environment alone will not establish equality of opportunity for the children from the different districts of the town. Unfit houses and unfit schools must be cleared together. Special services must be created to counteract the impact of poverty on the health and school attendance of the Middlesbrough children.

The high incidence of head infestations at the present time is a striking example of the ineffectiveness of piece-meal reconstruction. The complaint occurs mainly in the poorest and most blighted districts; the greatest concentration is in Cannon and Newport. However, uncleanliness is not confined to the old part of the town. A considerable proportion of the children on the Brambles Farm estate, which is notable for its poverty, suffer from it also.[31] In fact, if we compare the distribution of head infestations of school children with the distribution of other indices, such as age, rateable value and density of houses, and incomes of chief wage earners, the close relationship between poverty and "uncleanliness" is apparent, and it is clear, moreover, that this complaint is not due to bad housing alone. If families who have moved from the slums to the new estates, and who often have many children, can only spend a small part of their incomes on clothing and on the upkeep of the new home, it is not surprising that poverty diseases are still common among them. Furthermore, particularly on Brambles Farm, adequate facilities for shopping and recreation are lacking. Hence the tenants not only have an increased expenditure on fares, but they also tend to become indifferent towards their new environment.

The high incidence of head infestations in Middlesbrough is especially serious since it interferes with the general improvement of the health of school children.[32] The staff of the school medical service have to spend so high a proportion of their time in dealing with this complaint that many of their other duties have to be neglected. About four times a year the school nurses conduct special examinations of all school children to discover the incidence of uncleanliness and to keep careful records of all cases, although at the moment effective treatment is not possible. More than a third of all school children were found to be verminous at the last examination, but only a small proportion were, in fact, cleansed.[33] But the complaint cannot be eradicated without disinfesting all the family's clothes, their household goods and the dwelling itself. Even that is not sufficient, for such a widespread condition, which results from general environmental deficiencies, cannot be cured by piecemeal methods.

School Attendance

Irregular school attendance is also related to poverty. Since poor children are prone to frequent attacks of sickness, and often have to stay at home to help their mothers, the incidence of school absences tends to be especially high among them. These poor children can ill afford further interruptions in school attendance; they have already lost much time through evacuation, the closing of schools during the early months of the war, and through air attacks in 1940 and 1941. All these specific difficulties have affected the northern poor areas of the town far more than the remainder.[34]

Extracts from the school attendance returns from March 1943 to March 1944 show the average monthly proportion of all absences for each school and each district and also the proportion of "avoidable" absences, that is, those which are not due to illness. The schools in the poorest parts of the town have the highest proportion of all absences, and they also tend to have the highest proportion of avoidable absences. For instance, in the schools in district II, Cannon and Newport, which had the highest total absence rate, only 85·0 per cent. of all pupils were, on an average, in attendance, and almost half of the absentees were kept away through avoidable reasons.[35]

However, the monthly returns can be used only as an indication of trends. To interpret them, a detailed investigation of reasons for absences for the first 200 school sessions in 1944 was undertaken. Only a selected group of schools could be covered so that the results are not entirely conclusive. They indicate that absences are far more frequent among seniors than either among juniors or infants, and that the attendance records of senior girls are even worse than those of senior boys. Half of all absences of senior girls and more than two-thirds of all absences of senior boys remain unexplained. The parents had given no reasons, and the school attendance officers were often unable to contact them. In any case, attempts to investigate these cases are fairly rare. It is, therefore, likely that the incidence of avoidable absences is greater than it appears from the official attendance returns. From the reasons for absences given, and also from interviews with head teachers, it is clear that girls between the ages of eleven to fourteen are frequently kept away from school to do housework, to look after the younger children, or else to run errands.

School attendance is relevant to the attainment of educational equality. The older girls in the poorer areas who are kept away from school to help at home cannot easily reach the standard of their contemporaries in other areas of the town, or even that of the boys who are their class-mates. These girls might not be diverted from school if their mothers had more assistance in their daily job, if day-nurseries, nursery schools and home helps were available, and if shops were conveniently located, particularly on the new estates. Absences which are now regarded as "unavoidable", because they are due to sickness, could be reduced through improved housing conditions, proper nutrition and stricter supervision of the health of the school population. In fact, without the rebuilding of homes and neighbourhoods, the new education services, which are being planned, will be incomplete.

3. HIGHER EDUCATION[36]

Distribution of Pupils

Poverty problems affect the children who attend elementary schools; those who receive higher education come mainly from the newer and more well-to-do areas of the town. They are about a third of the total school population over 11 years of age. Three-quarters of them live in the outer residential ring, in the neighbourhoods of new private and municipal housing development. Only a few children from the poorest wards attend central, technical or secondary schools at the present time.[37]

School Environment

The school environment of the pupils in higher education compares also, on the whole, favourably with that of the children in elementary schools. All the five schools for higher education, which are administered by the local education authority, are equipped with halls and additional practical rooms or laboratories. All pupils attend playing fields though some of these are rather inconveniently located. There are, however, considerable variations in the structure and equipment of the individual schools.

EDUCATION: TABLE 5

AGE AND EQUIPMENT OF L.E.A. SCHOOLS FOR HIGHER EDUCATION

Name of School	Date of Opening	No. of Pupils March 1944	No. of Halls	No. of Laboratories, Practical Rooms, Libraries, etc.	Distance of School from Playing Field in Miles
Boys' High School	1877	398	1	12	1¾
Girls' High School	1877	356	1	4	1½
Acklam Hall Boys' Secondary School	1935	338	3	10	0
Kirby Girls' Secondary School	1911	410	2	5	0
Sub-total	—	1,502	7	31	—
Hugh Bell Central School	1907	609	3	15	1¼
Junior Technical School (Premises built in 1892)	1919	244			1¾
Grand Total	—	2,355	10	46	—

The two old school buildings in the northern area, the High School with separate boys' and girls' departments, and Hugh Bell Central School, which shares its premises with the Junior Technical School, are definitely inferior to the two more recent secondary schools in the south, Acklam Hall for boys, and Kirby School for girls. The High School buildings are out of date. On three sides, they are surrounded by residential and commercial buildings; on the fourth side, they back on to the Technical College. There is no room for playing fields, and indeed there is no room for further expansion on this site.[38]

The building used by both the Central and the Technical School, which is over fifty years old, covers a whole block in the midst of the densely built-up northern area. Although the two schools use the same premises, there is a strict division between them. Their pupils use playing fields at the outskirts of the town.

The two more up-to-date secondary schools are right at the border of town and countryside. They both have adjacent playing fields and are surrounded by additional open spaces. Acklam Hall is in an even more favourable position than Kirby School, and it is also rather better equipped, although before 1935 the main part of the building was an 18th century country residence. But practical rooms and halls have been built on at the back of the old mansion.[39]

Method of Entry into Higher Education

At present, the central and secondary schools are recruited through the general scholarship examination which is being held annually in all the elementary schools in the town, and which has been continued throughout the war years.[40] The children who pass the examination are divided, as a result of enquiries into the incomes of their families, into fee payers and "special place" pupils. All the children who pass the examination and for whom fees can be paid go to one of the secondary schools; those for whom fees cannot be paid go either to a secondary school or to the Central School, according to merit. Children who are offered places for secondary education can usually choose a school. The 1943 results show that Acklam Hall and Kirby School are definitely preferred to the High School.[41]

The Technical School is entered by means of an examination taken at the age of twelve years by boys in senior elementary departments. Boys remain at the Technical School until the age of fifteen and a half and are strongly recommended to continue their technical education through attending part-time courses after having left school.

Future Provision of Secondary Education

In future, secondary education will no longer be selective but universal. But the task of providing merely the physical framework of the new system is enormous in a town like Middlesbrough where so many school premises are obsolete. Less than half of the pupils who now receive higher education are in schools which are fairly up-to-date. The proportion of senior elementary school pupils in fairly adequate premises is far lower still; less than one-tenth of the total number have now a satisfactory school environ-

EDUCATION : TABLE 6

SECONDARY SCHOOL ACCOMMODATION REQUIRED

Present Type of Education	Present Number of Pupils				Approx. No. of New Places Required for Raising of School Leaving Age to 15	Total Number of Places Required
	In Fairly Adequate Schools	In Schools Requiring Reconstruction	In Obsolete Schools	Present Total		
	No.	No.	No.	No.	No.	No.
Higher Education	1,260	—	1,607	2,867	—	—
Senior Elementary Education	515	2,800	2,238	5,553	—	—
Total Number	1,775	2,800	3,845	8,420	2,800	11,220
Total Per Cent.	16·0	25·0	34·0	75·0	25·0	100·0

ment. Half of all seniors are in schools which require extensive reconstruction; two-fifths are in schools which will have to be demolished. Most of these schools do not even have separate senior departments, they have not been reorganised.[42] Even the fairly satisfactory senior elementary and secondary schools will require additions to meet the new standards. Moreover, there is not only the problem of obsolescence. The raising of the school-leaving age to fifteen years implies that the present school population of senior age-groups will be increased by about one-third.[43]

Therefore, if we assume that the size of the relevant age-groups will remain fairly constant in the immediate post-war years, we find that only about a sixth of the approximate number of secondary school places required are, in fact, immediately available. Accommodation for almost 60·0 per cent. of all secondary school pupils will have to be newly built, firstly, in order to replace obsolete schools; secondly, in order to implement the raising of the school leaving age. A fourth of all places are in schools which require extensive reconstruction. Consequently it has been estimated that, even if the utmost use is made of existing premises, seventeen new secondary schools will still be needed.[44]

A building programme of such magnitude is bound to have considerable repercussions. First of all, it will facilitate the re-organisation of primary schools. But even more important, if properly related to controlled population shifts within the town, it can transform the physical pattern of Middlesbrough. A group of four secondary schools requires a total site area of about 68 acres. Such large groups, with their varied buildings and open spaces, can be used as green wedges, linking the town with the country-side. Smaller groups of schools, distributed throughout the present densely populated areas, will introduce new amenities there.

But the building programme alone will not transform the social pattern of the town. At present, the cleavage between the two Middlesbroughs is perpetuated by the highly selective system of secondary education. And in the transition period, when the Act is being implemented, there may be a tendency to assume that the allocation of pupils to the new grammar, technical and modern schools will be proportionate to the present distribution between secondary, technical and senior elementary schools. Such a policy would imply that entrance to a grammar school would be as restricted and as highly competitive as it is now. Thus the new grammar school would inherit the superior social position of the present secondary school, and it would, in fact, help to maintain the existing social inequalities. To carry out the chief objective of the Education Act, it is essential to establish from the outset a considerably greater number of places in grammar schools than exist in the present secondary schools. The provision of multilateral schools, in which all three branches of the new secondary education are represented, and which facilitate the transfer of pupils from one to another, might help to obliterate the traditional differences in status.

V

EDUCATIONAL OPPORTUNITY IN DIFFERENT DISTRICTS OF THE TOWN

1. Variations in the Educational Standards of Elementary Schools

The present selectiveness of higher education is fully apparent when we consider the results of the scholarship examination in individual schools. The results of the 1942 and of the 1943 examinations have been analysed and as the picture is substantially the same in both these years, it is clear that the wide variations between the performance of individual schools and areas cannot be due to spurious causes.

Comparison of 1942 and 1943 Examination Results

On an average, there has been a slight improvement from 1942 to 1943. The number of children taking the examination, the number passing it and entering higher education, was proportionately slightly greater in the latter year.[45]

	1942	1943
	%	%
Proportion of 11–12 Year Age-Group Taking Examination . . .	92·0	93·0
Proportion of Those Taking Examination Who Passed . . .	20·5	22·5
Proportion of 11–12 Year Age-Group Who Entered Central and Secondary Schools	16·5	17·5

The improvement was not equally shared by all schools. In some of the badly equipped schools in the poorer districts, even fewer children entered the examination and fewer passed it in 1943 than in 1942; in other schools of this kind, the relevant proportions were equally low in both years. In two of the schools in the blighted district II (Cannon and Newport), for instance, no children passed the examination at all in either year. Improvement was most marked in the intermediate and newer parts of the town. In

Brambles School, for instance, on the new housing estate, 95·0 per cent. of the 11–12 year age-group sat for the examination in 1943, as compared with 88·0 per cent. in the preceding year, and almost every fourth child who took the examination passed it, as compared with every tenth in 1942. The improvement which was noticeable in 1943 was, therefore, so selective that it accentuated rather than obliterated the previous differences between the examination results of individual schools and districts.

Relation between Turnout and Performance

There was in both years a fairly close relationship between turn-out and performance. The schools in which only a comparatively small proportion of the relevant age-group participated in the examination were further characterised by the fact that few, if any, of the participants passed. Vice versa, a comparatively high turn-out for the examination was associated with a high proportion of successful results. Thus not a single child passed the examination in one of the schools which has been mentioned already and which, in 1943, had the lowest turn-out of all, i.e. 67·0 per cent. of the 11–12 year age-group. But Linthorpe school, which, in 1943, was on the top of the list for examination turn-out, since all but 1·0 per cent. of the eligible pupils participated, had also the best performance of all; 71·0 per cent. were, in fact, successful in the 1943 examination.

Reasons for Variations in Examination Turn-out

The wide variations between the examination turn-out of individual schools can fairly easily be explained. The incidence of absences from school is particularly high in the ill-equipped schools in the poorer districts. Moreover, it is unlikely that teachers would encourage backward children to sit for the scholarship examination, and as the schooling of many of these children has been interrupted during the war, it is probable that a higher proportion of children in these schools are considered backward than in the better equipped schools in the newer areas. And finally, parents in the poorer districts might be less anxious, for economic reasons, for their children to sit for the examination and if successful, to enter higher education than those in the more prosperous parts of the town. The last assumption is supported by the fact that non-acceptances of places offered for higher education are particularly frequent in those schools in which both turn-out for, and performance at, the examination are on a low level.[46]

Reasons for Variations of Performance

It is far more difficult to account for the even wider variations between the performance of the different schools at the examination. The assumption that these might be due to differences in intelligence is not very plausible in view of the fact that the range of variations is so very great: in three schools not a single child passed, whilst in four schools from 32·0 per cent. to 71·0 per cent. of all the children who sat for the examination were successful. Moreover, there is a definite pattern of variations. All the schools with the lowest record both for turn-out and performance are in the poorest districts; vice versa the schools with comparatively good records are in the newer and more prosperous parts of the town. Can we really assume that there is so close a correlation between intelligence and social status and, furthermore, that the consequent differences in intelligence are as great as shown by these results?

Educational Standards and School Environment

Before this assumption is followed up, it is worthwhile to observe the pattern of variations more closely. It is striking at first sight that the schools with the lowest record both of examination turn-out and performance also have the lowest rating for school environment, according to the indices previously employed. In fact, if schools are grouped according to their performance at the 1943 scholarship examination, the close relation, firstly, between examination turn-out and results, and secondly between performance and the level of school environment, is evident.

Educational Standards and Social Status

As, in Middlesbrough, the level of school environment is, in turn, related to that of home environment, it is not possible to establish precisely whether either conditions at home or at school influence examination results more effectively.[47] The particular importance of school environment is illustrated by the fact that in those districts where the physical standards of homes are alike, but where schools differ in equipment, examination results vary accordingly.[48] But in most parts of the town, the influence of home and school work in the same direction and reinforce each other.

However, not in all parts of the town is a comparatively good home environment, in terms of physical standards, also indicative of a comparatively high social status. The parents of the children

EDUCATION: TABLE 7

ELEMENTARY SCHOOLS, GROUPED ACCORDING TO THEIR PERFORMANCE IN THE 1943 SCHOLARSHIP EXAMINATION, BY EXAMINATION TURN-OUT AND SCHOOL ENVIRONMENT

Groups of Schools	Performance in Scholarship Examination: Proportion of Pupils Taking Examination Who Pass	No. of Schools in Each Group	Examination Turnout: Proportion of 11–12 Year Age Group Taking Examination	School Environment	
				Average Index No. for Each Group of Schools	Rating
	%	No.	%	No.	No.
I	0·0	3	78·0	43	1
II	3·0— 8·3	6	92·0	53	2
III	11·0—19·0	5	93·0	64	2
IV	21·5—30·0	7	96·0	107	3
V	32·0—71·0	4	97·0	238	5
TOTAL	21·5	25	93·0	100	3

on the new housing estates are on the same income level and follow the same occupations as the parents of the children in the slum-clearance areas from which they themselves have come. But as their children have exchanged a new house and school for the old blighted dwelling and unfit classrooms, their performance at the examination is incomparably better than that of the children who are left behind. There is no doubt that, other conditions being equal, improvements in the physical standards of home and school environment can produce a fairly rapid improvement in educational attainments.[49]

But even the children on the new housing estates have not had such excellent examination results as those in Linthorpe, the most prosperous district. Results for the elementary school in Linthorpe, and for the private and preparatory schools there, are the best in the town, even exceeding those of the two most up-to-date schools on the housing estates. Although the children on the new estates have a better school environment, the fact that their social status is inferior to that of the Linthorpe children appears to have been decisive.

By and large, therefore, the differences in educational attainment are associated, either directly or indirectly, with social inequalities. In the poorest areas of the town, where both home and school environment is totally inadequate, examination results are

EDUCATION : TABLE 8

RESULTS OF THE 1943 SCHOLARSHIP EXAMINATION IN ELEMENTARY SCHOOLS IN DIFFERENT DISTRICTS OF MIDDLESBROUGH*

Schools in Districts		Scholarship Examination				School Environment	
		Turnout: Proportion of 11–12 Year Age-Group Taking Examination	*Performance:* Proportion of Those Taking Examination Who Passed	*Higher Education*†: Proportion of Those Taking Examination Who Went Into: (*a*) L.E.A. Central and Secondary Schools	(*b*) L.E.A. Secondary Schools only	Index Number	Rating
		%	%	%	%	No.	No.
I and II	St. Hilda's, Cannon and Newport	85·0	3·3	1·5	0·8	48	1
III and IV	Vulcan, Exchange, North Ormesby, Cargo Fleet	94·0	20·5	18·6	9·2	69	2
V and VI	Cleveland, Acklam, Ayresome, North of Albert Park	97·0	21·0	18·4	8·3	80	2
VII, VIII, IX	The Municipal Housing Estates	94·0	27·0	22·5	13·2	211	5
X	Linthorpe	99·0	71·0	62·5	56·0	172	4
All Middlesbrough		93·0	21·5	18·5	10·6	100	3

* This table is based on the examination results in elementary schools only. A further 35 children of the scholarship age-group were in the Preparatory and Private Schools. All but one of those sat for the examination, and 80 per cent. passed.

† The proportion of children entering secondary schools from the outer residential ring is slightly higher than shown on this and the subsequent table. About 2·0 per cent. of those sitting for the examination refused central school places and had the intention of entering secondary schools as fee payers instead.

worst. Where the association between poverty and blight is broken, and where up-to-date schools exist, as on the new estates, there is a marked improvement in performance. But the best results are obtained in the district which has not only the most comfortable, but also the most prosperous homes.

Table 8 shows clearly the socio-geographical pattern of variations in examination results. In considering it, the special position of the new housing estates should be borne in mind. The social status of their tenants is similar to that of the people in districts I and II, from which the majority have come. But the physical standards of home and school environment are far better than in any of the northern parts.

Intelligence and Opportunity

The assumption that the differences in examination results, as shown by Table 8, reflect differences in intelligence is certainly not strengthened after consideration of the factors involved. This assumption cannot explain why one of five children on the new estates now has the chance of receiving higher education, and one in eight, of entering secondary schools, as compared with one in 77, and one in 154 respectively, of the children in districts I and II, from which the majority of tenants on the new estates have come.[50] This amazing transformation, and the whole pattern of variations in educational attainments, reflect primarily inequalities of opportunity. Where homes are poor and schools are out-of-date, so that educational differentiation is impossible, children cannot have the same chance to develop their abilities as in a more spacious, more healthy and more varied environment.

2. Entrance to Higher Education

Even when a child from a poor home and a blighted area has sat for, and passed, the scholarship examination, its chance to enter a central or secondary school is further limited. Only children who come out on the top of the list are awarded places in secondary schools, regardless of whether they can pay fees or not. Those who have passed the examination not quite so well are offered places in the central school, and they can be transferred to secondary schools only if their parents are able to pay their fees. Hence many places in the central school are not accepted; the poorer children continue in elementary schools; the children from the more prosperous homes are transferred to secondary schools as fee payers.

EDUCATION : TABLE 9

DISTRIBUTION OF THE 11–12 YEAR AGE-GROUP AND OF THE CHILDREN ENTERING HIGHER EDUCATION IN DIFFERENT DISTRICTS OF MIDDLESBROUGH, 1943

	Schools in Districts	Proportion in Each Area of :			
		11–12 Year Age-Group	Children Passing Scholarship Examination	Children Entering:	
				L.E.A. Central and Secondary Schools	L.E.A. Secondary Schools only
		%	%	%	%
I and II	St. Hilda's, Cannon and Newport	20·0	3·0	1·5	1·3
III and IV	Vulcan, Exchange, North Ormesby, and Cargo Fleet	18·0	16·0	18·0	15·0
V and VI	Cleveland, Acklam, Ayresome, North of Albert Park	27·5	26·0	28·0	21·0
VII, VIII, and IX	The Municipal Housing Estates	29·0	35·0	35·0	35·0
X	Linthorpe :—				
	(*a*) Elementary School	4·0	14·0	14·5	22·2
	(*b*) Private and Preparatory School	1·5	6·0	3·0	5·5
	TOTAL PER CENT.	100·0	100·0	100·0	100·0
	TOTAL NUMBER	2,286	478	400	236

Consequently, entrance to secondary schools is even more restricted and socially selective than entrance to central schools.

Table 9 shows the final results of the present system of competitive entrance to higher education. One of five of all the Middlesbrough children between 11 and 12 years of age attend schools, and mostly live, in the poorest parts, St. Hilda's, Cannon and Newport. But only one in 77 of those entering secondary schools come from these districts. Vice versa, one in eighteen of the relevant age-group belong to prosperous Linthorpe, but more than one in four of all those entering secondary schools live there.

These figures tell the story so plainly that no comment is required. Social inequalities are perpetuated by educational inequalities. The gap between the opportunities of children from different districts and social groups is so wide that no time should be lost in bridging it.

VI

THE PLACE OF THE SCHOOL IN THE NEIGHBOURHOOD

In recent town planning theory, it has been suggested that the size of a "neighbourhood unit" should be based on the number of households from which the population of a primary school is derived. The primary school should be conveniently placed in relation to other neighbourhood services, shops, clinics and the community centre. In terms of this theory, the primary school is the focus of the neighbourhood unit. But the elementary school of to-day plays a far less important role in existing neighbourhoods.

Neighbourhood Boundaries and School Catchment Areas

At present, the catchment areas of elementary schools are only rarely coincident with the boundaries of neighbourhoods, that is, of distinct territorial groups. Only the schools in the isolated parts of the town draw their pupils almost entirely from the neighbourhoods in which they are located. The schools in St. Hilda's, which is cut off from the rest of the town by the railway, in North Ormesby and Lower Marton Grove are neighbourhood institutions in that way. The catchment areas of two schools in the central part of the town are also fairly closely related to their respective neighbourhoods. But, on the whole, the school is not yet an integral part of the neighbourhood; its sphere of influence is not related to that of other social institutions.[51]

The Location of Schools in Relation to Other Neighbourhood Services

The present hapazard location of schools is, in fact, largely responsible for this lack of integration. The position of schools is usually not related to that of churches, clubs, shops and clinics. Schools are frequently at the edge of neighbourhoods, at a considerable distance from other services which, in turn, are scattered. Even on the new housing estates, which are the only examples of controlled development in Middlesbrough, the schools are apart from the very few social facilities which exist there. However, since there are hardly any buildings, apart from small church halls and huts erected by the Tenants' Associations, in which social activities can take place, two of these schools are also used as evening institutes and as club premises for school-leavers. They are, therefore, the most important institutions on the new estates. But their importance is not due to the fact that the school is regarded as the centre of social life; it is primarily derived from the lack of other facilities.

Some attempt at co-ordinated siting is visible only in the case of the denominational schools. These are usually located next to the churches from which they take their names. Their pupils are encouraged to participate in the social activities organised by the church, for some of which the school buildings are used. Therefore, a denominational school, and particularly a Roman Catholic school, is still in close contact with the social life of its parish, the boundaries of which, in turn, however, are only rarely coincident with those of a particular neighbourhood.

The Social Distance between Parents and Teachers

The fact that schools, by and large, do not influence the social life of their neighbourhoods is also partly due to the social distance between parents and teachers. The majority of local elementary school teachers are Middlesbrough people. But they do not usually live in the same area as their pupils. The homes of most of them are in the prosperous southern parts of the town, frequently rather far away from their school. Hence the teachers have no direct experience of the home conditions of their pupils and, in the poorer districts, the parents come only rarely to talk to them.[52] Visits are paid merely when the parents wish to make a complaint, or when the teacher's assistance is needed for filling out official forms. It is most exceptional for parents to discuss their children's future careers with the teacher. And there are now no Parents' Associations at Middlesbrough schools.

The local education authority have attempted to establish closer relations between schools and homes. Each school has occasionally an open day when mothers and fathers can come and watch their children at work. But it is doubtful whether so brief a contact has any lasting significance.

More can be done, and is being done, in the modern schools on the new estates. Their halls are large enough to give concerts and to stage plays to which parents can be invited. As social life is so barren in these neighbourhoods, the school performances are important events. The children are certainly proud of their new school and, particularly on such occasions, the adults share their pride.

The Future Place of the School in the Neighbourhood

There is no doubt that, in future, essential neighbourhood services, including the primary school, should be grouped rather than dispersed. But there is little evidence to suggest that the school should, in fact, be regarded as the focal institution in each neighbourhood. Such a conception bears no resemblance to its present role. Nowadays, the Middlesbrough schools on the whole do not help to produce neighbourhood integration; they hardly ever draw people together. There are only two exceptions. Firstly, the denominational schools, which have some influence in the religious communities whom they serve, by virtue of their relation to the parent church. Secondly, the modern schools on the housing estates, which are used by adults as well as by children, largely because these schools have a scarcity value and are in rather isolated areas. Since the role of these exceptional schools is due to specific circumstances, we cannot anticipate that their example will be universally followed in future. But when a convenient grouping of homes and institutions has been accomplished, and when parents and teachers have been brought into closer contact, it will soon be visible whether the primary school may not, after all, be capable of expanding its present function.

VII

THE BACKGROUND OF EDUCATIONAL RECONSTRUCTION

Middlesbrough's problems of educational reconstruction are not unique, they are shared by every local education authority in the country. But here they are accentuated by the specific social and physical structure of the town. Its rapid growth during the 19th century has left a legacy of obsolescence and lack of breathing space. Small houses were crowded together; the schools in the old mean streets were built on narrow sites; and no playing fields were provided. A large child population, which is predominantly working class, requires special care. Problems of poverty are always present. Because of ill-health, and because of domestic demands made on them, many children cannot even take full advantage of existing education facilities.

The sharp cleavage between 19th and 20th century Middlesbrough is accentuated by the corresponding inequalities between the opportunities of the children from these two parts of the town. Those in the old northern area have none of the advantages, either at home or at school, which the children in the outer residential ring possess. Consequently, their chances to obtain good results at school, and to reach higher education are far lower also. How much these children are penalised, simply because they happen to live in one part of the town rather than in another, is clear if we compare their opportunities in the scholarship examination with those of the children from the new housing estates who themselves have come from these same slum clearance wards. The transfer to an improved home and school environment has produced a corresponding drastic difference in examination results.

But so far, only a minority of the Middlesbrough children have been allowed to make progress. Piece-meal rebuilding, which has given them this chance, has at the same time exposed the educational waste which has been going on for so long and which is still continuing. The old problems have not been solved; they have merely been clarified.

It is now evident that the obsolete schools must be demolished, that playing fields have to be provided and that education services have to be redistributed and expanded. To make the new secondary education a reality, schools will have to change more than their names. The scope of child welfare will have to be widened, and facilities for those under and over school age will have to be established.

So vast a programme of educational reconstruction cannot be carried out unless the shifting and rebuilding of homes, of schools, and of health and recreation services is co-ordinated. There will be no equality of opportunity for the children of this town as long as there is a divided Middlesbrough.

PART IV

RETAIL TRADE

I

THE GENERAL DISTRIBUTION OF SHOPS

Inequality of Shop Distribution

The distribution of shops in Middlesbrough reflects the rapid and unplanned expansion of the town. Considering the town as a whole, there is certainly no lack of shopping facilities, but they are unequally distributed as between the north and the south. Shop development has lagged behind housing development, and whilst the centre of gravity has shifted, the major services and amenities of the town are still in their old position. Thus the division between the old and the new parts of Middlesbrough is just as striking if we survey its retail trade as if we consider any of its other aspects.

The inequality of shop distribution is illustrated by the Map of Shopping Centres and Isolated Shops. An invisible horizontal line runs through Albert Park, dividing the north from the south. In the north, there is an abundance of shopping centres and isolated shops, whilst in the south there is definite scarcity. Shop development started first in the oldest part, around the market place of St. Hilda's. From here, it spread all along Middlesbrough's "Main Street", Linthorpe Road, right up to its southern end, and extended into the subsidiary streets and side streets. As a result, these districts present an ugly picture of ribbon development of shops. It is only in the newer residential areas, where shopping facilities are on the whole inadequate, that shop development has taken the more convenient and more pleasing form of small co-ordinated groups.

A slight shift of retail trade and related amenities towards the present centre of gravity is visible. But this shift could hardly become more pronounced unless there is a radical overhaul of the town's physical structure. All the chief services of Middlesbrough, and, in particular, the railway and bus stations, are still at the northern tip of Linthorpe Road. The chief shopping centre must, of course, be in their vicinity, especially as Middlesbrough's retail trade does not merely cater for local demand. A large part of the surrounding area is included within its sphere of influence. Middlesbrough's position as a sub-regional shopping centre has accelerated the expansion of the local retail trade.

Shopping Centres

There are 22 shopping centres in Middlesbrough.[1] In observing the function, composition and spheres of influence of each of them, it became evident that there are four distinct types of centres.

(*a*) The Chief Centres, serving the whole town and even a considerable area beyond it; of which there are two, adjacent to each other.
(*b*) The Intermediate Centres, which to a lesser extent attract customers from all over the town; of which there are five.
(*c*) Local Centres, each of which is serving a group of neighbourhoods; of which there are four.
(*d*) Strictly Local Centres, each of which is serving one neighbourhood only; of which there are eleven.[2]

As the Map of Shopping Centres and Isolated Shops shows, all but two of the first three types of shopping centres are in the northern part of the town. The exceptions are centres Number 6, the Park, opposite Albert Park, and Number 7, Linthorpe Village, along the southern end of Linthorpe Road. Both of these are "intermediate centres". Linthorpe Village, particularly, represents the shift of shopping facilities towards the present centre of gravity of the town. It is already the most prosperous, and it is certainly the most promising, of the intermediate centres. In the remainder of the southern area and on the new housing estates, there are only strictly local shopping centres.

RETAIL TRADE : TABLE 1a

TOTAL NUMBER OF OCCUPIED AND EMPTY SHOPS IN MIDDLESBROUGH : IN SHOPPING CENTRES AND AS ISOLATED SHOPS

Location of Shops	Occupied Shops		Empty Shops		Grand Total	
	No.	%	No.	%	No.	%
In Shopping Centres .	772	62·0	245	63·0	1,017	62·0
Isolated Shops . .	484	38·0	144	37·0	628	38·0
Total . . .	1,256	100·0	389	100·0	1,645	100·0
Total . . .	1,256	76·0	389	24·0	1,645	100·0

RETAIL TRADE : TABLE 1b

TOTAL NUMBER OF OCCUPIED AND EMPTY SHOPS IN SHOPPING CENTRES AND AS ISOLATED SHOPS, PER AREA, AND POPULATION OF EACH AREA

Area	Population	Occupied Shops			Empty Shops		
		Total	In Shopping Centres	Isolated Shops	Total	In Shopping Centres	Isolated Shops
	%	%	%	%	%	%	%
Northern Residential Area	45·0	47·0	47·0	47·0	62·0	67·0	55·0
Town Centre	17·0	36·0	35·0	38·0	34·0	28·5	42·0
Outer Residential Area	19·0	12·0	12·0	12·0	4·0	4·5	3·0
Housing Estates	19·0	5·0	6·0	3·0	0·0	0·0	0·0
Total Per Cent.	100·0	100·0	100·0	100·0	100·0	100·0	100·0
Total Number	127,000	1,256	772	484	389	245	144

NOTE : The population as given here is that of the 1939 National Registration, excluding population in institutions. The proportionate distribution of the population over the different areas of the town has not changed since that year and is not likely to change in the immediate post-war period. The same population figures were used for all the subsequent tables. The area described as town-centre is the functional town centre, not the physical centre of the town. The areas were delimited as follows (see Map of Neighbourhoods) :

Northern Residential Area : Neighbourhoods A 1, A 2, A 3, A 5, A 9, A 12 i, A 14, A 16.
Town Centre : Neighbourhoods A 7, A 8, A 10–11–12.
Outer Residential Area : Neighbourhoods A 13, A 15, B 2, B 3, B 4, B 5, B 6, B 7, B 11.
Housing Estates : Neighbourhoods A 4, B 1, B 8–9, B 10, A 17–18.

Isolated Shops

Isolated shops form a considerable proportion of all Middlesbrough shops, almost 40·0 per cent., but they again are not equally distributed. All but 15·0 per cent of the isolated shops are in the same northern areas where the majority of shopping centres are situated.

Number and Location of Shops

Table 1a, which shows the total number of active and of empty shops in Middlesbrough, according to their location in shopping centres or as isolated shops, should be read in conjunction with Table 1b which gives a more detailed picture of shop distribution. We can see that although isolated shops are most needed in areas which are, by comparison, inadequately supplied with shopping centres, just in these areas there is a scarcity of isolated shops also. The town-centre has only 17 per cent. of the total Middlesbrough population, but 30 per cent. of all shops in shopping centres and 38 per cent. of all isolated shops. The housing estates have 19 per cent. of the total population, but as few as 6·0 per cent. of all shops in shopping centres and only 3·0 per cent. of all isolated shops.

At first sight, it appears as though the northern residential area has the correct number of shops, that is, it has roughly the same proportion of shops as of the total population. But many of the people living in this area use the adjacent excellent shopping facilities in the town-centre and hence the northern area has, in fact, too many shopping centres and too many shops altogether. As a result, as the second part of this table shows, 62 per cent. of the total number of the empty shops in Middlesbrough are in the northern area, and as many as 67 per cent. of all the empty shops in shopping centres are there.

Empty Shops

The number and distribution of empty shops clearly indicate the effects of uncontrolled shop development. There is no doubt that there would be fewer empty shops if shops were more equally distributed and, in particular, there would be fewer empty isolated shops. The town-centre has a disproportionately high number of all isolated shops, many of which suffer acutely from the competition of the shopping centres. Hence it has also a disproportionately high number of all empty isolated shops. Indeed, the problem of empty shops is almost entirely confined to the north of Middlesbrough; 96 per cent. of all the empty shops are here. Thus the failure to co-ordinate housing and shop development has led to acute scarcity of shops over a wide area of the town whilst, at the same time, almost every fourth shop in the town is empty.

Number of Foodshops and Non-Foodshops

In order to get a clear picture of the distribution of shopping facilities from the point of view of the customer, it is essential to differentiate between shops serving daily and those serving occasional needs. The former need to be in close proximity to homes, but people are usually prepared to go some distance to the latter. In fact, the two chief shopping centres of Middlesbrough, which offer a wider range of variety and choice than the other types of centres, and where the more specialised and more durable commodities can be bought, are used for these purchases by customers from all over the town, and even by people from the surrounding area. It is, therefore, misleading to allocate the number of non-foodshops in the town-centre to the population of this area only. On the other hand, although some people may prefer to travel a considerable distance to the major shopping centres for their daily purchases, it is clearly desirable that shops catering for daily needs, particularly foodshops, should be equally distributed throughout the town.[3] Hence the relation of the number of foodshops to the population of each area provides a fair comparison between shopping facilities in different parts of the town.

Area	Number of Persons per Shop			Foodshops as % of Total No. of Shops in each Area
	Per Foodshop	Per Non-Food-shop	Per Occupied Shop of all Kinds	
Town Centre	83	112	48	58·0
Northern Residential Area	136	335	99	71·0
Outer Residential Area	220	650	164	75·0
Housing Estates	460	1,550	355	77·0
All Middlesbrough	150	305	102	67·0

The inadequacy of shopping facilities in the outer residential ring and, to an even greater extent, in the housing estates, as compared with the northern residential area, is clearly established by these figures. The town-centre occupies a special position and would be expected to be at the top of the list. But it is surprising that there is so great a disparity not merely between the number of persons per non-foodshop in the town-centre and the other areas, but also between the respective figures of the number of persons per foodshop. Area differences in the number of persons per non-foodshop are the result of necessary centralisation; they cannot be eliminated. But in Middlesbrough, they appear to be so great that the need for some redistribution is indicated. However, the most important aspect in this context is the unequal allocation of foodshops to the different areas of the town.

The area differences in the number of persons per foodshop are particularly significant in view of intra-town variations in the ratio of foodshops to non-foodshops. The further we go away from the town centre, in any direction, the higher is the ratio of foodshops to non-foodshops. But although the proportion of foodshops increases in the northern residential area, and even more so in the outer ring and on the housing estates, the number of foodshops, in relation to population, decreases steadily. Hence the remedy is not a further increase in the ratio of foodshops to non-foodshops in certain areas, but a complete redistribution of shopping facilities: a decrease in the total number of shops in the north and a substantial increase in the south.

Number of Shops by Trade Types

A more detailed picture of the total number of persons per foodshops and non-foodshops of different trade types in Middlesbrough is provided by Table 2.

In Middlesbrough, as generally, a grocer's shop is the most frequent type of shop. Next in order of frequency are drapers and clothiers, many of which are small shops. "General shops", both those selling mainly food and those selling mainly other items, for instance, newsagents and tobacconists, are the second most frequent type in each of the two groups, foodshops and non-foodshops. The number of the more specialist foodshops, such as greengrocers, fishmongers and dairies, is comparatively small, chiefly for two reasons. Firstly, the more general foodshops, particularly grocers, also have outlets for these specialised commodities.[4] Secondly, Middlesbrough is essentially a working-class town, and the more expensive and more varied items of diet are, therefore, not bought to the same extent as in a well-to-do area. For this reason, the small number of fishmongers is partly offset by the large number of fried fish shops.

RETAIL TRADE : TABLE 2

TOTAL NUMBER OF MIDDLESBROUGH SHOPS, BY TRADE TYPES AND IN RELATION TO POPULATION

FOODSHOPS					NON-FOODSHOPS				
Shops by Trade Types	No. of Shops No.	No. of Shops %	No. of Shops per 1,000 People	No. of People per Shop	Shops by Trade Types	No. of Shops No.	No. of Shops %	No. of Shops per 1,000 People	No. of People per Shop
Grocer	246	29·0	1·94	515	Draper and Clothier	161	39·0	1·28	790
General Foodshop	156	19·0	1·20	815	General Non-Foodshop	105	25·0	0·80	1,200
Baker	118	14·0	0·90	1,080	Household Accessories	61	14·0	0·48	2,100
Butcher	117	14·0	0·90	1,080	Chemist	36	9·0	0·28	3,500
Fried Fish Shop	108	13·0	0·85	1,180	Junk Shop	21	5·0	0·16	6,100
Greengrocer	68	8·0	0·54	1,870	Furniture	20	5·0	0·16	6,350
Fishmonger	16	2·0	0·13	7,950					
Dairy	12	1·0	0·09	10,600	Department Store, Co-operative, Variety Bazaar	11	3·0	0·09	11,600
TOTAL	841	100·0	6·55	150	TOTAL	415	100·0	3·25	305

However, it is unlikely that the same reasons are responsible for the small number of two of the more specialist types of non-foodshops, household accessories (i.e. ironmongers) and chemists.[5] Shops of this kind should certainly be well distributed, and there appears to be a real shortage of them. Of the 22 shopping centres in the town, nine have no shop selling household accessories, and four shopping centres have no chemist. It is clear, therefore, that the existing ratio of shops of each type to population should not be adopted as the ideal ratio in planning future shopping facilities. There is certainly a scarcity of some, and an excessive number of other types of shops.[6] In any case, the specific needs of each area will have to be taken into account.

Staff Structure

The number of shops of different trade types indicates the distribution of selling points, but not necessarily the distribution of sales.[7] From the latter point of view, it would, of course, be misleading to put a draper's shop with one counter-assistant into the same category as one with thirty assistants. Therefore, to assess the relative importance of shops, in terms of the frequency of sales, a picture of their staff-structure is required.[8]

Trade Type and Size of Staff

This information for Middlesbrough relates only to non-foodshops, since foodshops were not included in the detailed questionnaire enquiry. The results show, first of all, that the range of variation in the total number of shop-workers for shops of each trade type is relatively narrow, that is, the size of the staff is closely related to the trade type of the shop. The shop with only one or two workers is most frequent among general shops and among shops selling household accessories. Three-quarters of the former and almost one-half of the latter are of that size. Only three of the 144 general shops interviewed, and only four of the 60 shops selling household accessories, have a staff of more than five persons. Drapers and chemists most frequently have a staff of three to five. Furniture shops are slightly more varied in size, but those with a staff of three to five workers are also most frequent. The small shops predominate in all these categories In fact, the only large shops in Middlesbrough are those in the group of department stores, co-operatives and variety bazaars. Of the eleven shops in this group, eight have a staff of more than 50, ranging from 59 to 345. There are no other non-foodshops of this size in the town.

Since, therefore, in Middlesbrough, significant variations in the number of workers per shop do not occur among shops of the same trade type, but are associated with differences in trade type, we can assume that the economic importance of shops of the same trade type does not vary widely either. Hence the geographical distribution of shops of the same trade type gives a fair indication of the distribution of sales.

However, it also follows that the comparison of numbers of shops by trade, in relation to population, is not indicative of the relative economic importance of the different types of shops. In order to obtain a rough index of economic importance, that is, of frequency of sales, the number of shopworkers per 1,000 people in each category of shops should be used instead.[9] These figures are set out below and contrasted with the number of shops per 1,000 people in each category.[10]

Trade Types of Non-Foodshops	Index I		Index II	
	No. of Shop-workers in Each Category Per 1,000 People	Rank Order According to Index I	No. of Shops in Each Category Per 1,000 People	Rank Order According to Index II
Department Store, Co-operative, Variety Bazaar	11·00	1	0·09	6
Draper and Clothier	5·00	2	1·14	1
Household Accessories	1·80	3	0·47	3
General Non-Food-shop	1·30	4	0·53	2
Chemist . .	1·20	5	0·27	4
Furniture . .	0·90	6	0·16	5
TOTAL . .	21·20	—	2·66	—

Economic Importance of Different Trade Types

We can now see that the position which the different types of shops occupy according to their economic importance differs considerably from that held according to the frequency of shops of each type. In the case of department stores, co-operatives, variety bazaars, the position is, in fact, entirely reversed. Compared with the other trade types, they have the smallest number of shops, yet they have the largest number of shop-workers. In fact, the rank of all the different types of shops is changed, except for the category of household accessories, which occupies the third place in the rank order of both indices.

The predominant position which the small minority of large non-foodshops in Middlesbrough hold in relation to all the others, is illustrated even more sharply by Table 3. Only 1·5 per cent. of the total number of non-foodshops interviewed have more than one hundred workers each, but these stores have 42·0 per cent. of the total number of shop-workers. The small shops, with one or two workers each, represent 46·0 per cent. of the total number of non-foodshops, but only 9·0 per cent. of the total retail staff covered are working for them.

Proportion of Counter-Assistants

Table 3 shows separately the distribution of each of the two major categories of shop-workers, of counter-assistants and of subsidiary staff. In comparing these, we find certain slight, yet important, differences. The few large shops, 1·5 per cent. of the total, have 36·0 per cent. of all counter-assistants, but as many as 54·0 per cent. of all subsidiary staff. Conversely the smallest shops, those with one or two workers only, employ 14·0 per cent. of all counter-assistants, but only 1·0 per cent. of all the remaining retail staff. We would assume that counter-assistants are a smaller proportion of the total staff in the larger shops, since these need, and can afford, subsidiary staff more than the smaller shops. Therefore, there might be an inverse straightforward relationship between size of shop, in terms of total staff, and proportion of counter-assistants. However, in fact, this relationship is not consistent; there are significant exceptions. (See Table 3, column 6.) The medium-sized shops, those with six to twenty workers, have a particularly low proportion of counter-assistants. This is due to the fact that some of the shops in this group sell furniture and thus require a comparatively high ratio of subsidiary staff. It is clear, therefore, that the proportion of counter-assistants varies not only with the staff size of shops, but also with their trade type. Hence the total number of counter-assistants is apparently a less reliable general index of the comparative size and economic importance of shops than the total number of shop-workers.[11]

RETAIL TRADE : TABLE 3

TOTAL NUMBER OF SHOP-WORKERS AND OF COUNTER-ASSISTANTS IN NON-FOODSHOPS INTERVIEWED, BY SIZE OF SHOP*

1	2	3	4	5	6
Total Number of SHOP-WORKERS per Shop	Proportion of SHOPS in This Category %	Proportion of All SHOP-WORKERS in This Category %	Proportion of COUNTER-ASSISTANTS in This Category %	Proportion of WORKERS WHO ARE NOT COUNTER-ASSISTANTS in This Category %	COUNTER-ASSISTANTS AS PROPORTION OF ALL SHOP-WORKERS in Each Category %
1	16·0	2·0	3·0	0·0	100·0
2	30·0	7·0	11·0	1·0	94·0
3	16·0	6·0	8·0	3·5	83·0
4	14·0	7·0	8·0	4·0	81·0
5	6·0	4·0	4·0	3·0	76·0
6 to 10	9·5	9·0	8·0	11·0	57·0
11 to 20	4·0	8·0	6·0	11·5	50·0
21 to 50	2·0	7·0	7·0	7·0	64·0
51 to 100	1·0	8·0	9·0	5·0	77·0
101 to 345	1·5	42·0	36·0	54·0	57·0
TOTAL PER CENT.	100·0	100·0	100·0	100·0	66·0
TOTAL NUMBER	337	2,701	1,785	916	—

* See also Appendix C, Retail Trade, Table II, p. 241, on staff-structure.

Proportion of Male Workers

One in five of the workers in the shops interviewed was male, but there was an even lower proportion of male workers in the chainstores, co-operatives and department stores, than in the independent shops and in the multiples. Chainstores have the lowest proportion of male labour, all but 5 per cent. of their total staff are women.

Part-Time Workers

Part-time workers are only 6·0 per cent. of the total retail staff covered, but the proportion of part-time workers is slightly higher in the independent and, therefore, in the smaller shops than in the larger ones. Family shops, as might be expected, have the highest proportion of part-time workers, almost 40·0 per cent. of their staff are in that category.

"Family Workers"

The employment of members of shopkeepers' families in the small independent shops is a traditional feature of retail trade. Every eighth member of the total staff of the shops interviewed was a "family-worker". Hardly any but the small independent shops employ family workers, every fourth of whom assists part-time only.

Economic Types of Shops

Since both the economic type and the trade type of shops determine the size and structure of their staff, the relevant distribution is summarised on Table 4. The most frequent type of non-foodshop in Middlesbrough is still the small independent shop. But although, on the whole, one branch shops, family and one-man shops predominate, these are not evenly distributed over the various trade types. In fact, each trade has also its characteristic economic type. Two-fifths of all furniture shops are multiples; two-thirds of all chemists are one branch independent shops. Family and one-man shops are particularly frequent among drapers, among shops selling household goods and, to an even greater extent, among general shops, the majority of which are of this type.

Although the small independent shops are most numerous, their economic importance is comparatively slight. Altogether, the many family and one-man shops employ only 6·0 per cent. of the total number of workers, whilst the few shops in the category of

RETAIL TRADE : TABLE 4

DISTRIBUTION OF NON-FOODSHOPS INTERVIEWED : TRADE TYPES BY ECONOMIC TYPES

ECONOMIC TYPE	TRADE TYPE						TOTAL
	Department Store, Co-operative, Variety Bazaar %	Furniture %	Chemist %	Draper and Clothier %	Household Accessories %	General Shop %	%
Department Store, Co-operative, Chain Store	100·0	—	3·0	2·0	—	—	4·5
Multiple	—	40·0	14·0	22·0	15·0	1·0	16·0
Independent :							
Multi-Branch	—	30·0	5·5	16·0	22·0	15·0	16·0
One Branch	—	15·0	63·0	37·0	32·0	24·0	33·5
Family and One-Man Shop	—	15·0	14·5	23·0	31·0	60·0	30·0
Total Per Cent.	100·0	100·0	100·0	100·0	100·0	100·0	100·0
Total Number	11	20	35	144	60	67	337

Definitions of economic types : MULTIPLE STORE, i.e. any firm with more than five branches.
INDEPENDENT, MULTI-BRANCH, i.e. an independent firm with two to five branches.
INDEPENDENT, ONE-BRANCH SHOP, i.e. any shop which is neither a one-man shop nor staffed entirely by the owner's family.

department stores and co-operatives employ just over half of the total number.

Age of Shops

The shops of the comparatively most modern economic type have by no means all been recently established. Three of the five department stores, and four of the eight co-operatives, are among the oldest shops in the town: they were established between 1850 and 1899. One department store was established in 1909, and the most recent one in 1923. Quite a high proportion of the multiples are also old firms: just over a third of them were founded before 1910.[12]

In fact, the average age of department stores, co-operatives and multiples is higher than that of the traditional types, particularly family and one-man shops. It may be assumed that most of the larger shops, except the co-operatives, started as independents, but being able to maintain themselves and to expand, they adopted new methods of organisation. Only a few of those which survived are still small independent shops. Hence the majority of the existing independent shops have been fairly recently established.

Considering all the shops interviewed, we find that about a fourth of them were established before 1900, the same proportion between 1900 and 1918, a fifth between 1919 and 1929, and the remainder, 30·0 per cent., since that time.

Premises

"Living over the shop" is very common in Middlesbrough. Almost a third of all the shops interviewed are in premises where shop and living quarters are combined. This happens, of course, chiefly in the case of one-man and family shops: two-thirds of the former and four-fifths of the latter are in premises of this kind. A few shops, 7·0 per cent. of the total, chiefly those of medium size, have combined workroom and shop premises. Lock-up shops are the most frequent type, being 38·0 per cent. of all shops, but a higher proportion of the medium-sized shops use such premises. The largest shops occupy the whole of the buildings in which they operate.

Area Variations

So far, we have chiefly considered the general picture of shop distribution in Middlesbrough. However, there are considerable variations in the different areas of the town, not only in terms of numbers of shops, but also in terms of staff-structure, trade type, economic type, age and premises. These variations, in turn, are associated with the differences in the type and function of the various shopping centres. Their distribution has, therefore, been observed in greater detail.

II

THE SHOPPING CENTRES

I. TYPES OF SHOPPING CENTRES

Differences in the Function and Type of Shopping Centres

The four types of shopping centres which exist in Middlesbrough are characterised by consistent differences in their catchment areas. These differences, in turn, are due to the fact that each type of centre fulfils a specific function. The Middlesbrough housewife buys her best clothes in one of the chief centres; some of the more frequently needed household appliances in one of the intermediate centres; once a week she may visit the nearest local centre, which has a wider variety of ironmongery and groceries than her own strictly local centre, where she buys daily her vegetables, her bread and her newspaper. This example is oversimplified, since it applies particularly to the housewives in the new parts of the town, but it expresses the chief differences between the functions of the four types of centres. The chief centres and the strictly local centres have the most clearly defined functions. The former serve specialised and occasional needs, the latter daily needs. The difference between the intermediate and the local centres is not so clear-cut; the co-existence of these two types is due to the lack of planning. The importance of some of these centres, particularly of those in the extreme north, has decreased, that of others has been accentuated as the result of the continuous exodus southwards. Thus Cannon Street is one of the oldest, and used to be one of the most important, centres of the town. To-day it is merely a local centre. In fact, this centre, and the other three of this type, all of which are in the old part of the town, would have been further reduced in status, but for the fact that some of the original inhabitants of these areas still return to do occasional shopping there. The tenants of the Brambles Farm housing estate, for instance, have no other choice but to frequent the local centre in North Ormesby. The shopping facilities on their own estate are inadequate.

The northern intermediate centres, located in the densest working-class areas of the town, provide similar shopping facilities as the chief centres but, on the whole, their customers are poorer and less widely distributed. Their shops also differ accordingly. The only intermediate centre which has not suffered from the southward shift, but which has, in fact, been established because of it, is Linthorpe Village, on the southern tip of Linthorpe Road. It meets a genuine need. South of it, there are only strictly local centres. Geographically also, it is in an intermediate position, being on the main road to the central shopping and administrative area of the town.

The differences in the functions of the various shopping centres are evident if we consider the types and the sizes of the shops they contain.

Types of Shops

The incidence of foodshops, of general shops and of specialist shops indicates the function and type of each shopping centre. The more local its character, the higher is the proportion of foodshops and also of general shops, and the smaller is the number of specialist shops.

Grouping of Shops	Food Shops As Proportion of Total Number of Shops in Each Group, Excluding General Shops %	General Shops[13] As Proportion of Total Number of Shops in Each Group %
Chief Centres . . .	28·0	6·0
Intermediate Centres . .	56·0	16·0
Local Centres . . .	77·0	18·0
Strictly Local Centres . .	81·0	22·0
Isolated Shops . . .	87·0	30·0
Total . . .	69·0	21·0

The ratio of foodshops to non-foodshops is the major index of the function of a shopping centre. The distribution of non-foodshops of different trade and economic types further clarifies the picture. Thus the higher the proportion of drapers and clothiers is in a shopping centre, the wider is its sphere of influence. More than half of all the non-foodshops in the chief centres are of that type, as compared with two-fifth in the intermediate centres, a third in the local centres and just over one quarter in the strictly local centres.

Whilst many of the non-foodshops in the chief centres have specialist outlets, most of those in the intermediate centres are general in character. They cater to a considerable extent for the poorer people in the town who, if they go to a draper or ironmonger, like to see a display of as many different kinds of goods as possible. A specific feature of the local centres are small general shops which are, in fact, the counterparts of the variety bazaars in the central shopping area. They sell hardware, stationery, toys and haberdashery. The shops in the strictly local centres cater entirely, though sometimes inadequately, for "daily needs". In addition to food, commodities usually available in a strictly local centre include hardware, bicycle accessories, haberdashery, chemist's goods, stationery and cigarettes. Odds and ends of women's and children's clothing are sold locally, but it is assumed that men prefer to shop in the larger centres. The range of outlets matters most and, unlike the larger centres, those of strictly local character usually have only one or at most two outlets of each type, apart from the general shops.

The distribution of non-foodshops by economic type in the different groups of centres follows the same pattern. The detailed survey of non-foodshops showed that 75·0 per cent. of all the non-independent shops, including department stores, chainstores, co-operatives and multiples, were in the chief centres. Vice versa, the local and strictly local centres were almost entirely composed of independent shops.

However, as Table 5 shows, a higher proportion of all the non-foodshops in the strictly local centres are of the multi-branch independent type than in the local centres. The reason is that all but two of the strictly local centres are at the outer periphery of Middlesbrough, in the districts which have only recently been opened up. These centres do not suffer from the competition of the numerous shops in the old northern parts of the town; they are prosperous, and hence the newer multi-branch firms are attracted to them. For the same reason, compared with the local centres, they have a relatively low proportion of one-man shops. A number of these, which had started as one-man shops in the strictly local centres, were able, in the absence of competition, to expand and to take on more staff.

Size of Shops

However, the average size of non-foodshops is smaller in the strictly local than in the local centres. The size of shops is, in fact, closely related to variations in the function of shopping centres.

RETAIL TRADE: TABLE 5

DISTRIBUTION OF NON-FOODSHOPS, BY ECONOMIC TYPE, IN SHOPPING CENTRES OF DIFFERENT TYPES.

Grouping of Shops	Percentage of Non-Foodshops Interviewed of Each Economic Type in Each Group					Total Number of Shops in Each Group	
	Non-Independent Type	Independent Type					
	%	Multi-Branch %	One Branch %	Family Shop %	One-Man Shop %	%	No.
Chief Centres . .	43·5	18·0	31·0	5·0	2·5	100·0	119
Intermediate Centres .	18·5	22·5	31·0	16·0	12·0	100·0	81
Local Centres . .	4·0	9·0	40·0	25·0	22·0	100·0	45
Strictly Local Centres .	2·0	18·0	38·0	29·0	13·0	100·0	45
Isolated Shops . .	0·0	6·0	34·0	30·0	30·0	100·0	47
Total . . .	20·5	16·0	33·5	17·0	13·0	100·0	337

The wider their influence, the larger is the average number of workers per shop. Hence, the chief centres have 35·0 per cent. of the total number of non-foodshops interviewed, but over 60·0 per cent. of all the workers employed in such shops.

Grouping of Shops	Proportion of Non-Food-shops Interviewed %	Proportion of Shop-Workers in These Shops %	Average Number of Workers per Non-Food-shop in Each Group No.
Chief Centres	35·0	61·0	14·0
Intermediate Centres	24·0	26·0	9·0
Local Centres	13·5	5·0	3·0
Strictly Local Centres	13·5	4·0	2·4
Isolated Shops	14·0	4·0	2·2
Total Per Cent.	100·0	100·0	—
Total Number	337	2,701	8·0

All but two of the non-foodshops with over 25 workers are in the chief centres. The exceptions are the two department stores in the intermediate centres. The largest shop in the local centres is one with eighteen workers, in the strictly local centres one with seven workers, and none of the isolated shops has more than six workers.

Number of Shops per Centre

The composition of a shopping centre in terms of types and sizes of shops appears to be a more definite indication of its function than the total number of shops it contains. On an average, the chief centres have the largest number of shops, and the strictly local centres the smallest number, but the average local centre has more shops than the average intermediate centre. This is largely due to the fact that centres of local or intermediate character are very varied in size. Several of them, which are in the old part of the town, are still very large. On the whole, these types of centres have more shops than is justified by their present function. Hence they have an excessively high number of empty shops.

Catchment Areas

The spheres of influence of the different shopping centres are illustrated by their catchment areas. The influence of non-food-

RETAIL TRADE: TABLE 6

DISTRIBUTION OF OCCUPIED AND EMPTY SHOPS IN SHOPPING CENTRES OF DIFFERENT TYPES

Types of Shopping Centres	No. of Centres of Each Type	Percentage of Shops in Each Category of Shopping Centres			Average Number of Shops per Shopping Centre of Each Type	
		Occupied Shops	Empty Shops	All Shops	Average No. of Occupied Shops	Average Total Number of Shops
	No.	%	%	%	No.	No.
Chief Centres	2	23·0	10·0	20·0	89	102
Intermediate Centres . . .	5	27·5	50·0	33·0	42	67
Local Centres	4	29·0	36·0	31·0	56	78
Strictly Local Centres . . .	11	20·5	4·0	16·0	14	15
All Centres	22	100·0	100·0	100·0	35	46

shops is more important in this context than that of foodshops, since it is the incidence of non-foodshops and their specific function that primarily determine the character of a shopping centre. Moreover, foodshops, no matter where they are situated, are likely to attract customers from the immediate neighbourhood.[14]

Despite these qualifications, the catchment areas for sugar-registrations of the foodshops in the different centres clearly indicate the varying range of influence. The chief centres have sugar-registrations from all over the town, the strictly local centres from their own neighbourhood only. In most centres, the catchment areas of foodshops, in terms of sugar-registrations, and those of non-foodshops, appear to have the same pattern.[15] Shopping for green-groceries, however, is usually done in close proximity to homes.

A sample of housewives were asked at which shops they were registered for sugar, where they bought their greengroceries and their best clothes.[16] The answers to the last question showed that almost all the important clothes buying was done in the northern parts of the town, in the chief centres, and in three of the long established intermediate centres which are situated in that area.

Further indications of the spheres of influence of all types of non-foodshops were derived from the replies of the shopkeepers who were interviewed. They were asked: "About what proportion of your customers come from the immediate neighbourhood?" The estimates given were, of course, no more than a rather vague indication of the proportion of strictly local custom, particularly since no fixed definition of "neighbourhood" was used. However, the results are entirely consistent with the classification of the different shopping centres which the survey had previously established.

Percentage of Customers from the Immediate Neighbourhood	Distribution of Replies from:			
	The Chief Centres %	The Intermediate Centres %	The Local Centres %	The Strictly Local Centres %
Under 25·0 per cent.	36·0	15·0	2·0	0·0
26·0 to 50·0 per cent.	14·0	17·0	9·0	2·0
51·0 to 75·0 per cent.	3·0	20·0	11·0	13·0
75·0 to 100·0 per cent.	2·0	28·0	62·0	76·0
Don't know	45·0	20·0	16·0	9·0
Total Answers	100·0	100·0	100·0	100·0

The proportion of customers from the immediate neighbourhood appears to increase steadily from the chief centres to the strictly local centres.[17] Furthermore, the higher the proportion of local customers, the lower is the proportion of "don't know" answers. Shopkeepers in the more central shopping groups, who depend largely on occasional passing customers, found it difficult to give even a rough estimate.

Shopkeepers were also asked from which districts of Middlesbrough they draw their customers. Merely districts were indicated, not the number of customers from each, so that the proportion of customers from each district is not known. The replies showed that non-foodshops in the chief shopping centres draw customers from widely scattered districts. The more local the character of the shopping centre, the fewer districts outside its immediate neighbourhood were mentioned.

2. LOCATION AND LAY-OUT OF SHOPPING CENTRES

The Chief Centres

The central shopping area, at the northern end of Linthorpe Road, has two parts, the "primary centre" and its southern extension, the "secondary centre". These were the terms used by a Linthorpe Road shopkeeper to distinguish them. According to reports from shopkeepers who know the district well, shops were first set up at the northern end of Linthorpe Road to "catch" potential customers going to and coming from the railway station. The stores did excellent trade on a Saturday evening when crowds of people would stop here on their way to the famous tea-gardens of the 1870's and 1880's. Even to-day, the majority of the cinemas, restaurants, hotels and the only theatre, are located in or near the chief centres. The people shopping here can take advantage of the best entertainment that the town can offer.

The focus of Middlesbrough's social and commercial life, at the northern tip of Linthorpe Road, is no longer in the town's geographic centre. For this reason, shopkeepers in the "secondary centre" hopefully anticipate a southward shift of retail trade from which they would benefit. So far, however, there has only been a slight movement in that direction, and it is likely that for the time being the primary centre will retain its status. As one of the oldest parts of the town, it has, of course, a higher proportion of long-established shops: a quarter of the present number of non-foodshops were founded between 1860 and 1899. But as the attraction of this centre is still very strong, there has also been a steady influx of new shops: one-half of the total present number have been established since 1919.

The comparatively favourable layout of the primary centre is one of the reasons for its continued pre-eminence. Its shape is like a cross, with short spurs which include shops just round the corners of side streets. This close grouping of shops does not persist in the southern extension, the secondary centre, which is characterised by long lines of shops on both sides of "Main Street".

On the whole, shopkeepers in the primary centre are well satisfied with their location. Such complaints as were made related to factors impairing the value of their central position. Some of these comments are typical of the general location problems of Middlesbrough shops. Shopkeepers dislike the interspersing of wholesalers' premises and of banks and offices with shops. They also complain about the lack of parking facilities for private cars and distributive vehicles. They lose trade through traffic congestion; for instance, people coming from the railway station tend to by-pass the extreme northern tip of Linthorpe Road to avoid the dense traffic there. Hence this section of the primary centre is less prosperous than the remainder.

Shopkeepers in the secondary centre expressed strong dislike of the generally dilapidated and unpleasing appearance of their road and shop fronts. Furthermore, this part of Linthorpe Road is considerably wider than that in the primary centre. Hence the road divides the shops instead of exercising a common pull. As a result, one side of the street was described as being "poor for business".[18] In fact, it was found that shopkeepers everywhere in Middlesbrough disliked wide shopping streets.

One feature which is appreciated by shopkeepers, and which is particularly marked in the primary centre, is the close grouping of shops of the same trade type. Most of the shoe shops, for instance, are located next to one another. It is believed that an unbroken line of the same kind of shops provides a special sales attraction to the customer, who can then look into all the shop windows before making his purchase.

The Intermediate Centres

The three intermediate centres in the extreme north, St. Hilda's, Newport Road and Corporation Road, have all suffered from the southward migration which, in turn, is the *raison d'être* of the other two intermediate centres further south, the Park and Linthorpe Village. Only the last of these five centres is prosperous.

Originally, the shopping centre in St. Hilda's, north of the railway, was the most important in the town. The shops here were grouped around the spacious market place which even to-day, in spite of its decay, has still a pleasant appearance. The market was then the chief attraction. Shopkeepers looked forward to market-days when customers came from north and south of the river. But the prosperity of this centre has gradually diminished, as did that of the market, with the town's shift southwards.

To-day, more than half of the total number of shops in the St. Hilda's centre are empty. Only a few open shops remain in the market place; the majority are in adjacent streets. The placing of shops around a square is no longer considered desirable; close grouping on both sides of a street of medium width is preferred. All the shopkeepers think that it would help them if the market could be rejuvenated. At present, the shops remaining in St. Hilda's are cut off from the rest of the town, and there is an urgent need for improved communications.[19]

The other four intermediate centres are examples of uncontrolled ribbon development. Newport Road, in particular, which is known as "poverty row", has suffered from it. Although still the most important intermediate centre in the town, it is rapidly developing into one of the chief problem shopping areas of Middlesbrough. There are two parts to Newport Road. One branches off from, and belongs to, the primary centre; then the road bends, and from this point on, it is the Newport Road shopping centre, a narrow high-way, with heavy traffic of passenger and distributive vehicles, which has one of the highest local accident rates. All side streets lead into the densest working-class residential area of the town. On each side of the road there is a line of almost unbroken shop property, including 43 empty shops. These are a third of the total number of shops in this centre.

Newport Road is famous for its "poverty shops": fried fish shops, pawnbrokers and junkshops. A number of the pawnbrokers are also general outfitters and drapers. Their goods, many of which are second-hand, are stacked on the pavement in front or hung over the shop door.

When the Newport Road shopkeepers were interviewed, a high proportion expressed dissatisfaction with their location. The decline in trade had been evident before the war. For many years, it had been necessary to launch considerable advertising and hire purchase schemes to attract customers. The future of this centre was viewed with scepticism and apprehension. Some of the shopkeepers thought that certain physical improvements might revive trade. They criticised the narrowness of the road, the noise and dirt due to heavy traffic, and the fact that the shops are too numerous, badly distributed and unattractively designed.

The Corporation Road intermediate centre is in lay-out very similar to Newport Road, but it has recently benefited from the establishment of a cinema and a department store, both of which have attracted new customers and have helped to revive trade.[20]

Linthorpe Village is the only definitely prosperous and promising intermediate centre.[21] Like Newport and Corporation Roads, it is also an example of unrestricted shop development along a main road. But, fortunately, the main road forks off south of this centre and, on the whole, its location, in the present centre of gravity of the town, is far more advantageous. It gains customers through being on the major bus route from north to south and, in particular, through having bus stops on either side of the road. The shopkeepers here are unanimously satisfied with their location. They approve of the grouping of shops and are particularly pleased because branches of one of the largest foodstores and of the co-operative society have been established here. They realise that they occupy a strategic position in the town which may become increasingly important. The catchment area of this centre is already very wide, for foodshops as well as for non-foodshops; it extends over the whole southern area of Middlesbrough.

The Local Centres

In location, lay-out and economic position the local centres are similar to the intermediate centres, with the exception of Linthorpe Village. They are all in the north. They also are examples of the uncontrolled ribbon development of shops. None of them can be described as being prosperous.

The local centre around the market place of North Ormesby has the same character and the same problems as the intermediate centre of St. Hilda's. As there is no longer a market here, except for a few occasional stalls, the chief attraction of this centre has now disappeared. The upkeep of the market site has been neglected, so that the square is now rather derelict. Here, as in St. Hilda's, the main group of shops was originally in the marketplace, but shops have gradually shifted into the side streets. In the wide market place the shops appear to be cut off from each other, and hence there is not sufficient mutual sales attraction.[22] Only one of the shopkeepers still in the market place did not complain of this feature. He is a pawnbroker whose shop front is so brightly painted that it hits the eye from every corner of the square.

The Cannon Street local centre closely resembles the adjacent intermediate centre of Newport Road. To-day, it is the poorest of the four local shopping centres, but is reputed to have been the "money-making thoroughfare of Middlesbrough" in the 1870's and 1880's. It was then one of the main highways of the town. In those days, Middlesbrough had a second railway-station at the south-west end of Cannon Street. Passengers who arrived at, or departed from, this station, or who changed stations, passed down Cannon Street. Hence, this was a proper place for the setting up of an important shopping centre. To-day, the second station is gone and Cannon Street, which passes through one of the densest and blighted residential areas of the town, lies well off the beaten track. It is by-passed by all but heavy traffic, and is frequented mainly by the people from the adjacent streets and by a certain number of faithful customers from the new housing estates who originally lived in the vicinity. Each side of the road is lined by a row of shops in much the same way as in Newport Road and Corporation Road. As 35·0 per cent. of the shops are empty, and most of the other shops are in need of repair, the street looks dismal and untidy. No new non-foodshops have been successfully established here in the last twenty years.

The local shopping centre in and around Parliament Road is a slightly improved version of Cannon Street. The street is less isolated and the surrounding residential district is less poor. A cinema and a large public house, which were established in the 1930's, have helped to revive trade and to attract customers from beyond the immediate neighbourhood.

Both Parliament Road and the fourth local centre, Borough Road West, which also contains a popular cinema, are in the vicinity of the chief centres. But in the opinion of several shopkeepers, this feature is rather a mixed blessing. Through it, they lose perhaps as many, if not more, customers than they gain.

On the whole, the position of the local centres is as precarious as that of the intermediate centres although they are more limited in scope and less dependent on customers from a wider area. They only maintain themselves because of the unequal distribution of shopping facilities and amenities throughout the town. They are within the "amenity zone", and for that reason they still draw customers from the less well-equipped southern districts. But they are also within the zone of acute competition; they have to hold their own against the numerous shopping centres and isolated shops in the north.

The Strictly Local Centres

The eleven strictly local shopping centres can be divided into three groups, according to their location:

(*a*) The "old" centres:
Beaumont Road, North Ormesby
Waterloo Road

Both are situated in the northern area of the town.

(*b*) The "suburban" centres:
Roman Road
The Longlands
Acklam Road South

These serve the southern districts of recent speculative development.

(*c*) The "housing estate" centres:
Marton Road, Marton Grove
Eastbourne Road, Marton Grove
Sutton Estate
Whinney Banks
Marshall Avenue, Brambles Farm
Kestral Avenue, Brambles Farm

These serve housing estates built either by the Corporation or by a housing trust.

The layout of the "old" strictly local centres is similar to that of most of the intermediate and local centres. They present the same picture of lines of shops on both sides of the road. They differ from the bigger centres only in two respects. Firstly, the line of shops is less continuous. The shops are more often at the corners of the numerous side streets than in the main street itself. Moreover, shops are interspersed with residential rather than with commercial buildings.

But the new centres, on the speculative and municipal housing estates, differ markedly from all the other shopping centres in the town. First, they are isolated in the outer periphery of the town, away from the numerous shops in the old parts, so that they enjoy a virtual monopoly in their districts. Secondly, these shopping centres have not grown haphazardly, but have been deliberately designed by the local authority or by building societies. Special blocks of buildings were set aside for shops and these were designed accordingly. Consequently, each centre forms a definite and co-ordinated group of shops. In some cases the shop premises are built a considerable way back from the road, and occasionally there is a narrow belt of trees between the road and the edge of the pavement.

On the whole, the shopkeepers in the strictly local centres were well satisfied with their location. Many of them felt that their role, serving the daily needs of the people in the neighbourhood, was almost a vocation of which they could be proud and which they could enjoy. Only a few specific complaints were, therefore, made. Shopkeepers on two of the housing estates regarded the shopping facilities provided by their own centres as inadequate. As a result, they said, people still preferred, whenever possible, to return to the northern area of the town to do their shopping.

It is certainly true that the Whinney Banks estate has barely a sufficient number and variety of shops. Brambles Farm, in special need of good facilities because of its isolated position, has certainly too few. For instance, it has only four non-foodshops all told in its two small shopping centres. There is no hardware store, nor a dispensing chemist. The nearest outlets of both types are in North Ormesby. Shopkeepers on this estate, who are now overworked, would welcome the establishment of more shops.

Even so, Brambles Farm and the other housing estates are now far better equipped than they were in their early period of settlement. For eight years, the only non-foodshop on Brambles Farm was one general store. Marton Grove had none for four years, and Whinney Banks none for over one year.[23] Hence the tenants were forced to continue to shop in the old parts of the town. Their habits changed only gradually as facilities on the estates improved.

The two "old" strictly local centres have a few empty shops, but all those in the outer residential ring work to full capacity. The neighbourhoods from which they draw their customers are entirely dependent on them for daily purchases. Therefore, the shops in these centres do not suffer from competition. In fact, in some cases, they might be even more prosperous if the group to which they belong were slightly larger, including a greater number and variety of outlets. Customers have more confidence in shops which do not appear to have a monopoly in their particular district, and in a shopping centre which offers them some degree of choice. It appears that controlled and more equal distribution of shopping facilities in Middlesbrough would, therefore, accentuate rather than diminish the prosperity of the strictly local centres.

3. PROSPERITY AND DEPRESSION IN SHOPPING CENTRES

Causes of Prosperity and Depression

The present poverty of certain types of shopping centres is due to the fact that shop development has been uncontrolled and not adjusted to the southward shift of the population.[24] The poor lay-out and design of shopping centres, a direct result of lack of control, has had a depressing effect on trade. A further result, the unequal distribution of shops, has led to acute competition between shops in the older part of the town, whilst shopping facilities in the newer areas are often inadequate, inconvenient and do not provide sufficient choice. The combination of the various ill-effects leads to poverty. Hence the shopping centres which are most exposed to competition, whose location is no longer favourable and which, at the same time, have an unfortunate lay-out, are most clearly marked by depression.

Neither the chief centres nor the strictly local centres show these symptoms. The status and the amenities of the chief centres place them beyond local rivalry, and most of the strictly local centres are outside the zone of competition. Moreover, both these groups have clearly defined functions. On the whole, they are, therefore, prosperous.

The functions of the intermediate and of the local centres are much less clear-cut, and hence they are more exposed to competition. These two types of centres only exist side by side because shop development has not kept pace with housing development. Their position is precarious. They have to compete with each other, with the chief centres, and also with numerous isolated corner and side street shops. Hence the poorest shopping areas in the town are either intermediate or local in character, and Linthorpe Village is the only one of the nine intermediate and local centres which is prosperous. Most of the others contain an admixture of conditions. Parts are already marked by decay, whilst there are still some prosperous patches.

The Map of Shopping Centres and Isolated Shops, which indicates the relative prosperity of each centre, shows the effects of competition. All but one of the shopping centres which are poor or tending towards poverty are in the northern area of the town.

RETAIL TRADE: TABLE 7

INDEX OF PROSPERITY AND DEPRESSION IN SHOPPING CENTRES

Shopping Centres	Index Number	Rating
The Primary Centre	15	6
The Secondary Centre	171	4
The Chief Centres	78	5
The Village, Linthorpe	71	5
The Park, Linthorpe	166	4
Corporation Road	188	3
Newport Road	224	3
St. Hilda's	366	2
The Intermediate Centres	229	3
Borough Road West	168	4
Market Place, North Ormesby	193	3
Parliament Road	257	3
Cannon Street	451	1
The Local Centres	308	2
Acklam Road South	0	6
Marton Road, Marton Grove	0	6
Eastbourne Road, Marton Grove	0	6
Sutton Estate	0	6
Kestral Avenue, Brambles Farm	0	6
Whinney Banks	66	5
The Longlands	79	5
Roman Road	88	5
Marshall Avenue, Brambles Farm	225	3
Beaumont Road, North Ormesby	237	3
Waterloo Road	250	3
The Strictly Local Centres	114	5
Grand Total	200	3

Classification: 6 Very Prosperous.
5 Prosperous.
4 Average; tending towards prosperity.
3 Average; tending towards poverty.
2 Poor.
1 Very Poor.

In fact, the only really prosperous centres north of Albert Park are the primary centre and the Longlands, a strictly local group of shops.

The Index of Prosperity and Depression

Two indices have been used to estimate the degree of prosperity in each shopping centre: the proportion of empty shops and the proportion of poverty shops.[25] The first reflects the degree of vitality of the shopping centre, the second indicates roughly the extent to which it caters for poor customers. The resulting rating of centres, shown above,[26] has confirmed the impressions gained during visits to the shops and in interviewing the shopkeepers. Old and shabby premises are prevalent in most of the centres classified as poor or as being on the verge of poverty. Complaints that trade was precarious, and pessimism and dissatisfaction with the location of shops, were also prevalent there.

The variations in prosperity among the chief centres and the strictly local centres respectively are of particular interest. The primary centre is, of course, definitely prosperous. But the secondary centre is not quite so fortunate. It is more exposed to competition, and it is also inferior in lay-out and location.

Three of the strictly local centres are considerably poorer in character than the majority of the group. These are the two "old" centres, Beaumont Road in North Ormesby, and Waterloo Road, which are both in the northern zone of competition, and one of the small centres on Brambles Farm. The last is too inadequate to be very successful, and the majority of its customers are poor.

Prosperity and Turnover

Prosperity exists, therefore, chiefly where the location, lay-out and composition of a shopping centre are suited to, and clearly define, its function.[27] The geographical distribution of shops is perhaps the most important factor. If there are too many groups of shops in one area, or if there are too few, the function of each of them is weakened.

Hence the shopping centres which are most prosperous are not necessarily those with the highest turnover, but those which have a definite *raison d'être* and thus a turnover appropriate to it. Evidence of comparative turnover in different types of centres confirms this point.

Turnover of foodshops, as indicated by the number of sugar registrations, is highest in the two most prosperous groups, the chief centres and the strictly local centres.[28] The rival attractions of these two types of centres adversely affects all but one of the intermediate and local centres whose own residential neighbourhoods have been severely depleted and which, in addition, have to compete for customers with each other and with the many isolated "pantry" shops in the old part of Middlesbrough. Linthorpe Village, alone among this group of centres, has a high average

AVERAGE NUMBER OF CUSTOMERS REGISTERED FOR SUGAR PER OUTLET IN EACH GROUP OF CENTRES

Grouping of Shops	No. of Registered Customers	No. of Grocers' Outlets	Average No. of Customers per Outlet
The Chief Centres	26,761	16	1,672·5
The Intermediate Centres	23,692	48	493·5
The Local Centres	19,492	57	342·0
The Strictly Local Centres	28,825	54	534·0
Isolated Shops	34,433	205	168·0
Total	133,203	380	350·5

number of sugar registrations, i.e. over 1,000 customers per outlet.

A different picture is presented if the available indices for the turnover of non-foodshops are considered; that is, the number of workers per shop and the turnover of clothing coupons. We then find that the strictly local centres, though prosperous, are at the bottom of the list. The number of workers per shop, as was shown previously, decreases steadily from the chief centres to the strictly local centres. The average weekly coupon turnover shows a similar pattern. The majority of all the clothing outlets are in the chief and intermediate centres, and all the outlets with the highest coupon turnover are there. Nine of the twelve shops with an average weekly turnover of 1,501 coupons and over are in the chief centres, three are in the intermediate centres. The strictly local centres have barely 2·0 per cent. of the shops with a turnover of 301–1,500 coupons weekly, although they have almost 8·0 per cent. of all the relevant outlets.

Yet the low level of coupon-turnover in the strictly local centres has not impaired their prosperity. They cater largely for daily needs and their turnover of such commodities, using sugar registrations as an index, appears to be satisfactory.

The chief centres, with the highest turnover both of food and non-foodshops, can also maintain themselves at their existing standards. But the same cannot be said of either the intermediate or the local centres. Since 56·0 per cent. of all the shops in the intermediate centres, and 77·0 per cent. of all those in the local centres are foodshops, the low level of turnover of foodstuffs, as indicated by sugar registrations, matters a great deal. The resulting loss is not sufficiently offset by the comparatively high turnover of the non-foodshops in these types of shopping areas. There are clearly too many of these centres. Most of them are out-of-date and beginning to decay. It is doubtful whether a town of Middlesbrough's size and structure can support more than three or four groups of shops which have neither a definitely central nor a strictly local function.

III

SPECIFIC ASPECTS OF DISTRIBUTION

1. Buying and Selling

Sources of Supply

Both before and since the war, the majority of the shops interviewed, and particularly the non-independent shops, have bought their stocks chiefly from wholesalers and manufacturers in other parts of the country. Shortage of staff, slow deliveries and other transport problems have slightly increased the scope of local buying since the war. But even now merely a few, one-tenth of the total number, rely upon local wholesalers, and most of these have done so only since 1939. About the same proportion of shops obtain some part of their supplies regularly from local sources.[29] All these are the small independent non-foodshops, such as general shops, drapers and shops selling household accessories. Most of the others use local supply sources only for occasional or emergency requirements.

Leeds, an important clothing distributive centre, was frequently mentioned as a source of supply but, on the whole, it appears that goods are bought as much from wholesalers and manufacturers in the south of England as from those in the north. The chainstores and multiples are mainly supplied from their own central depots, in or near London.

Supplies from local wholesalers are collected or delivered, by van or messenger, often by the shopkeeper himself. Goods from a distance are most frequently sent by rail, to a slightly lesser extent by road, and only rarely by post. Before the war, transport of the less bulky goods by road was increasing. The non-independent types of shops, particularly the multiples, often used their own vans for collecting goods. There were frequent complaints that rail transport was subject to delays and that some goods, particularly clothing, arrived in better condition when transported by road. However, it is unlikely that rail transport, which is still, in the opinion of many shopkeepers, the quickest and most efficient method, will be superseded by road deliveries in the near future.

Retail Deliveries

In Middlesbrough, as elsewhere, delivery services have been cut considerably since the war. The disparity between present and pre-war deliveries is particularly striking, since in the two years before the war, Middlesbrough's retail deliveries were, in the opinion of many shopkeepers, exceptionally extensive. This was probably in part due to the fact that the town had just recovered from a ten-year depression. Therefore, the stores were doing everything they could to make shopping as convenient as possible. About one-third of the shops interviewed had not undertaken deliveries at that time, and these were chiefly the small independent shops selling tobacco, stationery and small draper's goods. In 1944, more than two-thirds of all the shops interviewed have no delivery service at all. Most of the remainder deliver only a small proportion of their sales, and even these shops, the department stores, multiples and multi-branch independents, have given up most of their own facilities for sending goods. They rely instead chiefly upon the pool delivery organisation.

The pool, a war-time experiment in co-operative deliveries, was first set up in 1940 under the auspices of the Ministry of War Transport as a petrol economy measure. It is now run by a committee of representatives from three of the big department stores and from one multiple store selling furniture. These four shops and two others, not represented on the management committee, provide the twelve vans used by the pool. Any shop can employ its services for a small charge, which covers expenses only, but as the delivery of small parcels is not encouraged, principally the big furniture shops, department stores and a few of the clothing shops take advantage of the pool organisation.

However, the pool is regarded only as an emergency measure. Shopkeepers stated that they wished to re-establish individual delivery services as soon as circumstances make it possible. Judging from pre-war conditions, it is likely that there will be a considerable increase in deliveries soon after the end of the war, and that this will apply both to foodshops and non-foodshops, particularly to those in the chief centres which have extensive catchment areas, both in Middlesbrough itself and in the surrounding area.

The Credit System

Middlesbrough's trade has grown up on the credit system. Since the early growth of the town, the majority of the people have had no other income than their weekly wages, and hence it has always been difficult to find ready cash for anything but small purchases. A system that enabled people to pay for their clothes and household goods in small instalments was, therefore, welcomed.

The "tallyman" of the last century was the first credit agent. He walked around from house to house with his bundle of wares. A customer could have an article by giving a small deposit to the "tallyman", who would call back weekly for collections till the payment for the article was completed. Lady Bell in her book *At the Works*, written in the late 1890's, referred to the tallyman's trade, although by her time the modern ticket agent, who still uses the methods she described, was already a well-known figure.[30] To-day, the credit system is used extensively by shopkeepers and by a large section of the population. The depression in the '30's gave it a special impetus.

Five major methods have been developed. First, there are the mail credit companies, working from headquarters in London and elsewhere, which organise small clubs working on a 20-week contribution basis. Periodically, the clubs have ticket draws, and the lucky member gets his goods sent to him before the completion of payment, though he continues his weekly contributions to the end of the 20 weeks. This system was never very extensively used in Middlesbrough, and since the war it has become almost extinct. It is unpopular both with local ticket agents and retailers, who lose potential trade, and the customers themselves usually prefer to see and choose what they are buying.

Secondly, nationally organised credit companies establish local branches and agents. Their method is similar to that used by insurance agents who go from door to door, canvassing for customers, returning weekly for payments on the policies sold. Only one such company has a branch in Middlesbrough, but in 1939 it had over 100 agents working there, and it is estimated that it had 4,000 to 5,000 customers distributed throughout the town. Its "credit tickets" were accepted by twenty to thirty shops of different kinds. Lack of staff has reduced this business during the war, and the Board of Trade Order, limiting the agent's discount to 1/- in the £, has made it less profitable.[31]

Thirdly, there are three or four local companies, employing methods very similar to the national companies, which confine their activities to Middlesbrough and to the Tees-side area. One of these started as an Insurance and Friendly Society. It has gradually enlarged its field, but it still sells insurance policies as well. Between them, these companies employed about one hundred agents before the war, but they also have had to reduce their activities since 1939.

Fourthly, there are the many individuals who work on their own account, independently of any of the companies, each acting as agent for two or three shops simultaneously. They must first convince the shops that they have some amount of capital behind them. Widows who start with a small sum of savings often undertake this work. They also have to sell a certain minimum number of tickets, amounting to a minimum value, which is specified by each shop. Since these individual ticket agents undertake their collections entirely on their own, without help, the scope of their activities is rather limited. It appears that before the war there were about 80 to 100 such agents in Middlesbrough. Since then, many have had to discontinue their activities, chiefly again because of the Board of Trade Order limiting discounts.

Finally, many of the shops run their own clothing clubs and hire purchase schemes. Four of the department stores, the co-operative society, and five or six other shops employ their own agents, although not on a large scale, for they can also use outside agents. Others establish clothing clubs on their own premises to which customers come weekly to make payments.

As would be expected, the various credit schemes are mainly used for occasional and more expensive purchases such as furniture, radios, bicycles and clothing, including footwear. Before the war, when wages were generally lower and there were no restrictions on any form of the credit system, most of the larger stores made use of at least one of these schemes. Even in 1944, all the department stores, all but one of the co-operative branches, and almost half of the multiples and of the multi-branch independents have some such system. The chainstores sell only for cash and so do most of the small independent firms. Shops of this last type, small drapers, chemists or general shops, which cater for everyday requirements, have no real need to make use of the credit system. They sometimes have allowed their customers, particularly at the height of the depression, to buy on credit. But this was usually a personal and *ad hoc* arrangement. It was not organised nor done on a large scale.

Most of the shops which use the credit system are situated in the older and poorer part of the town. Yet the existence of such schemes in a particular shopping centre does not necessarily imply that it suffers from depression. Whilst many drapers and furniture shops in the Newport Road centre, which is known to be poor, depend almost entirely on clothing clubs, ticket agents and hire purchase, an equal number of multiples and department stores in the prosperous primary centre employ the same methods, though they do not rely on them to the same extent. In general, the use of the credit system depends largely on the function of shops, on their serving occasional rather than daily needs. For this reason, there are more shops selling by credit in the chief and intermediate centres, than there are in the local and strictly local centres.

Taking Orders

Most shopping in Middlesbrough is still done over the counter. Receiving orders by post or by telephone is relatively new and rare and confined almost entirely to the chief centres and intermediate centres. The shops in these centres sometimes receive telephone orders from their wealthier customers in the outer residential ring. Mail orders reach them chiefly from people living outside Middlesbrough. However, since deliveries and the sending of goods "on approval" have been restricted during the war, an increasing number of customers come into town to select and collect their purchases.

The use of credit systems and, to a lesser extent, the taking of mail and telephone orders, no doubt helps the chief and intermediate centres to maintain, and perhaps even to widen, their spheres of influence. The more a shop relies on these methods, the less tied is it to its present location. Consequently, the re-distribution of some of these shops and shopping centres, which appears to be necessary for the general benefit of local retail trade, might not in every case disturb their trade significantly.

2. Social Functions of Shops

A number of shops in Middlesbrough fulfil a social as well as a trade function. This is particularly true of the shops in the newer areas of the town, which are not adequately equipped with neighbourhood services. By taking on post-office duties, offering a variety of small services, using their windows for displaying advertisements or even acting in a limited way as meeting places, shops are helping to fill the gaps caused by the lack of social facilities in their neighbourhoods.

Post Offices

Ten of the 23 post offices in Middlesbrough are in shops, and all but three of these are in the parts of the town which are inadequately equipped with social facilities. A shop which undertakes post-office duties, and particularly one in an isolated or new district, occupies an important position in its neighbourhood. Through the Post Office Savings Bank, the payment of pensions and the issue of licences, the manager comes into continuous personal contact with his customers and is able to discover ways in which he can be of further service. He is usually well known in the district and especially popular with the shops near him, which benefit from being on either side of the most frequented store in the neighbourhood.

Services

Service is an essential adjunct to the trade of some shops. Shops selling musical instruments, bicycles or radios usually have repair departments. Shops that sell coats and gowns often have work-rooms where alterations or tailoring can be done. These kinds of services are offered by about a third of all non-foodshops in the old part of the town and by about a quarter of those in the newer areas. Shops of all economic types, except chainstores and one-man shops, provide such services.[32]

Personal service, unrelated to the trade of the shop, is much rarer and given only by some of the small shops in the isolated or outlying areas. For example, the manager of a small general shop in North Ormesby undertakes for a small sum to dispatch advertisements for his customers to the local newspaper and, if necessary, to collect the replies as well. As the only public call-box on the Brambles Farm housing estate has long ceased to function, the telephone in one of the general stores there is not only used by the customers, but the owner herself regularly makes urgent calls for them, at no more than the usual post-office price.

Notice Boards

A number of shops act as general information centres. Notices of lost property, goods for sale, rooms to let, are displayed on boards hung in a conspicuous place, either in the window or at the door-way. A few shops prefer to keep registers of information inside the shop. For instance, a newsagent has a list of rooms to let, and an antique dealer keeps a servants' register for his regular customers.

The majority of shops with notice boards are in the strictly local centres in the south, but every group of shops, except the primary centre, has at least one shop of this kind. However, many shops dislike displaying notice boards and refuse to do so even at the specific request of their customers.

Meeting Places

Some shops are used as informal meeting places, and not only by their customers. The cafés of the department stores, for instance, are frequented by many people who have no intention of buying anything in the store. The use of the smaller shops as meeting places is more often combined with a trade transaction, but many customers make a small purchase the excuse for a long gossip. In the poorer areas, they often buy goods in the smallest possible quantities to the annoyance of the shopkeeper, and visit the same shop three or four times a day. Once in the shop, they are sometimes joined by neighbours passing by, who come in merely to chat. At all hours, one can see little groups standing talking round the counter or at the doorway. Some even come and go without buying anything.

One in eight of the non-foodshops interviewed is used as a meeting place in that way. There are such shops in every part of the town, but they are more frequent in the poor and isolated parts than in the central districts.

The Role of the Small Shop

The village shop tradition is carried on chiefly by the small general shops, whose owners still know their customers personally and are, therefore, able to assist them in many different ways. With a few exceptions, shops which are used as meeting places, or which which display notice boards, are independent family or one-man shops. These do far more for their customers than merely supplying them with goods, particularly in the isolated and newer districts which are inadequately provided with social facilities. There is no doubt that the small shop is still an essential institution in every urban neighbourhood.

Yet the small shop can only help to meet social needs, it cannot adequately satisfy them on its own. It cannot take the place of the various neighbourhood services, the lack of which is clearly indicated by the social functions now performed by shops. Small information centres and places where housewives can meet informally appear to be required in each neighbourhood. It cannot be left to the shops to provide these facilities, the demand for which at the present time certainly exceeds the supply.

3. Customers from the Tees-side and Cleveland Area

Middlesbrough is generally regarded as the chief shopping centre for the Tees-side and Cleveland area. Though Stockton with its good market, and Darlington, at a major railway junction, are competitors, Middlesbrough as the largest town in the area, with a great variety of shops and frequent bus-services to and from the smaller towns and villages, plays the most important role.

The extent of custom drawn from the Cleveland area is indicated by the fact that over a quarter of all the Middlesbrough non-food-shops interviewed estimated that at least 25·0 per cent. of their customers came from outside the town. Most of these shops are, of course, in the chief centres. An additional substantial group of shops, one-half of the total number, have a small proportion of ouside customers. Non-foodshops which serve Middlesbrough only are definitely in a minority. Most of these are in the strictly local centres or isolated.

That Middlesbrough foodshops, too, attract people from the Cleveland area is indicated by the number of sugar-registrations at the town's shops in April 1944 which exceeded the total estimated Middlesbrough population by 12,000.

Shopkeepers gave a list of places from which their customers came regularly, which illustrated the scope of the town's sphere of influence. It ranges from Darlington, 15 miles to the west, West Hartlepool, 12 miles to the north, Stokesley, 10 miles to the south, towards the east, more than 30 miles along the coast to Whitby, and includes most of the intermediate towns and villages. The weekly time-table of the pool delivery service show a similar wide catchment area, and even the daily and bi-weekly round of the pool's vans extends far beyond the town itself, as is shown on the Maps of Middlesbrough's Spheres of Influence.

The local co-operative society, in particular, has promoted relations between Middlesbrough and the surrounding area. It has altogether some 51,100 members, 19,500 of whom belong to branches in the nearby small towns and villages.[33] Middlesbrough is the distributing centre for the society's branches and the major shopping centre of their members. The branches receive their groceries and dry goods from central warehouses in Middlesbrough. The society's Middlesbrough dairy distributes milk over an area which extends well beyond the town. Members from the Cleveland area, who come to Middlesbrough for guild meetings, visit the town's co-operative stores at the same time, particularly the large department store, the Emporium, which regularly sends goods, through the pool, to customers in Nunthorpe, Eston, Grangetown, Redcar and Saltburn. Since the co-operative society also runs a clothing club, the tickets of which are transferable from branch to branch, its Middlesbrough stores can always count on customers from Tees-side branches.

Middlesbrough's function as a shopping centre for the Cleveland area has to be taken into account in the replanning of the town's central shopping areas which are those most visited by outside customers. Provision should be made for adequate passenger and distributive transport, and for parking facilities, within easy reach of the chief centres. It is equally important to develop the amenities of these centres. Cinemas, restaurants and a great variety of shops, closely grouped together, are the main attractions for the people from outside the town.

4. The Impact of the War

The war does not appear to have altered significantly either the general distribution of shops or the relative importance of the various shopping centres. There have, of course, been some changes in the numbers and types of shops, in their staff structure, and in the goods they sell, but these changes have been general and have, therefore, not distorted the picture.

Numbers and Types of Shops

The total number of Middlesbrough shops appears to have decreased by about 10·0 per cent. since 1939. Shops had to close for various reasons: some premises were bombed; owners were called up for national service; it was difficult to get the necessary supply of goods or an adequate staff. The poorer intermediate and local centres suffered most, as many of their shops, which had barely managed to keep open before the war, were forced by these additional difficulties to close down. But in the chief centres most of the shops which were destroyed by bombs or fire were re-established in temporary premises. The strictly local centres have hardly any empty shops, and three new non-foodshops have even been established there since 1939.[34]

There have been no significant changes in the distribution of shops by economic type. The detailed survey of non-foodshops shows that all the larger shops, department stores, chainstores, co-operatives, multiples and multi-branch independents have retained their pre-war status. But a quarter of all the one-branch independent shops have, through shortage of staff, been reduced to the status of family shops or one-man shops, and about the same proportion of family shops have become one-man shops.

Trade Outlets

There is certainly less variety in trade outlets in 1944 than there was before the war. Over a quarter of all the shops interviewed[35] have either had to take on alternative trade lines or to restrict the range of their commodities. Fewer shops are able to specialise. Only limited supplies of the articles which they used to sell are now available, or such goods have even been entirely taken off the market. Drapers and clothiers, and shops selling household accessories, which normally specialise a good deal, have been most affected by the war-time shortage of goods.

Staff-Structure

Shortage of staff has affected the Middlesbrough shops more than any other war-time restriction. Apart from the general reduction in numbers, there have also been changes in staff-structure. The most important of these has been the increase in the proportion of female workers. Many shops, particularly those selling men's clothing, furniture, bicycles, radios and electrical equipment, have changed over from an all-male to an all-female staff.

Categories of Shop Workers	Categories of Shop Workers As Percentage of Total Staff in the Non-Foodshops Interviewed	
	1939	1944
Male Workers	36·0	21·0
Female Workers	64·0	79·0
Total	100·0	100·0
Counter-Assistants	62·0	66·0
Other Workers	38·0	34·0
Total	100·0	100·0
Full-time Workers	96·0	94·0
Part-time Workers	4·0	6·0
Total	100·0	100·0
Employees	88·0	88·0
Family Workers	12·0	12·0
Total	100·0	100·0
Average Number of Shop Workers per Shop	9·7	8·0

Counter-assistants were a lower proportion of the total staff in 1939 than in 1944. Wherever possible, their number has been maintained at the pre-war level, while the number of delivery, clerical and service staff has been reduced.

The slight war-time increase in the proportion of part-time workers is due to the fact that some employees now work part-time. Before the war, part-time work was undertaken by family workers only.

There has been no change at all in the proportion of family workers. Their number has decreased to the same extent as that of the total staff.

Transitory Changes

Most of the changes which the Middlesbrough shops have undergone since 1939 appear to be transitory, except for those cases in which war-time difficulties have aggravated latent poverty. It is probable that many shopkeepers now on active service will wish to reopen their shops when they are demobilised; more premises destroyed by bombs or fire will be rebuilt. Most shops will attempt to increase their staff as soon as possible and, as supplies become available, a greater variety of outlets and specialisation will be reintroduced. But although there may be expansion and more diversity, the picture of shopping facilities in Middlesbrough, in the immediate post-war years, is likely to resemble closely the one presented here. In the near future, significant changes can only be brought about through the planned redistribution of shops.

IV

CONCLUSIONS

1. Redistribution and Regrouping of Shops

Redistribution

A plan for Middlesbrough's retail trade has to solve two major problems. First, shops have to be redistributed so that each neighbourhood, and the Cleveland area as a whole, is adequately served. Secondly, a regrouping of shops is required.

The present unequal distribution of shopping facilities throughout Middlesbrough has caused inconvenience and depression. Where there are too many shops, a high proportion are forced to close down. As a result, there is not only an immediate loss of rates, but the poverty, represented by the empty shop-fronts in the street, is usually infectious.

Regrouping

There are too many isolated shops in the northern part of the town, and there are also too many shopping centres. Some of these appear to be redundant; their lay-out and location is out-of-date, and hence their function is no longer clearly defined. Only three types of centres appear to be required: first, one centre fulfilling a central function, which might be adjacent to a market; secondly, no more than three centres with an "intermediate" function; and thirdly, a number of strictly local centres, one for each neighbourhood, catering principally for daily needs.

The Siting of Shopping Centres

In shifting some of the existing centres or in establishing new groups of shops, two general principles should be applied. The distribution of shops has to be adjusted to the distribution of the population. Moreover, in each case, retail facilities should be related to social facilities. The chief centre should be near to the main cultural and recreational amenities of the town, since it is its function not only to attract the people from all parts of Middlesbrough, but also those from the surrounding area. A visit to the chief centre is something of an outing, many people wish to combine it with a visit to a cinema, restaurant or library. The grouping and scope of the amenities in or near the present primary centre would have to be improved in order to accentuate its status.

Centres with an "intermediate" function should be located so as to serve groups of neighbourhoods in the southern part of Middlesbrough. They should be closely related to the social centres of these districts. The present intermediate centre, Linthorpe Village, could well be retained and slightly enlarged and two further centres established, one in the south-east and one in the south-western area of the town.

A few of the local and intermediate centres in the north, which are now redundant, could be redesigned as strictly local centres. Some of the small strictly local centres in the south, which are now inadequate, should be enlarged. In each case, it is advisable to relate the group of local shops to the group of other neighbourhood services.

2. The Design of Shopping Centres

The Sorting Out of Land-Use

The principle of the alignment of shopping and social facilities does not imply, however, that there should be mixed land-use. On the contrary, this is, in the opinion of the shopkeepers, one of the major defects of the present lay-out of shopping centres, which should not be repeated in the new design of groups of shops. The intermingling of different types of buildings, residential premises, warehouses, banks or cinemas, with shops, conflicts with retail trade functions. Cinemas or banks on a corner site often stimulate trade, but they should not interrupt a sequence of shops.

Close Grouping

In fact, the close grouping of shops, which provides mutual sales attraction, is one of the most important aspects in the design of shopping centres. The whole group of shops must be closely connected but sufficiently spacious to avoid congestion. There should be enough room for people to move freely from one shop window to another. Too wide a street can effectively divide the shops that line it, while too narrow and crowded a street may lose its appeal. Ideally, a shopping centre should display its shops with as much care as each shop displays its goods. Both the size of the group and the design of each shop front should, therefore, be subject to control.

Variety of Trade Types

Shopkeepers in the larger centres prefer shops of the same trade type to be adjacent to each other. But each centre, large or small, should include, for the sake of mutual sales attraction, a variety of trade types, appropriate to its specific function.

The Composition of the Strictly Local Centres

It is particularly important to control the composition of a strictly local centre. Since it caters for a limited area only, the number of shops it can support is far less elastic than that of the other types of centres. At the same time, all daily needs should be served and some choice provided. The present standard of four foodshops to one non-foodshop could well be maintained. Sometimes as many as three grocers can be supported, a co-operative, a multiple and a small independent shop, but rarely more than one of each of the essential types of non-foodshops. There are usually two newsagents and tobacconists in the small Middlesbrough centres, but a second chemist, draper or ironmonger is seldom prosperous. However, additional outlets of these types are sometimes successfully provided by the co-operative and multiple grocers which are arranged on a semi-departmental basis. The small centres at present lack service shops, such as electricians, hairdressers, cleaners and cobblers. The demand for these varies according to the standard of living of the neighbourhood, but some provision for such services should certainly be made in each local centre.

Traffic Problems

Access to major traffic routes is of particular importance for the larger centres, but control and segregation of traffic is essential everywhere. The chief centre cannot maintain and widen its sphere of influence throughout the town and the surrounding area, unless the major bus and railway stations, now divorced from each other and restricted in space, are conveniently located and redesigned. Above all, traffic congestion must be avoided. The pedestrian should have priority in all shopping areas. He would gain it if through traffic were diverted and adequate service roads and parking facilities immediately behind the shops were provided.

At present, some centres suffer from being too far from the main stream of communications. Others, where through traffic is allowed, have a high accident rate, particularly so wherever numerous residential streets branch out from the main shopping road. The congestion in these centres is so notorious that it leads to loss of trade. People prefer to by-pass such a shopping area. Even a small centre gains from being near a bus stop, but if the route runs straight through it without a stop, the buses simply carry off potential customers to one of the central groups of shops. Proper allocation of transport routes and stopping places is essential if balance between the different types of shopping centres is to be restored and maintained.

3. Readjustment

It is evident that there is an urgent need to restore balance in the distribution of shops, in the composition of shopping centres and in their relation to each other. In fact, lack of balance is the dominant feature of Middlesbrough's retail trade, just as it is the keynote of every other aspect of present-day Middlesbrough. Maladjustment has spread from one sphere to another. The straggling shopping street, desolate or overcrowded, broken up by empty shop fronts and non-retail premises, is only one of its familiar symptoms. Mixed land-use has produced mixed traffic and consequent congestion, danger and depression. In one area, shops and social services are too numerous and hence too competitive, whilst in another, they are too scarce and hence inconvenient. One major cause, the uncontrolled growth of the town, has produced this universal maladjustment. There can be no other but a universal cure.

PART V

SURVEY AND PLAN

The General Theme

At every stage, the survey of Middlesbrough has led to the same general conclusions:

The contrast between 19th and 20th century Middlesbrough is ever present. The physical and social structure of the town, and the distribution of its services and amenities, all show the same division.

But while Middlesbrough is split, all its problems are interconnected. The health of the people is not dependent on the provision of health services alone; rehousing requires more than houses; equality of educational opportunity cannot be achieved merely through the building of schools; the fortunes of the town are bound up with those of the surrounding area. These relationships are only too obvious, and yet their specific implications need to be stressed at every point, for they determine both the principles and the programme of planning.

Moreover, they also determine the attitude towards the very concept of planning. For not only are Middlesbrough's problems now all intertwined, but they also all derive from one common cause: 19th century *laisser-faire*. Uncontrolled development has caused all the cumulative maladjustments; it has continually widened the social cleavages within the town. It cannot be allowed to persist.

The Nature of the Planning Proposals

While the need for planning is thus a recurrent theme, the detailed survey results point to specific planning proposals. All these have one object in common: to create a unified and balanced Middlesbrough; to eradicate inequalities and yet to assure diversity; to make change and growth compatible with adjustment. Therefore, although these proposals are often specialist in character, they are all based on the recognition of the town as a whole. Indeed, as the survey has shown, we cannot even tidily separate the physical from the social and economic aspects of town life. They all have to be fused in the plan.

Yet for this very reason, the completed town plan itself, and even the individual proposals, some of which have been stated here, may appear to be utopian. A short term and a long term programme can be developed; areas which need slum clearance most urgently can be indicated. But apart from specific requirements of this kind, no strict system of priorities can be developed. Industry, homes, schools, local and central services, all are equally important. In fact, it is their relationship to each other which matters most. Hence the town plan is, of necessity, based on the assumption of a large scale combined operation.

But although the plan may be ahead of the times and may not be fully implemented, it does provide a framework for reconstruction and new development. At the very least, its proposals are a measure of our shortcomings.

The Functions of the Planning Survey

The persuasiveness of planning proposals depends largely on the survey from which they are derived. But what sort of a survey is necessary to produce a considered plan which is not merely an exercise in design? And how is the application of survey to plan, in fact, to be achieved?

While our experience is still so limited, these questions can, at least tentatively, best be answered by examining the three different functions which a survey in the field of town-planning can fulfil. Each of these three, the technical, the theoretical and the political motive, is represented in the Middlesbrough enquiry.

The Technical Purpose of the Survey

First, and usually foremost, the survey has a technical purpose; that is, it has to provide facts on which immediate planning decisions can be based. Most of the familiar surveys of the physical aspects of town life are of this character, but it has increasingly been realised that certain social aspects are of equal practical importance. Not only the existing physical boundaries, but also social boundaries should determine proposals for realignment and regrouping. While the survey should delimit reconstruction areas, it must also identify neighbourhoods from which resistance to change might be expected; that is, for instance, neighbourhoods which are either closely integrated, or those where homes and workplaces are near to each other, or those which are almost entirely inhabited by owner-occupiers.

Hence the picture of the neighbourhood pattern was just as

useful in the formulation of the Middlesbrough plan as the picture of the road pattern. The survey showed the interrelationships of neighbourhoods and hence the broader sub-divisions within the town. While not all the existing neighbourhood boundaries were retained in the plan, the knowledge of the specific needs and characteristics of each distinct territorial group could be interpreted, particularly in the housing programme and in the proposals for consequent population shifts. It was suggested that neighbourhoods with inadequate institutional equipment, or those which were too small to support essential services of their own, should be rounded off or connected with new housing development. In proposing new transport routes, it was possible to avoid cutting across existing neighbourhoods, and to link more closely those which were already interdependent.

There are other examples of the technical function of the social survey. Most important, as long as official figures are not available, the housing requirements both of existing and of potential households can only be estimated on the basis of a specific sample enquiry, which shows the distribution of households by type and by size throughout the town. When this knowledge has been obtained, population shifts can be controlled so as to establish a balanced distribution of dwellings and of households in the neighbourhoods which should be reconstructed or newly developed.

Further, the survey has to provide material for the siting and grouping of services and amenities; for instance, for the proper allocation of the different types of shopping centres. Simple rules of spacing are clearly not applicable in every town, if indeed in any town. Middlesbrough could not afford a series of intermediate shopping centres, neatly arranged at intervals of half a mile.

The Theoretical Function of the Survey

While the technical parts of the survey are indispensable for every town plan, enquiries which have a theoretical function, that is, which help to formulate planning principles, need not and cannot be repeated in every case. At present, our knowledge of urban life and relationships is so deficient that a few comprehensive and comparable studies of a more theoretical character are urgently required. Their findings would make it possible to restrict the scope of subsequent planning surveys.

The Middlesbrough survey was not designed for the study of planning principles, but some of its technical enquiries were amplified so that their results are capable of theoretical interpretation.

Thus the spheres of influence of different types of institutions, and the patterns of movement within and between neighbourhoods, were observed in considerable detail. Two features in the final picture of Middlesbrough's neighbourhood structure can be assumed to be of general significance.

First, there is the fact that neighbourhood boundaries are determined by the physical characteristics of the environment and the social characteristics of the people, but that they are not boundaries of movement. Hence, though distinct territorial groups exist, which might be called neighbourhoods, these are never self-contained. Only a few, which are both geographically isolated and poor, show a considerable degree of self-reliance. It appears, therefore, that the interdependence of neighbourhoods should be emphasised in urban design, rather than the strict demarcation of each of them.

This conclusion is reinforced by the second and far more important general feature in the portrait of Middlesbrough; that is, by the fact that social stratification has been accentuated by geographical separation. People of different social groups live apart; by and large, the level of environment corresponds to the level of incomes; thus poverty is perpetuated. These persistent social divisions, in turn, have created persistent habits of social segregation.

How can democracy in town life be promoted? This is the major problem of urban grouping, which is present everywhere, and of which Middlesbrough is but a typical example. It applies to the planning of new towns as well as to the reconstruction of old towns, and yet it cannot be solved through the medium of town-planning alone. The mere shortening of the physical distance between the different social groups can hardly bring them together unless, at the same time, the social distance between them is also reduced.

Hence the solution of "social mixing" in residential units, which is so often advocated, appears to be rather unrealistic. According to this proposal, groups of expensive houses should alternate with groups of cheap houses in the same neighbourhood. But would the inmates of these different houses really get together? Would they use the same local institutions? Would not such a design merely create enclaves of the different social groups and thus reproduce the present pattern of socio-geographical differentiation, though on a smaller scale?

While these questions remain unanswered, it need not be assumed that the town-planner is incapable of contributing towards a solution of this problem of urban class-structure. Deliberate attempts at "social mixing" might fail. But the general raising of environmental standards, which is the very job of physical planning, is not less direct an approach and it might prove to be a far more effective one. People who live in slums and people who live in suburbs do not have very much in common. But they might get to know each other far more easily when the old contrasts have been obliterated, and when houses and amenities vary according to family size and need, rather than according to income.

Moreover, the very process of planning creates a common interest, as long as the people are consulted and are participating in the solution of their problems.

The Political Function of the Survey

The survey is the medium through which their views can be made known. Hence the survey has not only a technical and a theoretical, but also a political function; it is an instrument of democratic planning. Most of the time, the task of fact-finding itself implies that people's opinions are interpreted and that their interest is stimulated. But there are also occasions when it is necessary to prove the obvious in order to obtain public support.

A few instances should be quoted. Even a cursory examination might suffice to distinguish the obsolete from the up-to-date schools. But while a mere list of unfit schools can be laid aside, a detailed analysis of the schools, and of their impact on the children, cannot easily be ignored. One fact, in particular, which was brought to light in Middlesbrough, will not be forgotten. It was found that the chances of children of reaching higher education were multiplied fifteen times when they moved from the blighted areas to the new housing estates, and thus from the obsolete to the up-to-date schools.

Similarly, derelict houses are easily identified. But slum clearance appeared to be far more urgent a job when it was realised that the infant mortality rate was almost twice as high in the slums as in the suburbs.

The sociological part of the survey, in particular, brings the planner and the people together. Enquiries into the physical setting alone are rather impersonal; comparatively few contacts are made to carry them out. But enquiries into the needs and relationships of the people are everybody's concern; they cannot be undertaken without the co-operation of many individuals and of all the major organisations in the town. The local societies and officials, the housewives and the wage earners, the industrial employers and the shopkeepers, the teachers and the school children, all were asked in Middlesbrough to tell their story and many even carried out parts of the survey themselves. Therefore, most of them felt that they had a stake in the plan.

The Application of Survey to Plan

Of course, there are conflicting needs and interests, which have to be reconciled. Hence it is difficult to interpret all the facts which have been collected. Indeed, the limitations in the application of survey to plan should be stressed.

The survey can help to reduce, but it cannot eliminate the arbitrary element in planning decisions. The problems which the plan has to solve can, and should be, scientifically discovered and presented. But their final solution, which is rarely unequivocal, is at the discretion of an individual or of a group.

As it is essential, therefore, that the survey results at least be entirely reliable, specialised techniques of investigation have to be used, and several fields of enquiry have to be covered. Thus a new difficulty arises in the application of survey to plan. Different specialists should be consulted, but while their methods are necessarily varied, their approach to the problems of planning should be unified. Town-planners, architects, geographers and social scientists have yet to learn to synthesise their specific points of view, and they can learn it only through the experience of co-operative work.

But are all these efforts really worthwhile? Is not the usefulness of the survey inevitably impaired, simply because its results are time-bound and thus do not lead to accurate forecasts? This question is often raised, and yet, both in theory and in practice, it is hardly appropriate. In fact, it is based on a false interpretation of the function of planning.

Social change is neither unprecedented and sudden, nor automatic. Consequently, a reliable picture of existing conditions shows the outlines of potential developments, the direction and the substance of which yet remain to be influenced and controlled. Thus, while the survey can help us to anticipate, it does not allow us to predict, precisely because the future is not immutable, but can, and should, be planned.

Of course, a plan which is laid aside will soon be out of date. But if its proposals are being implemented, the essential observations will necessarily be renewed, and decisions will consequently be revised. As there are so many imponderables, both the design and the administration of each plan should be flexible. Planning principles can only be tested through a series of experiments, some of which will be attempts to assure continuity, while others may lead to a deliberate departure from the present.

Indeed, the process of planning cannot be regarded as a Cook's tour into the future; it is essentially our common journey of exploration and adventure. Therefore, it is important to co-ordinate the existing knowledge well in advance; to prepare the maps and charts; to establish communications; and, most of all, to get to know our travelling companions.

APPENDICES

APPENDIX A

THE GEOGRAPHICAL AND ECONOMIC BACKGROUND

BY A. E. SMAILES

I

THE PHYSICAL SETTING

1. THE VALE OF TEES

In its lower course the river Tees meanders across a flat or slightly undulating lowland, and just east of Middlesbrough opens out into a large estuary. Only a century ago it made its way to the sea across the tidal flats by three shifting channels, but the river is now confined within a single channel by training walls, and the estuary flats are in process of reclamation. Much land has been added since 1850, especially on the south shore where almost all the land lying north of the Redcar railway has been reclaimed by dumping slag.

In Durham the land rises from the river very gradually towards a low plateau, but a few miles south of the river the great Cleveland escarpment rises steeply from the plain to heights of over 1,000 feet. In the lowland the meandering river swings from side to side of an alluvial flood plain, and the present channel between Stockton and Middlesbrough is the result of two artificial cuts across the necks of large loops in the old river course. These cuts were made early in the nineteenth century with the object of improving navigation of the river to the port of Stockton.[1] Between the two main urbanised areas of Tees-side, the abandoned meander loops form an extensive tract of flat land uncovered by buildings.

Narrow strips of alluvium extend up tributary valleys, e.g. Billingham Beck and the series of parallel south-north becks which feed the Tees from Cleveland. There are also scattered patches of alluvium elsewhere in the lowland, but no extensive areas; and except in the Stokesley district where the Leven is liable to flood considerable areas, little of the region is seriously affected by river flooding.

The surface of the plain is formed by a layer of glacial drift which overlies a basis of Triassic rocks consisting of marls and sandstones. The drift is generally a heavy clay, and the soils, although moderately fertile, are difficult to work and suffer from impeded drainage. The clay, however, is relieved occasionally by patches of sand, notably in a discontinuous belt which extends from south-west to north-east along the line of the main road south of Middlesbrough. Some of the old villages, e.g. Lazenby, and Lackenby, are found on it, while Guisborough, Norton, and Wolviston are sited on other sand patches.

2. The Site of Middlesbrough

The older part of Middlesbrough is situated in the last great northward bend of the river before it enters the estuary. The port was established where, just below the river bend, the current of deeper water swings back to the south bank. Here, too, the river bank is approached by a spur of high ground, formed of glacial drift, which juts into the young alluvium. This was the site chosen for the original town, as laid out in 1830 by the owners of the Middlesbrough Estate; to the east the Dock was later easily excavated in the alluvium at the head of the estuary; and to the west the flat alluvial land in the river bend north of the railway has been occupied by the industrial works and railway sidings of the Ironmasters' District.

From its nucleus in the St. Hilda's Ward of the present Borough, the growing town spread outwards south of the railway on the plain of glacial clay. Beyond the advancing front of buildings the surface of this plain was pitted with numerous brick fields that provided the building material. Although the 100 ft. contour is reached within the southern limits of the Borough, most of the present housing of Middlesbrough lies below the 50 ft. contour line. Along the courses of the tributary becks the drift surface is slightly grooved by long fingers of lower alluvial land. That along Marton Beck separates Albert Park and Linthorpe from the Grove Hill and Marton Road districts. To the north it converges with the valley of the Ormesby Beck, followed by the Guisborough railway. North Ormesby occupies the northern end of a long low-lying spur of drift between this valley and the next, that of the Middle Beck. Beyond the Middle Beck, again on drift, is the Brambles Farm Estate. Yet another strip of alluvium, along the Spencer Beck, intervenes before South Bank is reached, and along part of the stream course here is the eastern boundary of the Borough.[2] On the west side of the Borough, beyond the Whinney Banks Estate, where an extensive tract of open land separates Middlesbrough from Thornaby, the boundary follows part of the old course of the Tees.

Only the upper parts of some of the valleys just referred to are now occupied by surface streams, but their lines are followed by some of the main sewers carrying the main drainage of the town into the Tees, and some of the ward boundaries follow the old drainage lines which marked the natural divisions of the town site.

3. The Cleveland Hills

Stretching south of Middlesbrough towards the foot of the Cleveland Hills, the lowland rises very gently at first towards a line of old villages which include Marton, Ormesby, Normanby, and Eston. In front of the main escarpment Eston and Upleatham Hills are outlying masses of the same hard Jurassic rocks. They present an abrupt face to the north where the summit of the escarpment dominates the plain and estuary from a height of 800 feet at Eston Nab. The dip slope southwards is more gentle towards the re-entrant valley in which Guisborough is situated. Slapewath Beck enters the eastern end of this vale by a channel which represents a diversion of the drainage since pre-glacial times, and provides a route for the railway towards the mining field further east.

South of Guisborough the main escarpment rises very boldly to heights of over 1,000 feet in Roseberry Topping and Highcliff Nab. Behind it the plateau surface has a general altitude of over 800 feet, and is free from glacial drift. The sandstones and shales give only thin and poor soils, and the surface of the plateau is open moorland. Nearer the coast, however, the plateau lies at a distinctly lower level (400 feet to 700 feet), and the rocks are coated with glacial drift. Here there is more and better soil, and most of this lower plateau surface is farmed. The moorland edge often corresponds very closely with the limit of the drift, the drift-free plateau being almost invariably moorland even where, as on Eston Hill, it lies at a somewhat lower level.

From Saltburn southwards the highland comes right to the coast, and the stretch of sands which extends from Teesmouth by Redcar and Marske is replaced by a rocky cliff coast. The cliffs attain a height of several hundred feet, and at Boulby provide the highest cliffs on the English coast (660 ft). They thus present exposures of a large section of the lower Jurassic strata, including the ironstone seam and the alum shales. The latter were extensively worked along the cliffs here as well as south of Whitby during the two and half centuries before 1870.

Narrow breaches in the cliffs, as at Skinningrove and Staithes, mark the mouths of the becks (Skelton, Kilton, Easinton and Roxby) which dissect the coastal plateau with deep, steep-sided and usually wooded ravines, called gills. The absence of any coastal plain, and the presence of these gills, which break the smoothness of the plateau surface, make communications along the coast difficult and give stretches of steep gradients along the main coastal road, e.g. at Loftus.

Farther south the Esk occupies a larger and more open dale in the highland, almost but not quite closed to the west. At Kildale there is a narrow opening, used by the railway, which leads to the embayment of lowland around Stokesley. The lowland here lies at the foot of the most imposing part of the escarpment.

4. Mineral Resources

The mineral resources which have contributed in large measure to the industrial development on Tees-side are the Cleveland ironstone, the Durham field of coking coal, and more recently the salt and anhydrite of Teesmouth.

The Durham Coking Coal Field

Although the coalfield does not lie within the area covered by this survey, it must be mentioned here as its importance to the Tees-side industrial area can hardly be over-emphasised. The modern port was created as an outlet for its coal, and for this purpose the famous Stockton and Darlington Railway (1825), with the Middlesbrough extension (1830), as well as the Clarence Railway (1834) were built. For the industries subsequently established on the Tees, the proximity of this coalfield, with pits within twenty miles of Middlesbrough, has always been of paramount importance.

The Cleveland Iron-Ore Field

The great iron-smelting industry of Tees-side dates from the beginning of exploitation of Cleveland's ironstone field in the middle of the last century. Although at several horizons the Jurassic rocks are ferruginous, it is the Main Seam, near the top of the Middle Lias division, which has played the dominant part in the history of local mining. It outcrops along the coastal cliffs, but its large-scale exploitation dates from its discovery inland along the face of the escarpment at Eston in September 1850. From its outcrop at Eston, where it was over ten feet thick, the seam dips southeast. In this direction the great Upsall Fault brings up the lower strata again, so that the outcrop of the Main Seam is repeated along the escarpment south of Guisborough. To the south and east it again passes under a cover of sandstones and shales and becomes more and more deeply buried and less accessible. At the same time it thins considerably and deteriorates in quality (in the early workings at Eston the ironstone showed a metal content of 31–33 per cent., but in the southernmost mines it is only 25–27 per cent.). What is even more important, however, is that in the south-east the seam is split by a shale parting. The shale thickens farther south at the expense of the ore, and where it is over a foot thick the ironstone may generally be considered as unworkable. The ironstone was first won from open surface workings and adits driven along the outcrop, but shaft mining soon became necessary as the ore-bed was pursued under the covering rocks in the direction of the dip. The deeper mines are found in the Loftus-Skelton area where, as the cross sections show, the strata are arranged in a shallow basin structure. In this basin, shafts to reach the Main Seam need to be several hundred feet deep; the deepest, North Skelton, is 720 feet. Except in this area, however, the reserves of workable ore have been practically exhausted. The ironstone in Eston Hill has been worked since 1850, and this mine is unlikely to survive the war conditions. It is expected that at most only four mines (Lumpsey, South Skelton, North Skelton and Loftus) can remain active. Operations are now concerned entirely with the recovery of ironstone from areas which have already been once worked over by the pillar and stall method. From the outer zones of the mining properties operations are withdrawing towards the shafts, and the final exhaustion of the remaining reserves cannot long be delayed.

There are undoubtedly reserves of untouched ironstone farther south-east beyond the limit of the area that has been mined, but the stone is of poor quality, besides being relatively inaccessible, and because of the thick shale parting it is reduced to two thin seams. Consequently, it is doubtful whether it will ever be worked. Certainly it cannot be expected to be an economic proposition under any conditions that can be envisaged as obtaining after the war.

The Teesmouth Salt Field

Since 1860 the existence of a salt field at the mouth of the Tees has been known, but it was not until the '70s that production was begun. The field was extensively explored by borings before the end of the nineteenth century, since when little has been added to our knowledge of it. The salt-bed, generally about a hundred feet thick, lies about a thousand feet below the surface. It is confined to the area east of a line shown on map 18 and which passes east of Greatham and Cowpen, and through Middlesbrough Dock, near which it was first discovered. Further west the salt-bed thins out rapidly and disappears from the succession of strata. To the east, however, it maintains its thickness and is presumed to extend far to the south-east in the direction of the dip. Up to the present, however, this extension has not been worked or proved much beyond the immediate vicinity of the estuary. Here at Lackenby the salt-bed, 1,672 feet below the surface, attains a thickness of over 130 feet.

Anhydrite

At a slightly higher horizon, above the salt, is a layer of anhydrite (calcium sulphate), which is now extensively worked by the I.C.I. on their Billingham site. Great reserves of both minerals are known to exist, and they provide a great store of raw materials for the newly established chemical industries.

Water Resources

Besides these valuable minerals, the rocks under the plain of the lower Tees contain huge quantities of water, which is available on tap by sinking deep wells, and some of the industrial works have already used this resource. Both the Keuper sandstones which outcrop in the plain west of Middlesbrough under the superficial cover of drift, and the Magnesian Limestone lower down, are waterbearing; but the higher formations, under which these older rocks pass farther to the east, are impermeable.

Other Minerals

Among other minerals, the alum shales and jet, once extensively worked in Cleveland, are no longer important. The glacial drift, however, provides clay which has been extensively used by the local building industry; it is now used at Billingham by the new cement industry. The glacial sands are also worked for use in the iron industry, but for its other essential requirements of raw material, limestone for flux, dolomite and silica for furnace linings, the industry must look slightly farther afield. The limestone quarries are situated in Weardale, middle Teesdale, and in Wensleydale, and are largely owned and operated by the big iron and steel companies themselves. Dolomite is obtained from quarries in the Magnesian Limestone outcrop in mid-Durham within twenty miles range. Silica bricks come mainly from the coalfield, where the chief centres for their manufacture are in the south-west round Crook, using the suitable stones provided by the local carboniferous rocks. Some ganister, however, is quarried in Cleveland near Commondale and Castleton, and at the western end of Eston Hill, south of Normanby, there are works which provide some of the silica bricks used on Tees-side.

Finally, among the mineral resources of the area, mention must be made of the Cleveland Dyke. This is an intrusion of an igneous rock, dolerite (whinstone), which traverses the area in a straight line from west to east. It crosses the Tees at Eaglescliffe and reaches the Cleveland Hills south of Roseberry Topping. At various points along its outcrop, especially at Ayton Stainton and Coatham Stob, it is quarried to provide stone for making "tar-mac" for surfacing roads.

II

THE PATTERNS OF LAND USE

I. Land Use

Against this background of physical conditions, a pattern of land use has been developed which clearly reflects the varied suitability of different types of soil and surface conditions for different purposes.

Moorland

On the plateau surface behind Middlesbrough there are extensive heather moors. Moorland prevails above the 800 ft. contour line and sometimes extends below this height, in fact, wherever the sandstone and shale rocks lack a cover of glacial drift to give deeper and better soils, for the weathering of local rocks themselves gives only thin and infertile soils.

Woodland

The steep slopes of the escarpment bordering the plateau moorlands, and the equally steep sides of the deep-cut gills which dissect the plateau, are extensively wooded with oak and birch. Indeed the distribution of woodland throughout the region is largely an expression of steep slopes. Where not wooded, the escarpment face is usually covered with a wild vegetation of bracken and gorse, with some bilberry. The great potential value of the hill country derives from its very emptiness. It provides great open spaces with sweeping views, bracing air, and attractive scenery for the recreation of the urban industrial populations who live within only a few miles distance from these amenities.

Farmland

On the lower drift-covered plateau of the coastal belt most of the land is enclosed in farms, but the physical conditions give land of only moderate quality. Before the war it was very largely laid down to permanent pasture of a second rate type, mainly agrostis.

On the plain the prevalent heavy clay soils and impeded drainage are much more suitable for pasture than for arable land, but comparatively little is really high quality farmland. The best is provided by patches of lighter sands, and the urban fence established by the Ministry of Agriculture seeks to preserve from urban extensions the strip of lighter, well-drained soils which extends eastwards from West Acklam to Yearby in front of the hills.[3] Little land is at present used for the more intensive forms of commercial cultivation, fruit-growing and market-gardening, though the size of the local market (over 300,000 people) suggests that these might be developed. Allotments, however, occupy fairly large areas in the vicinity of the tracts of workers' houses, both on Tees-side and in the ironstone mining area.

Industrial Sites

The tracts of lowlying land composed of young alluvium which mark the flood-plains of the rivers, and the reclaimed estuary foreshore have been avoided by housing, but in places are extensively occupied by industrial works, as in the Ironmasters' District at Middlesbrough, and farther east on the north side of the Redcar railway.

Housing Areas

This railway, built in 1846, follows the estuary shore as it then existed. It separates industrial works on reclaimed land to the north from housing areas which lie to the south on firmer ground formed of glacial drift. Most of the settlements of the region, being located in the lowlands, are of necessity built on glacial drift, which is predominantly clay; but it is noteworthy that sites on drier sand patches, where available, have been chosen for the older settlements.

2. Location of Industry

Heavy industries and mining dominate the industrial structure of the region, and their sites have been established with close regard to physical conditions. They belong to the category of fixed industries, whose siting is confined within relatively narrow limits of choice by compelling physical requirements, and which, once established, are more or less immobile.

Iron-Ore Workings

Although the early ironstone workings were naturally located along the outcrops of the Main Seam on the main escarpment and its northern outliers (Eston and Upleatham Hills), modern mining from shafts is largely confined to the plateau between Guisborough and the coast near Loftus. Here the mining operations, both active and abandoned, have been responsible for sterilising considerable patches of the upland surface from agricultural use.

Iron and Steel Works

The iron and steel works are found on Tees-side, where they claim extensive areas of land. They were originally established alongside the railways which brought them coal from South Durham and ore from Cleveland; and most of them enjoyed the further advantage of being alongside navigable water for disposal of their bulky products. Since 1870 the use of imported ore has operated with increasing force to tie the industries to these riparian sites. Smelting has thus tended to concentrate near the river mouth. The majority of its important units to-day lie east of Middlesbrough on the south side of the estuary.[4]

Secondary Metal Industries

Foundries and other industries dependent upon the iron and steel industry, with the notable exception of shipbuilding, are more scattered, but are invariably located by the railways.

Chemical Works

North of the river, the I.C.I. works occupy an extensive new site at Billingham. Its exceptional advantages for the layout of a great chemical works are dealt with elsewhere.

Light Industries

The reclaimed areas along the estuary shores, and the new areas now under reclamation on the northern side, offer an acreage of land suitable for heavy industry which is far in excess of the requirements of the region. As is pointed out elsewhere, it is not a further great expansion of the space-taking heavy industries which is Tees-side's primary need, but rather a balancing development of light industries to correct the excessive emphasis on heavy industries. The numerous sites in the industrial tracts abandoned by active industry or occupied at present by obsolete works, and dispersed sites elsewhere in situations accessible from the homes of the potential personnel who would work in the new factories, are quite adequate for the industrial developments envisaged. There is no need to use more than a fraction of the vast area of land zoned for industry in the existing planning schemes. Nor is there any reason why the sites of new "foot-loose" industries should not be chosen with primary reference to their convenience of access from residential areas. In other words, special considerations should govern the selection of factory sites from among the large number of economically suitable locations.

Land-Use Zones

The Map of Cleveland Typical Transects presents, in summary form, the sequence of land-use zones met in typical traverses over the area, and it draws attention to their physical bases. Thus from the estuary southwards the following zones appear in succession: industrial works on the reclaimed foreshore, the railway following the old shore-line, housing areas behind it on the drift-covered plain, farmland extending to the foot of the steep, wooded or bracken-covered escarpment, where old ironstone workings have left their scars, and heather moorland or poor enclosed grassland on the plateau.

3. Settlement

Agricultural Villages

Successive phases in the history of settlement in the area are reflected in its present-day settlement pattern. The old pattern of the agricultural occupation of the pre-industrial age is still represented by small villages dotted over the lowland area, interspersed with scattered farmsteads. On the plateau below the moorland edge is a sparser and more dispersed type of rural settlement. Straggling hamlets, such as Moorsholm and Liverton, are found at altitudes of five hundred feet or more.

Old Market Towns

The old market towns of Stockton, Guisborough, and Stokesley also date back to the pre-industrial age, as does the old port of Yarm. When the new town of Middlesbrough was being laid out in 1831, Stockton with 9,000 inhabitants, and Guisborough with over 3,000 were the chief settlements in the region.

Industrial Settlements

This pattern of agricultural settlement is in parts heavily overlain by the industrial settlement which has spread extensively during the course of the last hundred years.[5] Largely urban and concentrated in the immediate vicinity of the river, it also includes the mining villages which have been established in Cleveland. These latter have often been sited without regard to any consideration other than convenience of access to the mines and a cheap plot of land into which to crowd some houses. Thus we find drab rows of miners' cottages packed together, often in the midst of bleak open country. Some villages, associated with the establishment of individual mines, are entirely new and quite unrelated to the older villages;[6] but mining has also produced considerable accretions to the older settlements, such as at Guisborough, Loftus, Eston, Skelton and Brotton. Larger blocks of workers' houses alongside the iron and steel works represent the industrial communities of Tees-side. The typical nineteenth century lay-out was a succession of parallel rows, but some of the more modern housing estates stand out clearly by reason of their departure from this conventional grid-iron plan, e.g. Dormanstown and Billingham.

Away from the masses of industrial settlement that have spread back from the riverside, the rural pattern has been little affected except by the addition of the mining settlements. In an area such as the Vale of Stokesley the pre-industrial pattern is virtually intact. Redcar and Saltburn are later urban developments on the coast, and near Nunthorpe Station, on the Guisborough railway, an outer dormitory satellite of Middlesbrough has sprung up at Marton Moor.

4. Middlesbrough's Sphere of Influence

In an endeavour to determine as precisely as possible the range of Middlesbrough's influence as a area centre and focus of commercial and social life, a great many indices of a varied character have been examined. Of these the more significant and valuable have been made the basis of a series of maps.

It should be borne in mind that the extent of Middlesbrough's sphere of influence, as that of any other city, varies for different purposes. It depends upon the effective range that can be served, that is upon the accessibility to and from the city, as well as upon the strength of the competition of other neighbouring centres where a similar service is provided. In relation to Middlesbrough, Stockton is the most important rival in the provision of centralised services for the population of Tees-side.

Middlesbrough and Stockton

It will at once be apparent from the Maps of Middlesbrough's Spheres of Influence that Middlesbrough's tributary area is very largely in Yorkshire on the south side of the river. Middlesbrough's hold upon the communities of the north bank is comparatively slight, and at present is effectively confined for most purposes to settlements contained in Billingham Urban District.[7] Stockton can provide for its inhabitants and those of nearby places services hardly inferior to those offered by its much larger, but less well-established neighbour. No daily newspaper is published at Stockton, however, and the circulation area of the daily evening newspaper published from Middlesbrough embraces an extensive district in south-east Durham, which for most other purposes is served from Stockton. As a mecca for football enthusiasts, too, Middlesbrough is without a rival between Sunderland and Leeds, the nearest centres which support other First League teams. The home matches, on alternate Saturday afternoons throughout the winter, bring large crowds into Middlesbrough from districts on the north as well as the south side of the Tees.

Agricultural Market Centre

As the agricultural market centre of the district, however, Stockton reigns supreme. Middlesbrough has no agricultural market, and it is Guisborough which serves as the subsidiary centre for Cleveland. Nevertheless, Middlesbrough is an important shopping and entertainment centre for the agricultural as well as the industrial and mining populations of the Cleveland area. Again, it is itself an important consuming centre for local farm products, especially milk. This link is reflected by the area within which the farms are situated which supply the Middlesbrough Co-operative Society with milk for distribution in the industrial towns of south Tees-side.[8]

Wholesale and Retail Distribution

For wholesale and retail distribution, Middlesbrough serves an extensive area to the south and east, including primarily the steel towns and the mining settlements of Cleveland. Middlesbrough is "town" for the inhabitants of these settlements, whither they flock for shopping and entertainment.

The Boundaries of Middlesbrough's Sphere of Influence

It will be noticed that there is a remarkable correspondence between the outer limits of Middlesbrough's sphere of influence as defined for different purposes. The whole of the mining area, with a population of about 30,000, is quite definitely within Middlesbrough's sphere, but farther afield Middlesbrough's effectiveness as a distributing centre and focus is limited to the immediate vicinity of the main roads.[9] The rural settlements of Eskdale and the coastal tract beyond Loftus are rather out of range for the discharge of some functions.[10] To the south-west, Middlesbrough's region extends beyond Stokesley to the villages along the northern foot of the Cleveland escarpment, but it does not effectively reach Northallerton. On the western side, access to the rural area beyond the river Leven is hampered by the paucity of bridges over the river, and the villages farther to the west have better contacts with Stockton or Darlington than with Middlesbrough. Similarly, Yarm and the rural area to the north on the Durham side of the Tees have much easier connections with Stockton, and the influence of Middlesbrough on their life is slight. Thornaby is quite near enough to share fully the district services provided in and by Middlesbrough, but as most of these simply duplicate what Stockton offers even more conveniently, Thornaby must be reckoned within the sphere of influence of Stockton rather than of Middlesbrough.

Administrative Areas

Amid the somewhat bewildering complexity of the *ad hoc* divisions set up for different aspects of administration, the county boundary appears with great constancy. It is usually treated as sacrosanct, but Thornaby goes with Stockton for some purposes, which include the County Court organisation, Parliamentary representation and the Ministry of Labour's Employment Exchange organisation. These departures from strict observance of the county boundary as a line of territorial demarcation are logical and a recognition of the realities of the community organisation, for Thornaby is an extension or appendage of Stockton across the Tees, which owes its administrative independence essentially to being in another county.

Cleveland

From a comparative study of the various schemes of territorial division, a fairly clear conception of the extent of a composite Cleveland area emerges. It corresponds approximately with the sphere of influence of Middlesbrough that has been recognised above, the area within which the influence of Middlesbrough as "city" and focus of the district life and organisation is paramount.

Within this area, however, because of recognition of Middlesbrough's own special status as a County Borough, the town is for several purposes, besides local government, treated as an independent enclave, with separate administration, and as such does not share the offices and institutions of the district that completely surrounds it.

The undeniable capital of an area which may very appropriately be designated Cleveland, Middlesbrough rarely appears, however, as a centre for regional organisation on a larger scale.[11]

Middlesbrough in Relation to North-East England

For most aspects of regionalism, official and unofficial, Middlesbrough is only a satellite under the great provincial capitals, Newcastle and Leeds, on the borders of whose respective spheres of influence the vale of Tees lies. For different purposes Tees-side is grouped under the control of the one or the other centre. But by reason of its economic associations it belongs in the main to North-East England, the metropolitan region of Newcastle. The nucleus of this region is the industrial area commonly known as the North-East Coast, within which Tees-side is one of the main concentrations of activity. Inclusion of Tees-side in the Northern Civil Defence Region was the rational expression of these associations, as is its grouping with other parts of the North-East Coast in the North-East Development Area.

The belt of thinly-peopled and economically unimportant country which roughly corresponds with the southern watershed of the Tees drainage is the natural boundary of North-East England. It runs inland from the coast south of the Cleveland iron-mining area, and crosses the narrowing of the lowlands in the Northallerton district to reach the Pennine highlands between Teesdale and Swaledale.

III

THE ECONOMIC BACKGROUND

1. Industrial Structure

Occupational Structure

In its occupational structure the area is predominantly industrial, although it includes within a few miles of Middlesbrough some profoundly rural villages in the Stokesley Rural District. Nevertheless, considering the area as a whole, agriculture employs less than 2·5 per cent. of the working population, as shown by the 1931 Census. About one-third of the total occupied population are engaged in providing services of various kinds, and the remaining two-thirds are engaged in industrial production. How heavily weighted the industrial structure is on the side of heavy industries is suggested by the following statistics which have been computed from material provided by the Industry Tables of the 1931 Census. Heavy industries then employed more than 40,000 workers (37·0 per cent. of the total number of occupied males) as compared with only 4,000 (3·0 per cent.) in light industries. Most of the 30,000 males then recorded as out of work may also be regarded as being normally attached to the heavy industries, which were the most depressed.

These heavy industries employ males almost exclusively, and up to the present, there has been little scope for women and girls in industry. As compared with a ratio for England and Wales of 44 females per 100 males engaged in gainful occupations, the Tees-side and Cleveland figure was only 26 per 100 (that of Middlesbrough C.B. was 27 per 100), and three-quarters of the employed women and girls were engaged in services.

It is possible to estimate the reservoir of female labour available for industry in the Cleveland area at between 20,000 and 25,000. For many light industries this labour pool probably represents the major attraction that the area can offer.

The Narrow Scope of Cleveland Industry

Nor is it only that light industries are so poorly represented; the heavy industries that dominate the economic life of the region are themselves very few in number. Of the industrial workers in 1931, 27,000 (60 per cent.) were accounted for by the iron and steel and constructional engineering group of industries. Chemicals (7,160, i.e. 16 per cent.), ironstone mining (3,700, i.e. 8 per cent.), and shipbuilding and repairing (3,400, i.e. 7·5 per cent.), made up nearly all the remainder, leaving only 4,000 or less than 9·0 per cent. engaged in all other forms of industrial production.[12]

Even these figures do not fully reveal the narrowness of the industrial specialisation, since the important lighter branches of the metal-working and chemical industries are practically unrepresented. Blast-furnaces and rolling mills, foundries, constructional engineering shops, and shipyards employ the vast majority of the metal-workers. Industries such as electrical engineering, construction of vehicles, manufacture of cutlery and small tools, and of hardware and light metal goods generally, which elsewhere in the country employ large numbers of workers, are here of insignificant importance. The working of non-ferrous metals is quite unimportant too.

The specialisation of Middlesbrough's industrial economy was brought out clearly when we compared the occupational structure of Middlesbrough with that of five other towns of comparable size (i.e. Brighton, Norwich, Wolverhampton, Oldham, Rhondda). Since this comparison refers to 1931, a year of industrial depression, one of the attendant misfortunes of extreme specialisation upon heavy industries is emphasised, viz. an especially heavy incidence of unemployment.

Unemployment

The trend of unemployment at Middlesbrough has followed that of the United Kingdom. The ups and downs coincide as to date, but throughout the period since 1925 the incidence of unemployment was higher in Middlesbrough than in the country as a whole, and the bad years were felt very much more severely in Middlesbrough. Thus in 1932 unemployment locally reached 39·0 per cent., as compared with the national figure of less than 23·0 per cent.

2. Industrial History

The industrial history of this essentially young industrial area falls naturally into four main periods, the distinctive features of which are summarised below.

(a) Before 1850

The Beginning of Industrial Development

Before 1850, when the principal economic activity of Tees-side was the shipment of coal from the southern part of the Durham coalfield, there were small works for iron manufacture already established on Tees-side. These took advantage of the facilities available there for assembling pig-iron from Scotland and coal from Durham. Puddling furnaces and foundries were established, and included Bolckow and Vaughan's works set-up at Middlesbrough in 1840. A little shipbuilding was also carried on to provide colliers for the coal trade. Some engineering repairs were carried out for the railway company, and there was a pottery on the riverside which survived until 1887.

Such were the small beginnings of industrial development.

(*b*) 1850–1875

Pig-iron

After 1850 Tees-side experienced an industrial expansion the suddenness of which was almost unparalleled in our industrial history. It began when, following immediately upon the discovery of ironstone at Eston, blast-furnaces were set up on the Tees to smelt the local ore with coal from Durham. The district had previously been importing pig-iron from Scotland, but the tables were turned at once, and the river-side location of the blast furnaces greatly facilitated the distribution of the pig-iron turned out by the rapidly increasing number of furnaces. By the end of 1855 there were 35 blast-furnaces in the district, and that year the production of pig-iron exceeded 80,000 tons.

Wrought-Iron

The local production of large quantities of pig-iron gave a great fillip to the manufacture of wrought-iron, which was already established on the Tees, and especially after 1860 there was a rapid increase in the number of puddling-furnaces on Tees-side. From fewer than 200 in 1864, the number increased to over 1,000 in 1872, supplying more than one-third of the country's wrought-iron. Most of this large output was in the form of iron rails. There were also many foundries, like the puddling furnaces, established along the railways that served the area. Although waterside sites gave an added advantage for engaging in the export trade and for coastwise distribution of products, the iron industry was not by any means limited to such sites during this period when all its raw materials were received by rail. Not only was the Stockton-Thornaby area quite as important as the Middlesbrough area, there were also outlying units on the railways further north and west, e.g. Norton and Carlton ironworks.

Cleveland Iron Ore

The demands of the growing iron industry on Tees-side were as yet met entirely by the expansion in local ore production, which proceeded apace as the ironstone field was feverishly opened up. By 1856 the annual output of Cleveland ore had reached a million tons, and the number of mines was increasing every year.

Railway companies vied with each other in providing the necessary transport facilities to handle the lucrative freight of ironstone. The first workings had been along the outcrop of the Main Seam on its northern outliers at Eston, Normanby and Upleatham and on the main escarpment south of Guisborough, with a little from the coast. But shaft mining soon became necessary as the most easily accessible tracts were opened up, and by the '70s shaft mining was being extensively carried on in the basin of deeply buried ore between Guisborough and the coast. Nearly 10,000 miners were employed at about 40 mines. By 1880, when the production had reached six million tons per annum, the Skelton-Loftus area had become the main centre of mining, although the Eston and Upleatham mines were still the most important individual undertakings.

(*c*) 1875–1918

Steel

Steel production was begun on Tees-side in 1876, shortly after commencement of another new feature, the import of foreign ore, the first cargo of which was landed from Spain in 1867. The increasing ascendancy of steel over iron, and the increasing use of imported ore were the outstanding features of the period from the late '70s until the first World War.

The '70s saw the victory of the steel rail, and between 1872 and 1878 the number of puddling furnaces at work on Tees-side was reduced by half. By 1903 the wrought-iron output was reduced to only 119,000 tons.

While production of wrought-iron declined, and that of pig-iron did not show any further significant increase, the production of steel was greatly expanded.

Import of Ore

Production of local ore reached its peak (6¾ million tons) in the early '80s, and thereafter fell off as supplies were steadily exhausted. On the other hand, the consumption of foreign ore increased rapidly in its place. Not until 1877 did imports exceed 100,000 tons, but by 1893 they were more than one million tons, and in 1913 they exceeded two million tons, a figure again reached in 1936 and 1937. It is an amount greater than the production from Cleveland, and very much greater when measured in terms of the content of metal that is represented by the crude ore.

The increased importance of imported ore made the advantage of tide-water sites for the blast-furnaces more and more decisive. When new furnaces were established, sites were chosen in immediate proximity to the water-front, with facilities for unloading ore at jetties. The inland works, at a serious disadvantage, progressively dropped out of production, as their plant became obsolete.

Shipbuilding

Shipbuilding was another expanding industry which was even more definitely tied by its nature to the river. The output of the shipyards varied much from year to year, but it was generally considerably greater in the '90s than it had been in the '80s and greater again during the first decade of this century.

Salt-Production

Salt production was another new feature in the industrial economy of the region which appeared during this period. It began in 1875, but in 1883 was still only 3,000 tons. By the middle '90s, however, over 300,000 tons were being produced. Between 80 per cent. and 85 per cent. of this was derived from brine wells located on the north shore of the estuary, and the remainder from the Middlesbrough and the south shore farther to the east. Most of it (about 200,000 tons) was being exported, and chemical industries remained undeveloped. However, by the end of the century, salt production had diminished considerably, and from then until the Great War, it oscillated about 200,000 tons per annum, about half of which was exported.

(*d*) The Modern Period Between the Wars

Chemicals

Since the 1914–18 war, an addition of outstanding importance to Tees-side's industrial economy has been made by the establishment of Imperial Chemical Industries at Billingham. The north side of the river opposite Middlesbrough was able to offer exceptional advantages for a great undertaking producing heavy chemicals. The industry uses great quantities of bulky materials and the cost of assembling them is a decisive factor in its economics. The facilities offered by the Billingham site may be summarised as:

(1) Proximity to the Durham coalfield, and direct rail connections with it.

(2) The salt-field, which lies immediately east of the site, supplies brine by pipe-lines.

(3) Anhydrite is available on the spot; it is actually obtained from under the site.

(4) A frontage on the navigable waterway gives facilities for cheap import of raw materials that are not locally available (principally potash and phosphate rock), as well as for cheap distribution of the heavy products, both coastwise and overseas.

(5) Waste effluents can be discharged directly into tidal water.
(6) Adequate supplies of water, which is used in great quantities in the manufacturing processes, are available.
(7) A tract of flat land, not previously built over, gives ample space for expansion.

On a site offering this quite remarkable combination of advantages, I.C.I. have undertaken since 1923 the manufacture of fertilisers and other heavy chemicals on a great scale, and in 1935 they established a large plant for the hydrogenation of coal. Cement manufacture has appeared as a dependent industry, using local clay together with calcium carbonate derived from the chemical works, where it is a by-product of the manufacture of ammonium sulphate from anhydrite.

The Ascendancy of Steel

Besides the new development of the chemical industries, there have also been important changes since the first world war in the established industries. Especially noteworthy among these has been the increasing emphasis upon the production of steel rather than of pig-iron. Foreign markets for pig-iron have fallen off, and there has also been a growing tendency to use pig-iron direct for steel-making by feeding it into the steel-furnaces in a molten state and so effecting an economy of fuel. Wrought-iron production, once the basic industry of the area, is now a thing of the past, the last puddling furnace having ceased in 1922. There has recently been a decline in foundry work, but this may not be a permanent feature.

Steel remains important. During the inter-war period, variations in the local steel output closely followed the national trend. The North-East Coast region, in which all the producing units except Consett are now concentrated on Tees-side, has maintained a remarkably constant share of the national output, about 20 per cent. of the total.

Decrease in Local Ore Production

Large quantities of the necessary raw material continue to be imported, but meantime the decline in local ore production from Cleveland has become more rapid as the field nears final exhaustion. In the present penultimate stage, the burden of heavy costs incurred in winning the ore is not sufficiently offset by transport economies, and Cleveland cannot compete with other sources of supply. In 1944, of course, ore is being produced under the protected conditions of a time of national emergency, and production is not governed by purely economic factors. At no time during the last twenty-five years have more than eight mines been at work simultaneously, and production has fallen to less than two million tons. The exhaustion of the northern tract of ore, where the Main Seam was thickest, richest and most accessible, is virtually complete.

While imports of foreign ore have been maintained at a high level, they have not increased sufficiently to compensate for the decrease in local ore production. There has, however, been a notable increase in the use of scrap metal, which is not only brought into the area from other parts of the country by rail, but which has also become a significant item in the port's inward shipments.

Concentration of Production

These changes in the iron and steel industry have a significant bearing upon its location. The rapid decline of local ore production, by emphasising the dependence of the industry upon imported sources of ore-supply, has reinforced the tendency of the industry to concentrate east of Middlesbrough along the estuary shore, where adequate facilities for assembling the raw materials exist. The increasing use of molten pig-iron in steel-making has tended to concentrate production upon the units where this is possible, and the process of concentration has been further powerfully assisted by changes in the organisation of the industry. The latter have been in the direction of its large-scale integration. The difficult economic conditions which have faced the industry in the inter-war period have demanded rationalisation of the industry, and have accelerated the process of integration. As a result of amalgamations, Dorman, Long and Co. now control most of the remaining ore output, and the company is a large producer of coking coal from pits owned in Durham, and also has extensive limestone quarries. Integration of control has had as its corollary the concentration of production upon the best-located and best-equipped works, and the abandonment of obsolescent plant.

The concentration of the smelting industry in the area east of Middlesbrough at the present time as compared with its spread in the early years is striking. Of 29 blast-furnaces established before 1860, the Stockton-Thornaby area had 11, and the area east of Middlesbrough had 14. Of 22 furnaces in blast just before the outbreak of war in 1939, the Stockton-Thornaby area no longer had any, and the area east of Middlesbrough had 12. The Stockton-Thornaby area retains a share in the steel-rolling industry, and has important foundries and constructional engineering works. The main centre of the last-named industry is the Ironmasters' District in Middlesbrough.

Shipbuilding

Rationalisation has left its mark on another associated industry, that of shipbuilding. The output of ships reached its maximum just after the last war in the years of replacement after the heavy wartime shipping losses. But the industry slumped after 1930, and the activities of National Shipbuilding Securities Limited resulted in discarding several yards, so that at the outbreak of war in 1939 there were only two yards at work on the river, that of Furness and Company at Haverton Hill and that of Smith's Dock Company at South Bank. At the present time, the industry is more active, but it is difficult to forecast what its post-war position will be.

Utilisation of By-Products

A trend already evident in the earlier period, which has assumed much greater importance recently, is the increased utilisation of by-products. About three-quarters of the steel is manufactured by the basic process, and the basic slag produced in great quantities has become an important marketable by-product for use as a fertiliser. There are large slag-crushing mills at several places on Tees-side, where the slag is prepared. Rough slag is also sold for use in road-making. Besides these by-products of the steel industry, there are those of the coking plants. Instead of buying coke from furnaces on the coalfield, more of the coking is being done at up-to-date plants on Tees-side, notably at Grangetown. They provide great quantities of gas, which is not only used extensively by the steel industry, but which also provides the area with the cheapest domestic gas supply in the country. The distillation products, tar, benzole, pitch, creosote, as well as ammonium sulphate, are available in quantity, and provide the basis of a chemical industry. One firm in Middlesbrough itself, for example, is engaged in processing coal-products.

Light Industries

The establishment of a large clothing factory at Middlesbrough in 1934 points to the district's greatest industrial need, as well as indicating one of its opportunities to help meet this need. Light industries are badly needed to diversify the lop-sided local industrial structure, and to produce consumers' goods which are in universal and relatively constant demand in order to offset the narrow dependence upon capital goods, the production of which is so notoriously sensitive to the booms and slumps of the trade cycle. These light industries are also needed to correct the almost exclusive emphasis on male industrial work by providing factory work for women and girls. The recent development of a local clothing manufacture appears to have taken place largely in response to the existence of the large reservoir of female labour. At present, it employs about 2,000 workers in two factories, both of which are located in Middlesbrough. It is almost the only significant representative of light industries which the whole district so desperately needs for the establishment of a healthier industrial life.

Expansion of the existing clothing industry and new developments in this field, together with the attraction of some of the prosperous light industries which use steel as raw material, e.g. motor-vehicles, and pioneer development in the promising new field of industrial opportunity offered by plastics, all these suggest themselves as possibilities.

Coal Derivatives

The establishment of the great hydrogenation plant of the I.C.I. at Billingham, and the increase of coking by-products noted above, serve to emphasise the importance of coal in the modern world as a raw material for the production of valuable derivatives, and not merely as a source of power. Tees-side is favourably situated to be in the vanguard of developments in this field, and to share in new forms of industrial production, e.g. coal-tar plastics, as well as in the further expansion of those already established.

The Industrial Giants of Tees-Side

One cannot leave the subject of the industrial economy of the area in its relation to planning without drawing attention to a feature of governing importance. A large proportion of Tees-side's industrial population are employed by two firms, Dorman Long & Company and Imperial Chemical Industries. Their decisions regarding the siting of new plants and the abandonment of obsolescent works or mines are of far-reaching importance. The very existence of a means of livelihood within daily access sometimes depends upon them. They determine to a considerable extent the work-places and therefore a large measure of the convenience or inconvenience of life for Tees-side's resident population, as well as the organisational problems of the local authorities, for instance, as regards provision of the necessary passenger transport facilities.

All planning by local authorities on Tees-side depends upon knowledge of the policies and prospects of these giant private undertakings. Planning cannot succeed unless it has their fullest co-operation, both in the provision of factual information and in the formulation of policies. Granted this co-operation, however, the very concentration of control of the regional industry simplifies the task of regional planning.

3. The Tees Ports

Specialised Functions

The Tees ports are highly specialised and have no important general cargo trade. Their imports are dominated by the requirements of the iron and steel industry; more than 80 per cent. consist of ore. Products of the iron and steel industry figure very prominently among the exports also, though two other important groups of commodities appear, coal and coke and chemicals.[13] In 1938 the Tees imported one-third of the iron ore received by Britain from abroad, and nearly that proportion of the manganese ore. It accounted for one-sixth of the country's coal exports, more than two-thirds of the exports of fertiliser, and one-eight of the exports of iron and steel products.

Trade in Chemicals

The coal trade was the *raison d'être* for the creation of Middlesbrough and the construction of its dock in 1842, and it is still an important feature. On the other hand, the trade in chemicals is new. It began with the export of salt, but since the establishment of the I.C.I. works at Billingham there has been a greatly increased trade in chemicals, especially in fertilisers. Indeed, in 1938 the tonnage of fertilisers shipped from the Tees exceeded that of iron and steel products.

Coastwise Shipments

Coastwise shipments are much more important out of the river than is the incoming coastal trade. They account for half the outward bound cargoes as compared with only a tenth of those which enter the port. Large quantities of slag, fertiliser, coal and coal products, pig-iron and steel are distributed from the Tees by coasting vessels. The chief incoming items of the coastal trade are scrap metal and corn, which is still the chief import at Stockton.

Corresponding with the phases of industrial history described above, the trade of the ports has undergone important changes in constitution.

Changes in Coastal Trade

At the beginning of the nineteenth century the trade was small and the conditions of navigation exceedingly difficult. The river was obstructed by sandbanks and shoals, such as the notorious Jenny Mills island below Stockton, where vessels were regularly grounded; and below Cargo Fleet the river wandered uncertainly to the sea across the estuary by three channels, which were constantly changing both in their position and depth.

When a stone bridge was constructed in 1769 at Stockton, an effective barrier was presented to navigation farther upstream, and Stockton captured Yarm's trade. Stockton exported some agricultural products from the surrounding district, and lead from the Pennine dales; and it imported timber, lime for agricultural use, and coal for local domestic consumption. Coal began to be exported from the Tees only when the construction of the Stockton and Darlington Railway in 1825 gave Stockton railway connection with the Durham coalfield. From then on until 1850, the coal trade was the chief activity on the Tees. As outlets for the household coal producing districts of South Durham, Middlesbrough and Port Clarence came into being after 1830 at the termini of early railways. The trade increased rapidly, and in the years immediately after the opening of Middlesbrough Dock, in 1842, coal shipments from the Tees reached their peak, over half a million tons in 1846. But they were not maintained at this high level for two reasons. First, the household coal trade declined once railways had brought the Midlands coalfields into contact with the markets in London and the south. Secondly, shipments from Durham were diverted to newly developed ports, notably the Hartlepools, more directly accessible from the mines.

Port Improvements

Even before the creation of Middlesbrough as a coal-shipping port by the railway company in 1830, the difficulties of navigating the channel up to Stockton had made it necessary for much of the loading and unloading of vessels to be done lower down the river, at Cargo Fleet (Port Cleveland) and at Newport. Early in the nineteenth century, the Tees Navigation Company obtained Parliamentary authority to make cuts through the great meanders below Stockton, and these improvements were reflected by the increase in Stockton's trade. Prior to 1830, however, nothing had been done below Cargo Fleet to fix the uncertain channel, to remove the rock obstruction known as Cargo Fleet Scarf, or to provide lighting to guide ships in their hazardous passage through the estuary. In 1852, however, just after the establishment of the iron industry on Tees-side, control of the river was vested in the Tees Conservancy Commission, the subsequent work of which has transformed the physical conditions of navigation.[14] The enormous expansion of trade which followed the establishment of the iron industry called for the measures of port improvement which have been carried out.

Increase in Trade

As a result, from a modest 300,000 or 400,000 tons in the early '50s, the trade increased rapidly and almost without interruption to more than four million tons in 1913.

During the first twenty years of this period it was largely an export trade in pig-iron and wrought-iron, in place of the much reduced coal trade, which by the '70s had dropped in some years to figures of less than 100,000 tons. The first cargo of imported ore arrived from Spain in 1867, and thereafter imports of foreign ore began to balance the exports of manufactured or semi-manufactured iron and steel. The trade of the Tees ports continued to be dominated by the raw materials and products of the iron and steel industry, in spite of the appearance of salt among the exports from the middle '70s. Although very much reduced, compared with its dimensions before the middle of the century, the coal trade continued to be a significant item. In the years prior to the 1914–1918 war it amounted to about a quarter of a million tons per annum.

Pig-iron exports reached their peak in 1907, when they were 1·6 million tons. They have greatly decreased since then and in 1938 amounted to no more than the production of a single blast-furnace. Whereas, in the 1904–08 period, they were about half of the total export trade, in 1935–39 they were relatively insignificant, only 3·5 per cent. of the total exports. The trade in wrought-iron has completely vanished, and steel products have come increasingly to dominate the metal exports.

Modern Developments

Besides continued large imports of ore this century has seen the appearance of considerable imports of manganese ore for use in the modern steel industry, and imports of scrap metal have begun to be a significant item in the import trade.[15]

The rise in the importance of by-products, and the expansion of the chemical industry are other modern developments which have introduced new considerable items into the trade of the Tees, giving it greater diversity. Basic slag is now one of the great bulk cargoes which leaves the ports.[16] Coking by-products, for instance, creosote and pitch, are also important.

Some revival of the trade in coal and coke has further lessened the dependence of the export trade upon iron and steel products. Since 1918, the coal trade has usually amounted to over 400,000 tons per annum, i.e. about one-quarter or one-fifth of the outward shipments from the river. Much of this is loaded at Middlesbrough Dock.

Decline in the Importance of Middlesbrough Dock

But the importance of the Dock is declining. Since the principal producing units have a water-front, they find it advantageous to load and unload their heavy cargoes at their own wharves, and to dispense with the services of Middlesbrough Dock. Whereas during the 1820–24 quinquennium the Dock handled 65 per cent. of the outward shipments from the Tees, the 1935–39 period saw the proportion reduced to 27 per cent. The rise of the chemical trade, which belongs to the north bank of the river, is partly responsible for the diminution in the relative importance of the Dock trade.

But its decline has also been absolute and not merely relative.[17] Trade has been diverted from it in the same manner, if not to the same degree, as the trade moved first from Yarm to Stockton and later from Stockton to Middlesbrough. After superseding Yarm in the latter part of the eighteenth century, Stockton for a time handled most of the Tees trade, until it became urgently necessary to develop outports farther east. In time these daughter ports amassed almost all the trade. Middlesbrough was recognised as an independent port in 1861, by which time Stockton itself was already unimportant. How complete Stockton's eclipse is to-day may be judged from the fact that the average value of its trade during the ten years before 1939 was only a little over £300,000 as compared with £10,750,000 for the Tees as a whole. The shift of trade downstream, however, has not stopped at the head of the estuary. Like industry, trade is gravitating eastwards to the estuary itself, and to-day there are shipping facilities at Redcar Jetty right at its mouth. When the stretch of river-bank adjacent to the Dock, the Ironmasters' District to the west and the riverside above Cargo Fleet to the east were the chief seats of the iron industry, the Dock discharged an important function. But now, as smelting and coking are carried on mainly at plants located farther east, the Dock has become of much less importance for the regional industry. And it must be remembered that the Tees handles little general merchandise. The chief cargo that is not related to the immediate Tees-side industries is coal from the Durham coalfield, and naturally enough it appears as the chief item in the Dock trade. Coal provided more than 40 per cent. of the outward cargoes from the Dock in 1937, and coal is much more important in the trade of Middlesbrough Dock than in that of the Tees ports generally, with iron and steel products correspondingly less so.

Thus the Tees trade has passed through successive phases related to changes in the industrial activities of the towns on its banks. These industrial towns constitute the essential hinterland of the Tees ports, which thus have a strictly local function, except for the fact that they share in the Durham coal trade. Accompanying the changes in the constitution of the trade of the ports, there has been a geographical shift, as a result of which the centres of trade have migrated eastwards towards the estuary. This trend dates back to the eighteenth century when Yarm was superseded by Stockton; in modern times it has involved the eclipse of Stockton, the rise of Middlesbrough, and now the decline of Middlesbrough Dock in favour of shipping points in the estuary mouth itself.

IV

CONCLUSION

Tees-side's industrial greatness has been built upon the iron and steel industry, and has arisen in direct response to special features of its geographical setting. Advantage has been taken of the local resources, in particular the mineral wealth and the presence of a tidal river, to establish a great concentration of heavy industries, with their dependent communities. In the course of the rapid rise of this industrial agglomeration, the face of the countryside has been profoundly altered, and the special aptitudes of various localities and zones have been developed to produce the present differentiation of land use.

Throughout the modern industrial period certain dispositions have proved remarkably stable, but changes in the industrial structure have enhanced some site values and reduced or cancelled others. Examples are the abandonment of early iron works scattered along railways away from tidewater, and the increasing concentration of iron and steel works east of Middlesbrough on the south shore of the estuary.

Alongside this trend, another modern development of major importance has been the rise of the chemical industry, sited upon the saltfield. In consequence, the industrial importance of the eastern part of the area, bordering upon the estuary mouth itself, has been emphasised. The post-war plans of Imperial Chemical Industries for a large-scale development of the Wilton Estate will doubtless tend farther to draw workers and trade to the area east of Middlesbrough.

The future of Middlesbrough itself as a producing centre in the steel industry seems to be in expansion of secondary, rather than primary processes. At present, constructional engineering is the chief representative of these.

The industrial evolution of Tees-side, as well as the special vicissitudes of the past twenty-five years and the industrial reorganisation carried out to meet them, have left considerable tracts of Middlesbrough's industrial quarter, the Ironmasters' District, unused by active industry. If the space at present occupied by obsolete works is not required for the expansion of the industries already established in the Ironmasters' District, it should be freed to accommodate new light industries, which make comparatively moderate demands upon site space.[18]

The ill-balanced industrial structure of the whole area is certainly badly in need of an infusion of such industries. They are sorely needed not only to provide a measure of insurance against a recurrence of severe depression in the staple industries, but also to provide more scope for the employment of women and girls in respect of which the established heavy industries are deficient. The economic analysis shows that the introduction of light industries producing consumers' goods is a prime requirement for the future economic social well-being of the Tees-side communities.

Expansion of the existing clothing industry, and of the promising new field of manufacture, associated with coal-tar plastics, together with the attraction of some of the prosperous light industries which use steel as raw material, e.g. motor-vehicles, all these may be suggested as possible lines of development. It must be admitted that these industries are of a type for which nearly all British towns are clamouring as they prepare their plans for the future. The claims of Middlesbrough and of Tees-side, however, are particularly urgent. It can hardly be denied that few industrial regions stand in greater need of such industries to balance their industrial structure. If the case seems compelling on the score of relative need, it is supported also by the economic advantages which Middlesbrough can offer, especially for the industries specifically referred to.

After its century of growth, Middlesbrough may be expected to pass from the narrow specialisation of a typical industrial town to the diversity of activities which would help the town to consolidate its status as the capital of Cleveland. By reason of its size, location and of its established services, Middlesbrough should increasingly develop its functions as an organising centre, in the fields of business and administration, and in the fields of shopping and entertainment. In this development, the town will be assisted by recent improvements in its transport connections with the surrounding area.

In this context, however, even from the narrow standpoint of Middlesbrough's own self-interest, a disquieting change in the industrial fortune of the area is the imminent complete exhaustion of the supplies of workable iron-ore. It will affect the single-industry mining towns and villages of Cleveland most directly and most disastrously, but it is bound also to affect Middlesbrough, both because of its bearing upon the location of smelting, and because the mining communities, whose livelihood is directly threatened, are within Middlesbrough's sphere of influence. Middlesbrough's prosperity cannot remain unaffected by the fortunes of Cleveland, with which the town has been so intimately associated throughout its development.

Indeed, this is but one illustration of the fundamental unity of interest which makes it essential, especially in the sphere of planning, to treat Tees-side and Cleveland as a whole. At present, the area is divided among ten separate urban authorities for the purpose of local government. But, in fact, the area is an indivisible economic unit, and in every aspect of its life an association of interdependent communities. Thus it cannot be too strongly urged that the local authorities of the whole of Tees-side and Cleveland should co-operate to produce integrated plans for the future development of their area. Furthermore, since planning is a continuous process, permanent machinery should be provided to ensure the continuance of co-operation and the taking of co-ordinated action for the welfare of the whole Tees-side and Cleveland community.

APPENDIX B

HOUSEHOLD DISTRIBUTION AND HOUSING REQUIREMENTS IN MIDDLESBROUGH

1. Household Classification

An estimate of the total number of dwellings needed, and of their distribution by size and by type, was derived in Middlesbrough from the results of the household sample enquiry, which had been carried out by the Wartime Social Survey. In order to prepare this estimate, a household classification had been drawn up, which made it possible to sort out "concealed" or potential households, and in terms of which the relevant results were analysed.

Definitions

The following definitions were used for the classification of households:

(*a*) A Household:

A Household is a person or group of persons occupying one separate dwelling (either a house or flat) and also having separate catering facilities and arrangements.

A separate dwelling is distinguished by its physical separateness (e.g. the top-floor of a house with separate cooking and washing facilities) and usually also by the fact that rent is paid directly to the owner or manager of the building. Even when there is sub-tenancy, the physical separateness of the dwelling and its separate facilities are the decisive criteria.

A lodger, or boarder, or domestic servant is part of a household. The presence of lodgers, boarders, or servants, therefore, does not affect the definitions of household types. However, the number of lodgers, boarders, or servants in each household was recorded.

(*b*) The Family:

Husband and wife only, or two generations: e.g. parents, or one parent, with one or more sons/daughters. (The age of the children does not affect the household type.)

(*c*) The Kinship Group:

Not a family as previously defined, but a group of persons related by blood or marriage; the relationship not being one of husband and wife or of parents and children: e.g. two sisters living on their own, without a parent or parents.

Abbreviated List of Chief Household Types

A summary of the detailed list of household types is set out below. The chief distinction to be made is between "single household units", which are not likely to split, and "multiple household units", which may contain one or more concealed households.

Single Household Units:

1. A Family or a Kinship Group.
2. One Person Household.

Multiple Household Units:

3. One Family or Kinship Group with one or more additional Related Person or Persons.
4. Two Related or Unrelated Families or Kinship Groups.
5. Two Related or Unrelated Families (or Kinship Groups) with one or more additional Related Person or Persons.
6. Three or more Related or Unrelated Families (or Kinship Groups) with or without one or more additional Related Person or Persons.

The analysis of these household types by number in household, number of rooms inhabited, and by age composition, particularly with reference to one-person-households, showed their housing requirements in considerable detail.

2. Distribution of Households by Type and Size

Tables Ia and Ib summarise the distribution of households by type and size in Middlesbrough during the period of the enquiry, in June 1944.

Table II shows a comparison of the existing and post-war distributions of households by type. The post-war distribution is based on the assumption that all household members, who were temporarily absent, either in the Forces or on war work, will return to their households of origin.

Table III shows a comparison of existing and post-war distributions of households by size, based on the census definition of households.[1] But as, according to Table II, 17·5 per cent. of all post-war households will be multiple household units, which include "concealed" households, it is clear that the number of small households is potentially considerably larger than is shown by the distribution of households based on the census definition.

TABLE Ia

EXISTING HOUSEHOLDS BY TYPE AND SIZE, MIDDLESBROUGH 1944
Based on the Household Classification

Household Type	Number in Household, excluding lodgers						Total
	1 %	2 %	3 %	4 %	5 %	6 or more %	%
SINGLE HOUSEHOLD UNITS:							
One Family	—	93·0	85·0	72·0	70·0	72·0	75·0
Kinship Group	—	7·0	1·0	1·0	—	—	3·0
One Person Household	100·0	—	—	—	—	—	8·0
Sub-Total	100·0	100·0	86·0	73·0	70·0	72·0	86·0
MULTIPLE HOUSEHOLD UNITS:							
One Family or Kinship Group with additional related members	—	—	14·0	19·0	17·0	14·0	10·0
Two or three Families or Kinship Groups with or without additional related members	—	—	—	8·0	13·0	14·0	4·0
Sub-Total	—	—	14·0	27·0	30·0	28·0	14·0
Grand Total: Per Cent.	100·0	100·0	100·0	100·0	100·0	100·0	100·0
Grand Total: Number	107	418	358	237	144	123	1,387

TABLE Ib : EXISTING HOUSEHOLDS BY TYPE AND SIZE, MIDDLESBROUGH 1944
Based on the Household Classification.

Household Type	Number in Household, excluding lodgers						Total
	1	2	3	4	5	6 or more	
	%	%	%	%	%	%	%
SINGLE HOUSEHOLD UNITS :							
One Family	—	37·0	29·0	16·0	9·5	8·5	100·0
Kinship Group	—	83·0	11·0	6·0	—	—	100·0
One Person Household	100·0	—	—	—	—	—	100·0
MULTIPLE HOUSEHOLD UNITS :							
One Family or Kinship Group with additional related members	—	—	37·0	32·0	18·0	13·0	100·0
Two or three Families or Kinship Groups with or without additional related members	—	—	—	36·0	34·0	30·0	100·0
TOTAL	8·0	30·0	26·0	17·0	10·0	9·0	100·0

Table II : Existing and Estimated Post-War Distribution of Households by Household Type

(assuming that absent household members return)

Based on the Household Classification

Household Type	Existing Distribution	Estimated Post-War Distribution
	Percentage of Households	Percentage of Households
SINGLE HOUSEHOLD UNITS:		
One Family	75·0	75·0
Kinship Group	3·0	3·0
One Person Household	8·0	4·5
Sub-Total	86·0	82·5
MULTIPLE HOUSEHOLD UNITS:		
One Family or Kinship Group with additional related members . . .	10·0	11·0
Two or three Families or Kinship Groups with or without additional related members	4·0	6·5
Sub-Total	14·0	17·5
GRAND TOTAL . . .	100·0	100·0

Table III : Existing Distribution of Households by Size, Excluding Lodgers, Compared with Estimated Post-War Distribution of Households by Size

(assuming that absent household members return)

Based on Census Definition of Household

No. in Household	Existing Distribution %	Estimated Post-War Distribution %
1	8·0	4·5
2	30·0	19·4
3	26·0	25·5
4	17·0	20·0
5	10·0	14·6
6 or more	9·0	16·0
TOTAL	100·0	100·0

3. Estimates of the Post-War Number and Distribution of Households in Middlesbrough

In order to estimate the potential number and distribution of post-war households by size, the following considerations were employed.

The number of existing households in Middlesbrough, as estimated on the basis of the Household Sample enquiry, was 35,800.[2] Additions to this number of households may occur for three reasons:

(*a*) Immigration; an unknown factor that could not be taken into account.

(*b*) The splitting-up of present multiple household units. This could be estimated on the basis of the distribution of households by type, as shown by the Household Classification.

(*c*) New Marriages of single people of marriageable age groups; this could also be estimated on information from the Household Sample Enquiry.

Reductions in the number of households occur for two reasons:

(*a*) Emigration; again an unknown factor that could not be taken into account.

(*b*) Existing households may become extinct through death or other causes; this is also an unknown factor.

As possible reductions in the number of households could not be forecast, only the potential increase was considered.

Three estimates of the post-war number and distribution of households could then be made: a minimum, an intermediate and a maximum estimate.

The Minimum Estimate is based on the assumption that existing "doubling-up" of households will continue and that only the single males, aged 25 to 45, who are away in the Forces or on war-work, are likely to marry on their return and set up households of their own.

The Intermediate Estimate assumes that only extremely complex multiple household units will be likely to split and that the same number of single males between 25–45 will wish to establish households.

The Maximum Estimate is based on the assumption that all multiple household units will split and that all single males, aged 19 to 45, both those who were in Middlesbrough in 1944, and those who were absent on war service, may wish to establish households of their own. Therefore, this last estimate shows the maximum number of households (i.e., 53,990) that could exist in Middlesbrough during the first few years after the war, irrespective of possible immigration.[3]

The minimum and intermediate estimates are as follows:

1. *Minimum Estimate*

Total number of existing households . .	35,800
Absent single males aged 25–45 who might wish to set up new households on their return .	2,580
Total number of post-war households . .	38,380

2. *Intermediate Estimate*

Post-war single household units . . .	29,500
Post-war multiple household units:	
(*a*) 3,900 (10·7 per cent. of total not to be split)	3,900
(*b*) 2,400 (6·8 per cent. of total) to be split into two households each . .	4,800
Absent single males aged 25–45 who might wish to set up new households on their return	2,580
Total Number of post-war households .	40,780

Table IV shows the application of the Intermediate Estimate of the potential number and distribution of households. It is worthwhile to compare the size-distribution of all existing households (second column) with that of all possible post-war households (last column). In the latter, the proportions of two and three person households is substantially larger than in the former, while the proportions of large households, of five and more persons, is considerably smaller. This last column gives the basis for an estimate of housing requirements.

TABLE IV: ESTIMATED DISTRIBUTION OF POST-WAR HOUSEHOLDS BY SIZE, INCLUDING ALL HOUSEHOLDS, i.e. BOTH EXISTING AND POTENTIAL HOUSEHOLDS

BASED ON THE INTERMEDIATE ESTIMATE.

Number of Persons in Household, excluding Lodgers	All Existing Households		Existing Household not to be split		Potential Households		All Post-War Households	
	No.	%	No.	%	No.	%	No.	%
1	1,600	4·5	1,600	5·0	48	0·6	1,648	4·0
2	7,000	19·4	7,000	21·0	4,730	63·4	11,730	28·8
3	9,200	25·5	9,200	27·4	1,800	25·0	11,000	27·0
4	7,100	20·0	6,700	20·0	730	10·0	7,430	18·2
5	5,200	14·6	4,550	13·6	72	1·0	4,622	11·4
6 or more	5,700	16·0	4,350	13·0	0	0·0	4,350	10·6
TOTAL	35,800	100·0	33,400	100·0	7,380	100·0	40,780	100·0

NOTE: Existing households not to be split (third column) include: (*a*) all single household units (see Table II) and (*b*) certain multiple household units which were assumed not to split. Potential households include: (*a*) complex multiple household units which were assumed to split into two households each and (*b*) absent single males, aged 25–45, who are likely to marry and set-up two-person households of their own. The final column includes both these groups and provides a moderate estimate of the immediate post-war number and distribution of households by size.

4. Estimate of the Required Distribution of Dwellings by Size

A housing programme to meet these requirements should, of course, allow for flexibility, that is, the distribution of dwellings by size has to reflect the successive stages of family life within a given population. Moreover, if a replacement birth-rate is to be achieved, the proportion of large families will have to increase, and an appropriate proportion of large dwellings will have to be provided.

For these reasons, the estimate of the proportion of dwellings (either houses or flats) of different sizes required does not correspond exactly to the proportions of households of different sizes, as shown in the last column of Table IV. The general ratio of one habitable room per person, regardless of sex and age, has been applied. But for the purpose of future adjustments, this ratio has been slightly raised for certain categories of households. For half of the estimated number of three person households, and for all households of subsequent sizes, one additional room per household has been allocated.

The result is as follows:

Estimated Distribution of Households by Size*		Estimated Distribution of Dwellings Required by Size	
No. of Persons in Household	Proportion of Households %	No. of Rooms per Dwelling	Proportion of Dwellings %
1–3	59·8	1–3	46·0
4 and 5	29·6	4 and 5	32·0
6 or more	10·6	6 or more	22·0
Total	100·0	Total	100·0

* As shown on Table IV, last column.

APPENDIX C

SUPPLEMENTARY TABLES

Appendix C: SUPPLEMENTARY TABLES

Appendix—Neighbourhoods: Table Ia

Indices of Living Conditions in Neighbourhoods: Basic Figures

Neighbourhoods		Indices					
Group	Neighbourhood	1 Net Population Density	2 No. of Houses per Acre	3 Percentage of Houses with Rateable Value of less than £11. 0s. 0d.	4 Percentage of Non-Owner-Occupiers	5 Percentage of Chief Wage Earners with Incomes of Less than £5. 0s. 0d. per week	6 Number of Poverty Shops per 1,000 people
1.	A 2	138	35·7	96·4	98·5	95·0	1·8
	A 7	104	29·4	80·7	93·8	92·0	3·0
	A 16	107	32·2	80·6	90·6	82·0	2·5
	A 1	100	22·8	77·6	98·4	82·0	2·6
	A 12i	126	33·7	80·4	97·0	91·0	1·2
	Group-total	120	31·1	87·0	96·9	91·0	2·1
2.	A 6	103	28·5	67·6	90·6	90·0	1·9
	A 14	104	31·2	79·0	89·0	95·0	1·2
	A 8	111	35·2	64·5	79·7	82·0	1·3
	A 9	101	27·5	60·3	73·1	87·0	1·3
	A 10, 11, 12	86	23·8	55·5	86·8	78·0	1·6
	Group-total	100	29·5	66·3	83·4	87·0	1·4
3.	A 5	98	30·1	25·5	66·7	90·0	1·1
	A 3	112	29·7	29·8	70·1	72·0	0·5
	Group-total	103	30·0	27·0	67·8	84·0	0·9

4.	B 8, 9	71	17·1	16·8	100·0	86·0	0·2
	A 17, 18	74	15·4	15·1	100·0	85·0	0·2
	B 6	69	21·2	25·5	39·0	49·0	0·8
	B 5	66	20·7	12·7	52·5	68·0	0·6
	B 10	56	11·7	0·0	100·0	86·0	0·3
	A 4	57	12·8	11·7	71·9	90·0	0·0
	B 1	52	11·6	11·8	75·6	85·0	0·0
	A 13	46	11·9	6·5	40·1	61·0	0·3
	Group-total	60	14·9	12·9	74·0	76·0	0·3
5.	A 15	45	12·5	0·0	26·5	46·0	0·0
	B 2	41	17·1	0·0	7·5	47·0	0·0
	B 3	30	10·0	0·1	13·0	39·0	0·5
	Group-total	35	12·0	0·08	12·9	43·0	0·3
6.	B 7	26	8·8	1·5	0·0	60·0	0·0
	B 11	25	7·6	0·0	6·0	37·0	0·0
	B 4	19	6·0	0·0	11·4	23·0	0·0
	Group-total	23	7·1	0·4	6·6	35·0	0·0
	ALL MIDDLESBROUGH	71	19·5	46·0	73·4	78·0	1·1

Appendix—Neighbourhoods: Table Ib

Example of Computation of Index of Living Conditions in Neighbourhoods

Indices	All Middlesbrough		e.g. Neighbourhood A 2, Newport	
	Index	Index Number	Index	Index Number
1) Net Population Density	71	100·0	138	194
2) Number of Houses per Acre	19·5	100·0	35·7	183
3) Per Cent. of Houses with Rateable Value of Less than £11. 0s. 0d.	46·0	100·0	96·4	210
4) Per Cent. of Non-Owner-Occupiers	73·4	100·0	98·5	134
5) Per Cent. of Chief Wage Earners with Incomes of Less than £5. 0s. 0d. per week	78·0	100·0	95·0	122
6) No. of Poverty Shops per 1,000 People	1·1	100·0	1·8	164
Total	—	600·0	—	1,007
Average	—	100·0	—	168
Rating	—	3	—	1

APPENDIX—EDUCATION: TABLE I

EXAMPLE OF COMPUTATION OF INDEX OF SCHOOL ENVIRONMENT

Indices	All Middlesbrough		e.g. St. John's School	
	Index	Index No.	Index	Index No.
1) Average Number of Classes per Age-Group . . .	1·50	100·0	1·0	66·0
2) Number of Halls per Department	0·70	100·0	0·0	0·0
3) Number of Additional Rooms per Department . . .	0·31	100·0	0·0	0·0
4) Proportion of Pupils Attending Playing Fields . . .	34·00	100·0	20·0	59·0
TOTAL	—	400·0	—	125·0
AVERAGE	—	100·0	—	31·0
RATING	—	3	—	1

Appendix—Retail Trade: Table Ia

NUMBER OF SHOPS AND NUMBER OF OUTLETS BY TRADE TYPES

Distribution of Non-Foodshops Interviewed

Trade Types	No. of Shops	No. of Outlets
I Department Stores		
Department Store	5	5
Co-operative Store	4	4
Variety Bazaar	2	2
Total	11	11
II General Shops		
General Shop	18	18
Books	6	9
Lending Library	2	3
General Stationer	7	20
Unclassified (selling mainly food)	11	11
Unclassified (selling mainly non-food)	23	41
Total	67	102
III Furniture Shops		
Furniture and Bedding	15	19
Bedding Specialist	2	4
Nursery Furniture	1	1
Second-hand Furniture	1	15
Perambulators	1	2
Total	20	41
IV Chemists		
Photographic Goods	8	8
Chemists	27	35
Medical and Surgical Appliances	—	2
Total	35	45
V Drapers and Clothiers		
General Draper	38	42
Household Linen and Piece Goods	2	4
Wool and Needlework	17	18
Women's and Maids' Tailors	6	7
Women's and Maids' General Outfitters	17	23

APPENDIX—RETAIL TRADE: TABLE 1a—*continued*

Trade Types	No. of Shops	No. of Outlets
DRAPERS AND CLOTHIERS—*continued*		
Women's and Maids' Specialist Outfitters	17	24
Women's and Maids' Underwear .	3	7
Women's and Maids' dress piece goods .	1	1
Women's and Maids' Millinery . .	3	3
Men's and Youths' Bespoke Tailors .	2	9
Men's Outfitters	18	24
Men's and Youths' Hatters . . .	—	5
Furriers	—	1
Footwear	20	21
Children's and Infants' Wear . .	—	25
Baby Linen Wear Specialist . .	—	6
Children's Wear Specialist . . .	—	2
Women's Handbags	—	3
Total	144	225
VI HOUSEHOLD ACCESSORIES		
General Ironmonger	19	19
Specialist Ironmonger	3	5
China and Glass	—	4
Leather Goods	2	4
Jewellers, Goldsmiths and Silversmiths .	8	13
Toys, Games and Sports Goods . .	1	3
Children's Toys	—	3
Sports Goods Specialist	2	3
Cycles and Accessories	17	23
Music	4	4
Radio and Gramophone	2	18
Electrical Goods	—	10
Pictures	1	2
Antiques	1	3
Junk	—	1
Total	60	115
GRAND TOTAL	337	539

APPENDIX—RETAIL TRADE: TABLE 1b

SINGLE TYPE AND COMPOUND SHOPS BY TRADE TYPE

Distribution of Non-Foodshops Interviewed

Principal Trade Type	Total Number of Shops of Each Principal Trade Type		Single and Compound Types of Shops						Outlets					
			No. of Single Type Shops in Each Group		Number of Compound Shops in Each Group									
					No. which have Outlets of Principal Trade Type only	No. which have Subsidiary Outlets as well	Total No. of Compound Shops		Total No. of Outlets in Each Group of Shops		Total No. of Outlets of Principal Trade Type in Each Group of Shops		Total No. of Subsidiary Outlets in Each Group of Shops	
	No.	%	No.	%	No.	No.	No.	%	No.	%	No.	%	No.	%
Department Store	11	100·0	11	100·0	0	0	0	0·0	11	100·0	11	100·0	—	—
General Shop	67	100·0	45	67·0	16	6	22	33·0	103	100·0	84	81·0	19	29·0
Furniture	20	100·0	3	15·0	9	8	17	85·0	46	100·0	21	46·0	25	54·0
Chemist	35	100·0	25	71·0	8	2	10	29·0	48	100·0	42	87·5	6	12·5
Draper and Clothier	144	100·0	76	53·0	56	12	68	47·0	234	100·0	204	87·0	30	13·0
Household Accessories	60	100·0	32	53·0	19	9	28	47·0	97	100·0	77	79·0	20	21·0
Total	337	100·0	192	57·0	108	37	145	43·0	539	100·0	439	81·0	100	19·0

APPENDIX—RETAIL TRADE: TABLE II

STAFF-STRUCTURE OF NON-FOODSHOPS INTERVIEWED

(A)

Sex	Staff Groups								Grand Total	
	Employees				Family-Workers					
	Full-time %	Part-time %	Total No.	Total %	Full-time %	Part-time %	Total No.	Total %	Number	%
Male Workers	15·3	0·2	416	15·5	4·5	1·0	158	5·5	574	21·0
Female Workers	69·7	2·8	1,951	72·5	4·5	2·0	176	6·5	2,127	79·0
Total	85·0	3·0	2,367	88·0	9·0	3·0	334	12·0	2,701	100·0

(B)

Nature of Work	Staff Groups				Grand Total	
	Counter-Assistants		Other Shop-Workers			
	Number	%	Number	%	Number	%
Full-time	1,631	60·5	901	33·5	2,532	94·0
Part-time	154	5·5	15	0·5	169	6·0
Total	1,785	66·0	916	34·0	2,701	100·0

APPENDIX—RETAIL TRADE: TABLE III

INDEX OF PROSPERITY AND DEPRESSION IN SHOPPING CENTRES, SHOWING THE GROUPS OF SHOPPING CENTRES

Shopping Centres	Indices		Index Numbers			Final Rating
	Empty Shops as % of all shops	Poverty Shops as % of all occupied shops	Index for Empty Shops	Index for Poverty Shops	Total Index	
The Chief Centres	13·0	1·8	54	24	78	5
The Intermediate Centres . . .	37·0	5·7	154	75	229	3
The Local Centres	28·0	14·6	116	192	308	2
The Strictly Local Centres . . .	5·4	7·0	22	92	114	5
Grand Total . . .	24·0	7·6	100	100	200	3

NOTES TO PART I

1. Lady Bell, *At The Works: A Study of a Manufacturing Town*, 1911 edition, p. 40.

2. "Obsolete" houses are those which show three adverse blight factors: more than 50 houses to the acre; over seventy years of age; no baths. "New Households" will be set up, if the supply of houses meets the demand, because existing households which are doubled up will split and because single people returning from the Forces will marry.

3. This definition might be criticised on the grounds that it is too mechanical, that it does not take the quality of the social life of a neighbourhood into account. This is, of course, an aspect which should not be ignored. But the essential characteristic of a neighbourhood is participation in local organised and unorganised social activities which, in turn, is indicative of their quality.

4. It will be noticed that work is not included in this list of primary social activities although it is the most important of all. But since workplaces and homes are now usually geographically separated, we cannot measure the concentration of social activities in terms of an aspect for which unavoidable dispersal is the norm.

5. This was based on the results of the household sample enquiry carried out by the Wartime Social Survey.

6. See map A of Neighbourhoods.

7. The same method, based on census tracts, the American equivalent of enumeration districts, is often used in the United States. But whilst the boundaries of census tracts are fixed so that changes between census dates can be studied, in this country a new *ad hoc* sub-division into enumeration districts is carried out at each census. Their usefulness as statistical units is thus seriously impaired.

8. See map B of Neighbourhoods.

9. These maps are based on the results of the Wartime Social Survey enquiry.

10. Most of the indices employed can be assessed either on the basis of maps or tables. The former method is quicker when all the relevant maps are available, but it will, of course, tend to be less precise. This more speedy method was originally used to discover the major variations between the characteristics of Middlesbrough's neighbourhoods. The results were found to vary only slightly from those obtained through the application of statistical indices which were later used wherever possible and which are here presented. But, of course, contrasts within Middlesbrough are very sharp so that even the cruder method of classification is bound to reveal them. By and large, statistical indices are certainly more satisfactory.

11. This is the only index which is derived from sample information, i.e. from the Wartime Social Survey household enquiry.

12. See appendix, Neighbourhoods, Table 1a, pp. 234, 235.

13. These are Neighbourhoods B 8, 9; A 17, 18; B 10; A 4 and B 1.

14. Day-nurseries and infant welfare centres should be included in this list. But these are not yet neighbourhood institutions in Middlesbrough since there are only five nurseries and seven infant welfare centres altogether.

15. I.e. number of elementary schools per 1,000 of the age-groups 5–15; number of clubs per 1,000 of the age-groups 5 and over; number of pubs per 1,000 aged 20 and over; number of post-offices, surgeries, churches and foodshops per 1,000 of the total population. The index was obtained through contrasting the respective numbers in each neighbourhood with those for the whole of Middlesbrough.

16. The number of foodshops per neighbourhood had to be computed separately since the location of a shopping centre is often quite independent of the particular needs of the neighbourhood in which it is situated. Consequently, whenever a shopping centre extends over more than one neighbourhood, only a proportionate share of its total number of shops was allocated to each of the participant neighbourhoods. But all the isolated shops were alloted to the neighbourhood in which they are located. Only the number of foodshops, not the total number of shops, was considered, since the number

of non-foodshops is particularly great in all the shopping centres which fulfil a central or sub-central function. On the whole, the catchment areas of non-foodshops tend to be wider than those of foodshops. For details see part IV, Retail Trade, pp. 158, 159.

17. See Part III, Education Services, pp. 109–116.

18. The classification for inflow has been multiplied by the index of outflow in order to give each factor equal weight.

19. It is interesting in this context to compare the catchment areas of post-offices with those of other types of institutions. The post-office is the only completely standardised institution at the present time, and it is, therefore, also the only one in Middlesbrough which has always a strictly local catchment area.

NOTES TO PART II

1. From 1881 to 1931, Middlesbrough's rate of natural increase, i.e. the excess of births over deaths, has been consistently higher in each decennial period than that either for the North Riding of Yorkshire or that for the whole of England and Wales. Between 1921 and 1931, for instance, Middlesbrough's natural increase amounted to 11·4 per cent. of the 1921 population, while the comparable figure for England and Wales was 6·0 per cent.

2. Lady Bell *At the Works: A Study of a Manufacturing Town*, 1911 edition, pp. 23, 24.

3. Annual Report of the Medical Officer for Health, 1906.

4. M.O.H. Reports. 1898, 1899, 1900.

5. M.O.H. Annual Report, 1906.

6. Lady Bell, quoted *ibid*, p. 82.

7. Lady Bell, quoted *ibid*, p. 22.

8. In 1905 the pneumonia death rate for some comparable towns in the North of England was 1·5 per 1,000 population; in Middlesbrough it was 3·7 per 1,000.
M.O.H. Annual Report, 1905.

9. Demolition by private enterprise also took place, usually where the site had been bought for business or commercial use.

10. About 12,000 houses, just over a third of all the houses in Middlesbrough to-day, have been built since 1914. Hardly any of these are in the old northern areas.

11. The latter figure is based on the 1939 National Registration which has been corrected for evacuation and call-up.

12. The history of the Brambles Farm estate is a case in point. People were moved in the 1930's from insanitary and overcrowded houses, mostly in North Ormesby and St. Hilda's, to this very isolated and bleak estate, which lacked most amenities. Comparatively little was done to help settlers to adjust themselves to the new environment, and their old habits continued. It soon became evident that diseases connected with their old environment were reoccuring: many of the houses became infested, and the derelict aspect of the gardens on the estate, and the verminous condition of the children led many people to say that "Brambles is becoming a slum". However, all the recent evidence shows that the tenants, and particularly the children, have adjusted themselves to the new environment, though the lack of amenities is still a source of complaint.

13. There is also at present a shortage of public baths in the town. A few slipper baths have been installed on the premises of the Public Swimming Baths and also at two subsidiary branches.

14. The crude birth-rate is, of course, a rather unreliable standard of comparison as the proportion of women of child bearing age-groups may differ considerably as between the different county boroughs. The general fertility rate, i.e. number of live births per thousand women between fifteen and forty-five years of age, provides a far more reliable comparison. But the material for the computation of the fertility rates for the county boroughs was not readily available. The same difficulty of the variations in the age-composition of different towns, makes it impossible to use crude death rates for an inter-town comparison of the incidence of deaths from different causes. A far more detailed analysis would have to be made. Since such an analysis is not essential for our purpose, it has not been undertaken. Middlesbrough's crude death rate has, since 1898, been consistently higher than that for England and Wales.

15. For birth rates and infant mortality rates see Registrar General's Annual Reviews, Part I, 1935–1939.

16. Only the official evacuation could be covered, as neither the number nor the addresses of those who were privately evacuated were known. This omission is not likely to be serious as only the northern and poorer wards of the town were scheduled as an evacuation area.

17. As the new housing estates were considered as a separate area, wards in which housing estates are located were divided accordingly. The areas referred to consist of the following wards or housing estates:

Area I.	St. Hilda's, Cannon, Newport, Vulcan, Cleveland, Ormesby (excluding Brambles Farm estate).
Area II.	Brambles Farm, Whinney Banks, Marton Grove.
Area III.	Acklam, Exchange, Ayresome.
Area IV.	Grove Hill (excluding Marton Grove estate), Linthorpe (excluding Whinney Banks estate).

18. We have used this quinquennium rather than the preceding quinquennium for the intra-town comparison chiefly because settlement on the new estates was not complete before 1939. The rates were computed from the births and infant deaths records of the public health department. A separate analysis was made for the wards which include housing estates, in order to separate the births and infant deaths on the estates from those in the remainder of their respective wards. There is no doubt that an analysis in terms of neighbourhoods rather than wards would have shown an even sharper differentiation of infant mortality rates, but it was not possible to undertake so detailed an analysis for the whole 5 year period. Area I includes all the poorest neighbourhoods and area II is also clearly defined. A more detailed differentiation would have been particularly important in the case of area IV, which includes the Grove Hill and Linthorpe wards which extend beyond the really prosperous neighbourhoods of the town.

19. See Part III, Education Services, Chapter V, pp. 124–131.

20. Neither the fertility rates nor the crude birth rates, as shown here, are entirely accurate since they had to be based on the population figures of a specific date, i.e. September 1939. The average population figures for the whole year, which provide a more suitable basis, were not available.

21. These details are recorded on the birth enquiry cards which are kept by the health visitors. Every child whose birth has been notified is supposed to be visited by a health visitor approximately a fortnight after birth and subsequently at regular intervals after that, until it is five years old. A record is made of the place of confinement, the condition and the care of the child, the number of previous pregnancies of the mother, whether she worked during pregnancy and whether she attended an ante-natal clinic. Further details are given about the home condition and the husband's occupation. Unfortunately, the age of the mother is not recorded on the Middlesbrough birth enquiry card. On this card, subsequent visits of the health visitor, and attendance at child welfare centres are also recorded, together with a brief account of the health and care of the child. This detailed information, together with a complete register of all births and infant deaths, was the basic material of our enquiry. It was supplemented by visits to the Municipal Maternity Hospital, to the child welfare centres and war-time day-nurseries, and by talks with the medical officer for maternity and child welfare, the superintendents of the health visitors, and of the municipal midwives.

22. Among these, there were ten multiple births, i.e. a total of 980 infants born.

23. In the remaining 11·0 per cent. of all cases, the fathers were either dead, unemployed, or their occupations were unknown.

24. The proportion of domiciliary confinements has only recently decreased. During the five-year period 1939–1943, only a third of all confinements took place in institutions. However, the proportions varied considerably from area to area. One-quarter of all births in the poor area I took place took place in institutions, as compared with one-half in the prosperous area IV.

25. A recent Ministry of Health Circular suggests that a maximum of twenty visits a day should be aimed at, since health visitors cannot give adequate attention to more cases.

26. The midwives are, of course, prepared to give ante-natal advice when they are consulted, but they do not pay periodic, i.e. monthly, routine visits to the expectant mothers who have booked with them.

27. A much larger group of cases would have to be studied in order to analyse the relative effect of social status and of hospital influence on the use of ante- and post-natal services.

28. These conclusions are only tentative, particularly since it was not possible to study the influence of health factors on the use of maternity services. Neither the information recorded on the birth enquiry card, nor the size of the sample, were sufficiently adequate for such an analysis. This is an important omission to which attention should be drawn.

29. From general records of all births, confinements, and attendances at clinics and centres in 1943, it could be seen that the use of maternity services was limited to the same extent in 1943 as in 1944.

30. Similar schemes were also operated in other parts of the country.

31. The total staff of 71 consists of 25 trained nurses, 10 other trained workers, and 36 untrained or part-time helpers. Each of the latter is only regarded as half a worker in considering the number of children per member of the staff.

32. As in all other parts of the country, a flat rate of one shilling per day is charged.

33. A discussion of the school medical service is included in Part III, Education Services, pp. 101, 102.

34. The results of the 1939 National Registration showed, for instance, that almost 40·0 per cent. of the men over 55 years, living in St. Hilda's ward, were single.

35. While the Maternity Hospital is in a fairly modern building, its site area is too small to allow for the addition of 100 further beds, the number which the Medical Officer of Health considers to be necessary.

36. Cases coming from the North Riding of Yorkshire, beyond the limits of the former Cleveland Poor Law Union, are charged full fees. A special agreement exists between Middlesbrough Corporation and the North Riding of Yorkshire County Council for the collection and transfer of these fees. Before January 1944, expectant mothers living outside the borough boundary were taken into the Municipal Maternity Hospital on the same conditions. After that date, however, only emergency and complicated cases from outside the Borough could be admitted.

37. The Medical Officer of Health in Middlesbrough is also the Chief Medical Officer of the Tees Port Health Authority, and the Port health services operate as a part of the Middlesbrough health services.

38. The scheme is also in operation at I.C.I. at Billingham.

39. If we take the Food Office figures for the week ending June 24th, 1944 and assume that each worker going to a work's canteen has five meals per week there, we find that only 3,000 workers received meals at canteens, a figure which represents approximately 5·0 per cent. of the total insured population.

40. These figures were obtained for the week ending 24th June, 1944. Whilst it is possible to calculate the number of persons served in British Restaurants, i.e. just over 2,000, and in industrial canteens, i.e. 3,000, it is not possible to obtain a comparable figure for commercial catering establishments. There are altogether 34 of these in the town, most of which are small cafés and snack bars.

NOTES TO PART III

1. In 1931, 25·0 per cent. of the population of the 83 county boroughs in England and Wales were between the ages of five to nineteen years. The same age-groups were 28·5 per cent. of the total Middlesbrough population.

2. See J. R. and U. K. Hicks: *Standards of Local Expenditure*, 1943.

3. See C. Postgate: *Middlesbrough*, 1898.

4. These and subsequent details of Middlesbrough's 19th century history of education, are referred to in J. H. Drury's thesis: *The History of Education in Middlesbrough*, 1935.

5. The term "elementary school" is here used throughout according to its definition prior to the Education Act of 1944. When that Act is implemented, the old elementary school will be transformed into the "primary school", and the term "primary" instead of "elementary" education will be applicable. "Primary" education will be given in L.E.A. schools for children between the ages of five and eleven years only. But at the time of our enquiry, the old system was still in force and hence the old definition was still valid.

6. The schools in North Ormesby and Cargo Fleet, originally under the supervision of the North Riding of Yorkshire, were transferred to the Middlesbrough education authority in 1913 when North Ormesby was incorporated in the Middlesbrough County Borough.

7. The exception is Fleetham Street school in the northern area, originally dating from the 1870's, which was entirely rebuilt on its old site. Because of the small acreage of the site area, and the present lack of play-space in its neighbourhood, this school is not as well equipped as the contemporary buildings on the new estates.

8. Since the local education authority only pays the fares of children who live three miles or more away from their schools, the fares of the children on the new estates were not covered. The greatest distance between homes and schools was approximately two miles.

9. Both Whinney Banks and Marton Grove have each also a Roman Catholic elementary school. St. Francis, on Whinney Banks estate, was established three years earlier than the local authority school, but St. Joseph's, Marton Grove, one year later than the first local authority school.

10. A good deal of information included in this section is referred to in J. H. Drury's thesis on *The History of Education in Middlesbrough.*

11. One further institution, the Preparatory School, should be mentioned here, which is run by the L.E.A. and classified as a Secondary School. This School does not fit into any of the usual L.E.A. categories as it takes children from five to eleven years, and at the present time, before the provisions of the 1944 Education are applied, fees have still to be paid for their education. The object of providing this school was to satisfy the requirements of professional and black-coated workers who did not want their children to be educated in the non-fee-paying elementary schools.

12. The Roman Catholics also run a private school, the only one in Middlesbrough.

13. The present minimum standards required are stated in the "Regulations Prescribing Standards for School Premises, Draft, dated November 3, 1944". Middlesbrough's minimum needs, of 16·8 acres per 1,000 pupils, are estimated on the basis of the present school population, excluding the Technical College, and through applying primary school standards for all those under 11 years of age, and secondary school standards for the remainder.

14. In addition 32 Middlesbrough children suffering from serious mental or physical defects are now in residential schools or children's hospitals in various part of the country.

15. The part-time specialists are dentists, a consultant oculist, a consultant aurist, an orthopaedic surgeon, a speech therapist and an educational psychologist.

16. Since 1943, the school medical service in Middlesbrough is administered by the public health department and thus co-ordinated with all the other health services.

17. By the end of 1943, it was estimated that 68·0 per cent. of all school children had been immunised.

18. In the summers just before the outbreak of war in 1939, the local education authority also organised a residential school for delicate children at Marske, a small sea-side village near Redcar. Children between the ages of twelve and fourteen years were selected by the school medical officers and sent there for either a fortnight or a month. The school was housed in an old hangar used by the Royal Flying Corps in the 1914–1918 war. Nowadays the medical officers still send debilitated children to a convalescent home in Cleveland; 235 children were sent there in 1943.

19. Education (Provisions of Meals) Act, 1906.

20. The Middlesbrough education authority supervised approximately 50 cases of legal adoption per annum during the war years 1940–43.

21. There is only one private school, which takes about 50 pupils, not all from Middlesbrough, and the Preparatory School, run by the local education authority, which has accommodation for about 200 children between the ages of five and eleven, all of whom pay full fees. This school is rather oddly classified as a secondary school.

22. The total number of elementary school children in March 1944 is 19,771. In addition, some 400 Middlesbrough children are still evacuated at the time of the enquiry and are attending elementary schools elsewhere.

23. There is, however, a considerable difference between the standards of the modern non-denominational schools and those of the R.C. schools. The former are far better equipped than the latter which have, for instance, no adjacent playing fields and do not use communal playing fields either.

24. We have used number of classes per age-group, which is indicative of educational differentiation and dependent on the amount and quality of space available, as one of the indices instead of class-room space per child. The latter cannot be reliably assessed at present. Since there is a shortage of teachers, and because some class-rooms are in disrepair, not all the available space is used in every school. On the other hand, in some schools, classes are also held regularly in halls and additional rooms.

25. An example of the method of computation of the index of school environment is shown in the appendix, Education, Table I, p. 237.

26. See Part II, Health Services, p. 54.

27. But, as previously stated, this applies only to the modern non-denominational schools.

28. The L.E.A. is obliged to provide free transport in cases where a school is more than two miles distant from the playing field. But since the longest distance in Middlesbrough is 1¾ miles, the seniors walk or use public transport at their parents' expense.

29. In addition, many children, and not only those aged nine to eleven, go swimming after school hours. For those in the densely populated areas, who only rarely go out into the country districts, swimming is a major recreation. It is, therefore, essential that swimming facilities should be improved.

30 See *Middlesbrough Survey and Plan*, published by Middlesbrough County Borough, 1947.

31. These details are derived from a map showing the addresses of children found to suffer from head-infestations in the summer term of 1943.

32. It appears that the incidence of head infestations has increased during the war. The proportion of all school children found to be verminous was 13·4 per cent. in 1936 and 38·0 per cent in 1942 and 1943. These percentages should be treated with caution, however, as the definition of "uncleanliness" may vary in different years and even with different nurses.

33. The only cases for which definite evidence of cleansing was available were those of children whose parents had been summoned before a court for persistent uncleanliness. There were ten such cases in 1943.

34. Only the northern part of the town was scheduled as an evacuation area and, therefore, mainly the children attending schools in that part were evacuated. During the 1939 evacuation, about one-fifth of these children left the town, if only for a short period. Those who remained behind received very little education in the first months of the war. Air attacks in 1940 and 1941 again affected chiefly the northern part of the town.

35. In serious cases of frequent absences from school without reason, the L.E.A. may ask the Juvenile Court for a school attendance order, or else take judicial action against the parents under the bye-laws. From the map showing the distribution of these cases throughout the town, it was clear that children summoned before the courts for irregular attendance come mainly from the poorest homes.

36. The terms "higher" and "secondary" education are used here throughout according to their meaning prior to the Education Act of 1944. As the old system of education was still in force at the time of our survey, the old definitions were still appropriate.

37. These details are derived from the catchment area maps of the individual schools which were based on our school census of the summer of 1944. In addition, an analysis of the results of the scholarship examination, which is referred to in Chap. V, was undertaken.

38. Before the war both boys and girls used a playing field which has since been temporarily requisitioned for military use and which is about ¾ of a mile distant from the school. It is hoped that the High School will be able to use this field again after the war.

39. In addition to the schools for higher education, administered by the local education authority, there are two "Direct Grant" secondary schools, both of which are Roman Catholic. They have just 500 pupils, not only from Middlesbrough, but from quite a wide area in Cleveland and South Durham. Since fees are paid for all but 5·0 per cent. of these pupils, they do not have to sit for the general scholarship examination. A few special places are awarded, however, to Roman Catholic children who pass the examination.

40. The examination is also held in the Roman Catholic Private School and in the Preparatory School which is being run by the L.E.A. The latter draws its pupils entirely from the prosperous neighbourhood in Linthorpe where it is situated. The school is accommodated in a large converted house standing in its own grounds. By comparison with the most modern elementary schools, its premises are poor and its classes are crowded. Yet since only fee payers are admitted, its social status is regarded as being superior.

41. A number of pupils come to the High School from outside the Middlesbrough municipal boundary. In 1943, there were altogether 49 entrants from the North Riding of Yorkshire, most of whom came as "special place" pupils on the basis of a specific arrangement. On the other hand, a few Middlesbrough children who are unable to pass the examination, or whose parents wish them to go to a boarding school, attend schools for higher education outside Middlesbrough. Altogether 48 Middlesbrough children attended such schools in Stockton, Redcar and Great Ayton in 1944, either as boarders or day pupils.

42. Only one of the sixteen elementary schools which are attended by seniors can be regarded as being adequate. Nine schools are completely out of date and seven of these do not even have separate senior and junior departments.

43. This is only a rough estimate, based on the present size of the school population. Although there may be slight shifts in the proportionate strength of the different age-groups, we can assume that the size of the senior school population as a whole will not change significantly in the immediate post-war years when the implementation of the 1944 Education Act will begin.

44 These are, in substance, the proposals of the Director of Education which have, however, been related to other aspects of the Middlesbrough Plan. According to these proposals, Acklam Hall, Kirby School, the two Roman Catholic direct grant secondary schools, as well as several senior departments in elementary schools, should be retained and enlarged. Since the building programme will, of course, be spread over a number of years, it will have to be adjusted to changes in the size of the school population.

45. However, the improvement in the number of children entering higher education is not proportionate to the improvement in examination results. As the number in the 11–12 year age-group was about 4·0 per cent. lower in 1943 than in 1942, and as, furthermore, a slightly higher number of places in the Central School was available, examination marks could be more tolerant in that year. Yet the available number of places in secondary schools remained the same in both years. Therefore, since there is a general reluctance to accept places in the Central School, the number of non-acceptances was proportionately higher in 1943. Under the present system, as long as secondary school accommodation remains static, general improvements in educational attainments cannot possibly be rewarded, unless there is a substantial decrease in the number of children of the relevant age-groups.

46. The non-acceptances here referred to are those of children who continue their education in elementary schools. Refusals of central school places occur also in the more prosperous areas, but merely because the parents prefer to send their children instead to secondary schools as feepayers.

47. If we had been able to obtain the addresses of all the children in the relevant age-group, and of those who failed in, or passed, the examination, it would have been possible to undertake a more detailed analysis along these lines.

48. This applies particularly to a comparison of the examination results of non-denominational and of Catholic schools on the new estates. The former schools are far more adequately equipped than the latter and their examination results are also substantially better. Whilst the physical standards of home environment on the new estates are the same for Catholic children as for the remainder, it is, however possible that the income and social status of Catholic parents is slightly lower.

49. This is further indicated by the outstanding improvement from 1942 to 1943 in the examination turn-out and performance of the school on Brambles Farm estate.

50. I.e. these are the proportions of the 11–12 year age-group from each of the areas mentioned who enter higher education. Table 8 shows the proportion of those taking the examination who enter higher education.

51. In the case of provided schools, the school attendance officers attempt to control the extent of school catchment areas. Wherever possible, they try to persuade parents to send their children to the nearest school. No control of this kind, however, is exercised over the denominational schools, and on the whole the catchment areas of these schools, particularly of the Roman Catholic schools, are more extensive than those of the non-denominational schools.

52. For instance, a head teacher in one of the poorest schools said that she found it difficult to understand the mentality of her pupils' parents and hence to establish contact with them in any way. Another head teacher said that she was surprised to find such pleasant children coming from such a poor environment.

NOTES TO PART IV

1. Apart from distinct geographical groupings, any collection of shops which, although slightly scattered, appears to be interdependent was defined as a shopping centre.

2. The area of each of the "neighbourhoods" here referred to is not necessarily identical with the neighbourhoods as defined in Part I. We are here concerned with the neighbourhoods of the shopping centres which are delimited in terms of the location of centres. This point is illustrated by the map showing the generalised catchment areas of the strictly local shopping centres.

3. The town-centre has, in fact, a wide catchment area even if we use the index of sugar registrations. (See the map of Generalised Catchment Areas of the Chief Shopping Centres). But this is largely due to the unequal distribution of shopping facilities. People are forced to go a considerable distance if they want to choose from a fair range of commodities, and this applies to choice of groceries as well.

4. The number of dairies need not be large in any case as milk is being delivered.

5. See Appendix, Retail Trade, Tables Ia and b, showing the number and detailed classification of shops and outlets under each of the major trade types. The largest proportion of shops in the "household accessory" group are ironmongers and shops selling sports goods.

6. This is still true if we consider the distribution of outlets rather than of shops. Whilst for some trade types there were twice as many outlets as there were shops, just for those trade types, which were represented by only a small number of shops, there were few or no additional outlets.

7. Although, strictly speaking, outlets not shops are selling points, we are using this term here since the detailed survey of non-foodshops showed that the comparative frequency of the different trade-types, in terms of outlets, differed only very slightly from their comparative frequency in terms of shops.

8. In the absence of detailed turnover figures, the number of shop workers, or that of counter-assistants, is generally regarded as the best index of economic importance.

9. Alternatively, the number of counter-assistants might be used. Since, however, the number of counter-assistants in each category of shops per 1,000 people showed the same rank order for the different trade types as the respective number of shop-workers, only the latter index is here inserted.

10. The numbers of non-foodshops in each category here shown refer only to the shops interviewed and hence differ slightly from those on Table 2. However, the rank order of the different trade types remains the same. All shops in the categories of department stores and furniture shops were interviewed and all but one each in the categories of household accessories and chemists. A further 17 drapers' shops and 38 general shops were omitted, the majority of these were small corner-shops in and around the town-centre where shops of this kind were deliberately excluded from the detailed survey. Of the remainder, two were refusals and ten could not be contacted. Junkshops also were excluded from the survey. However, some outlets of this type were found in other shops interviewed.

11. This point should be stressed since the opposite assumption is usually made, i.e. that the number of counter-assistants is a more, or at least equally, reliable index than the total number of shopworkers. It would, therefore, be worthwhile to make similar comparisons in further studies of retail trade.

12. There are only two chainstores, both of which were established since 1918.

13. Both types of general shops are included here, those selling chiefly food and those of the newsagent and tobacconist variety. Both types were excluded in calculating the ratio of foodshops to non-foodshops.

14. This can be seen in all those centres which are part of a residential area. The chief centres, which are in the main business and administrative district of the town,

can draw only comparatively few customers, for foodshops and non-foodshops alike, from the immediate neighbourhood.

15. Three of the northern intermediate centres are an exception. Their foodshops depend largely on customers from the vicinity, but their non-foodshops, among which are furniture shops and department stores, have a far wider range of customers.

16. These questions were a part of the questionnaire enquiry conducted by the Wartime Social Survey among a sample of Middlesbrough households. The maps showing the generalised catchment areas of the chief centres and the strictly local centres, based on sugar registrations, are derived from these results. These two maps illustrate the points here made.

17. The catchment area of each group of shops depends, of course, on the trade types of the shops which it contains. The higher the proportion of food shops, the more definite is the neighbourhood character of a centre. Furthermore, there are differences according to the types of non-foodshops which are located in a given centre. Department stores, furniture shops and the larger clothing shops have the widest catchment areas, and the majority of these shops are in the chief centres and the intermediate centres. General non-foodshops, chemists and small drapers shops derive the largest proportion of their customers from the immediate neighbourhood, and these shops predominate in the strictly local centres.

18. This statement by the shopkeepers was confirmed through a study of the catchment areas of the foodshops in this centre.

19. The principal entrances to the North Side are two subways, the first of which has a short flight of steps and is, therefore, very inconvenient for mothers with prams. The second is little used by pedestrians, as it is cold and dark, but principally for heavy traffic. The only other entrance to the North Side is the level crossing, which is only open during three or four hours of the day. Market stall-holders believe that this lack of a suitable entrance to the North Side for mothers with prams is one of the chief causes for the continued decline of the market, which slum-clearance has already deprived of many local customers.

20. This department store moved to Corporation Road when its original premises in the primary centre were destroyed by fire. A branch may remain, but the main store will move back to the primary centre as soon as the premises have been rebuilt.

21. The fifth intermediate centre, the Park, is situated just north of Linthorpe Village. It is not particularly prosperous.

22. Yet another reason for the shift of shops from the square to the side streets was that, before the establishment of the bus service running through North Ormesby, people who wished to go into the centre of Middlesbrough had to go through these side streets to catch the tram at its terminus. This stream of passers-by encouraged shop-keepers to establish themselves along these roads. With the introduction of the through bus-route trade has declined and, in fact, all the existing shops were established before that date.

23. In each case, this is the interval between the first year of settlement on the estate and the first date of the establishment of a non-foodshop.

24. So far the southward shift of retail trade has been slight, but where it has occurred, as the example of Linthorpe Village shows, it has led to prosperity. Only 87 of the 337 shop-keepers who were interviewed had moved their premises since their shops were first established and in practically every case the move had been only a few doors up or down the same street.

25. The number of empty shops was perhaps temporarily inflated at the time of our enquiry since small shops may have had to close when the owners were called up for the Forces. But this factor has not influenced the picture of comparative prosperity as those centres which contain a high proportion of small shops and which are, therefore, more likely to contain shops which are temporarily closed, have, in fact, the lowest proportion of empty shops. Moreover, the centres which now have a high ratio of empty shops are reputed to have had them even before the war.

26. For a more detailed presentation of these indices, see Appendix, Retail Trade, Table III, p. 242.

27. Prosperity exists under these conditions as long as purchasing power is available. Even a shopping centre which has a definite function may be poor if it relies almost exclusively on poor customers. But the only case of that kind which we encountered, the small strictly local centre on Brambles Farm, had additional shortcomings. Being so inadequate, it has to rely chiefly on the smaller purchases of its poor group of customers.

28. The number of sugar registrations at each foodshop in the town was obtained for the week ending on the 29th April, 1944.

29. There are about 90 wholesalers in Middlesbrough, distributing food and other commodities. Some of these are manufacturers as well.

30. Lady Bell, *At the Works*, 2nd edition, 1911, pp. 110 and 111:

"Most of the women buy their clothes ready-made and pay for them and for their boots on the £1 ticket system. I do not know whether this obtains in other parts of the country. These £1 tickets are sold by men who buy them for cash down at certain shops in the town, getting the tickets for 18/– or even less; and the women, who buy these from them, in their turn pay 21/– payable in instalments of not less than 1/– weekly and usually 2/6 for the first week. These tickets are available either for one shop or two; sometimes 10/– goes to a bootshop and 10/– to a draper. The advantage of this system over that of buying from the 'tally-men,' or hawkers is that, although in each case the woman has to make a weekly payment, in the case of the £1 tickets she goes to the shop in the town, and can get the goods that she sees at the prices marked in the windows, whereas by the other system she is at the mercy of the tallyman, who may palm off on her at a given price something which is usually sold far below it. She has, besides, to buy the thing unseen from a sample shown to her."

31. Before the war both credit companies and private ticket agents were allowed to charge what discount they pleased. The usual sum was 2/6 in the £. As the shop-keepers also paid the agent or company a discount for every credit customer, the real value of the customer's ticket was several shillings less than its title value.

32. Less than 1·0 per cent. of the one-man shops interviewed provided such services, whilst more than half of the department stores, co-operatives and multiples did so and two-fifths of the independent multi-branch, one-branch and family shops.

33. The pool delivery area and the branches of the co-operative society, as well as its milk delivery area, are shown on two of the maps of Middlesbrough's Spheres of influence, in pocket at end of book.

34. Altogether seven shops have been established since the war; three in the strictly local centres, one, a co-operative branch, in the Corporation Road intermediate centre, and three as isolated shops. Except for the co-operative, all are small independent shops.

35. This, of course, refers only to those shops which had been established before the war. Of the 337 shops interviewed, seven have been established since, and a further seven just before, the war. In an additional 17 cases, the present manager had not been there before the war and could not, therefore, answer all the relevant questions.

NOTES TO APPENDIX A

1. The stone bridge at Stockton marks the limit of navigation. Its erection in 1769 killed the trade of the old port of Yarm higher up-stream. The river is tidal as far as Worsall, above Yarm.

2. The physical distinctness of the several concentrations of working-class homes on the east side of Middlesbrough here noted is clearly reflected in the neighbourhood structure.

3. The detailed Land Use map, which is not included here, showed the pattern of farm boundaries, at least for the part of the farmland area that lies adjacent to the towns of South Tees-side. It is highly important that account should be taken of these boundaries in the planning of future land use, and that where alterations are proposed, the territorial units which the farm boundaries provide should be followed as far as possible. For efficient farm management may be jeopardised or rendered quite impossible by the subtraction of certain key fields. Uneconomic patches of land, which are of little use for farming or anything else, can all too easily be produced by drawing new and arbitrary lines in the land-use pattern.

4. Skinningrove works are an outlying centre, located on the coast farther south at the mouth of Kilton Beck. They use local ore obtained from the mines surviving within a few miles range.

5. The population of the area increased during the century 1831–1931 from a mere 20,000 to nearly 350,000.

6. As mining was extended south-eastwards, mining villages sprang up, especially during the '60s and '70s, e.g. Margrove Park, Boosbeck, New Skelton, North Skelton, and Lingdale, which all appeared at this time.

7. The Transporter Bridge now gives Middlesbrough direct access to the north side of the estuary and the Hartlepools, as well as to Haverton Hill. The new bridge at Newport built in 1934 is even more important in improving Middlesbrough's access to the north. It leads to Billingham and through Billingham greatly strengthens Middlesbrough's communications with large areas of Durham and farther north. It has destroyed the dominance of Stockton as the regional route-centre, and has given Middlesbrough the possible opportunity of extending its area influence northwards at the expense of Stockton. The volume of traffic on this road approaching Middlesbrough from the north is already very much greater than that on the road which comes into Stockton from the north-west via Sedgefield.

8. Messrs. Brunton, who are the other chief milk distributors in Middlesbrough, also draw their supplies from the northern part of Stokesley Rural District.

9. The moorland road which runs south-east from Guisborough to Whitby keeps to the high ground north of the Esk valley, and does not pass through any villages.

10. Bus transport has greatly improved the accessibility of the mining villages of Cleveland, now provided with frequent services to and from Middlesbrough. All the mining settlements are within about an hour's journey of the city—Loftus, the most distant, is a 67 minutes' bus journey away.

The villages nearer Whitby along the coast road, and those of Eskdale, are more than an hour's distance from Middlesbrough by either form of public transport service, and Middlesbrough is of correspondingly less use and importance to their inhabitants.

11. However, some exceptions to this are worth noting. Middlesbrough is the head of a Roman Catholic diocese which embraces most of Durham and North Yorkshire. In the district organisation of the Methodist Church, the joint Middlesbrough and Darlington District includes all the southern part of Durham and most of the North Riding. In the new regional organisation of the Post Office, Middlesbrough appears within the North-Eastern Region as the headquarters of a telephone area which includes all the southern part of Durham County and most of the North Riding.

12. In 1944, about 42,000 were engaged in metal-working industries and over 15,000 in chemical industries. Of the former group nearly 17,000 work in Middlesbrough and Haverton Hill; 14,000 in the works situated east of Middlesbrough on the south side of the estuary; and about 11,000 in the Stockton-Thornaby area.

13. The former are about one-quarter, the latter about one-third of all exports from Tees ports.

14. Dredging operations have removed the bar where in 1863 there was still only 3½ feet of water available at low tide, and together with the construction of training walls have led to the establishment of one fixed and deep channel. Breakwaters and river-lighting have been provided, and since 1858 extensive reclamation of the foreshore has been carried out.

15. In the three years 1936–38 they averaged 60,000 tons per annum.

16. Between 1935 and 1939 slag represented 17 per cent. of the total out-shipments.

17. Exports from the Dock were usually more than a million tons per annum in the 1920s, but after 1930 they fell rapidly to less than half this amount. Imports are far less important in peace-time.

18. Within the Middlesbrough borough boundary, besides the Ironmasters' District, there are other scattered sites, especially in the eastern part, which would be quite suitable for the establishment of factories for the type of industry suggested.

NOTES TO APPENDIX B

1. According to the census, a household or "private family," is any existing household, including boarders, but excluding lodgers, regardless of whether it is a single or multiple household unit.

2. As the sample covered one in 25·8 of all Middlesbrough households, the sample figures were multiplied accordingly for the purpose of these estimates.

3. One category of potential households was, however, omitted, that of people who now live as lodgers, and who might also wish to establish separate households. This category was not included since there were comparatively few lodgers in Middlesbrough, i.e. lodgers were only 2·0 per cent. of the total population in households.

ADDITIONAL PUBLICATIONS ON THE MIDDLESBROUGH SURVEY AND PLAN

1. MAX LOCK: *The County Borough of Middlesbrough Survey and Plan:* Published by the Middlesbrough Corporation, Yorkshire. 1947.

2. DENNIS CHAPMAN: *The Social Survey of Middlesbrough:* Wartime Social Survey, New Series No. 50. September 1945.

3. GRISELDA ROWNTREE: *Maternity Services in Middlesbrough:* Association for Planning and Regional Reconstruction: Report 40. April 1946.

INDEX

KEY

INDUSTRIAL AREAS ....

CENTRE OF BUSINESS AND ADMINISTRATION ....

UNDEVELOPED SITES AND FARM LAND ....

RESIDENTIAL AREAS

Houses let on weekly or similar tenancy ....
predominantly in private ownership

Houses in private ownership ....
86 *per cent. owner occupied,* 14 *per cent. let on yearly or similar tenancy*

Housing Estates ....

Note :
Areas of retail trade are not shown on this map

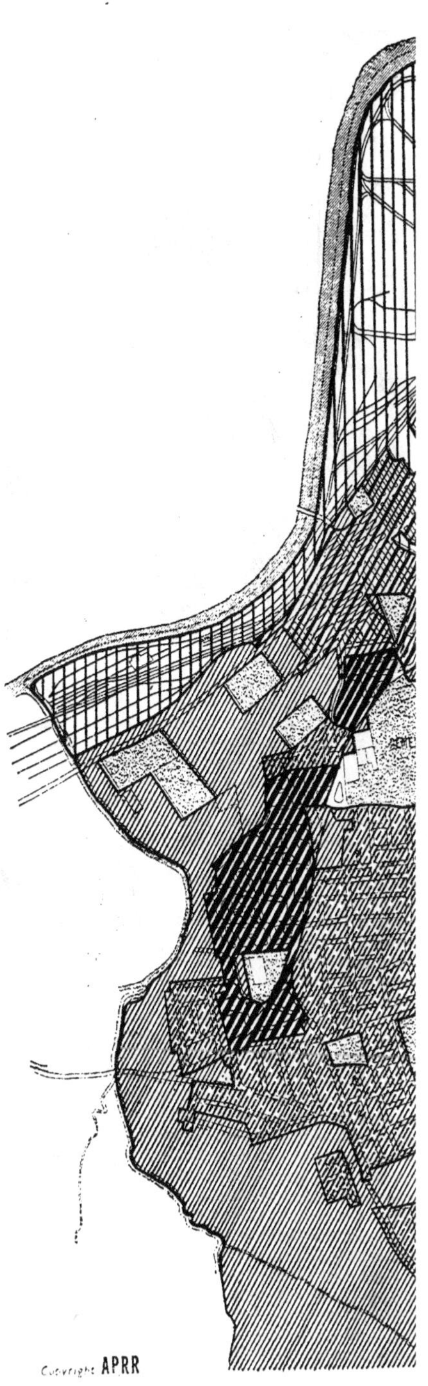

RIVER TEES
L.N.E.R. DOCKS
ALBERT PARK
CEMETERY
PALLISTER PARK
HOSPITAL GROUNDS
STEWART PARK

MAP I

MAJOR LAND USE

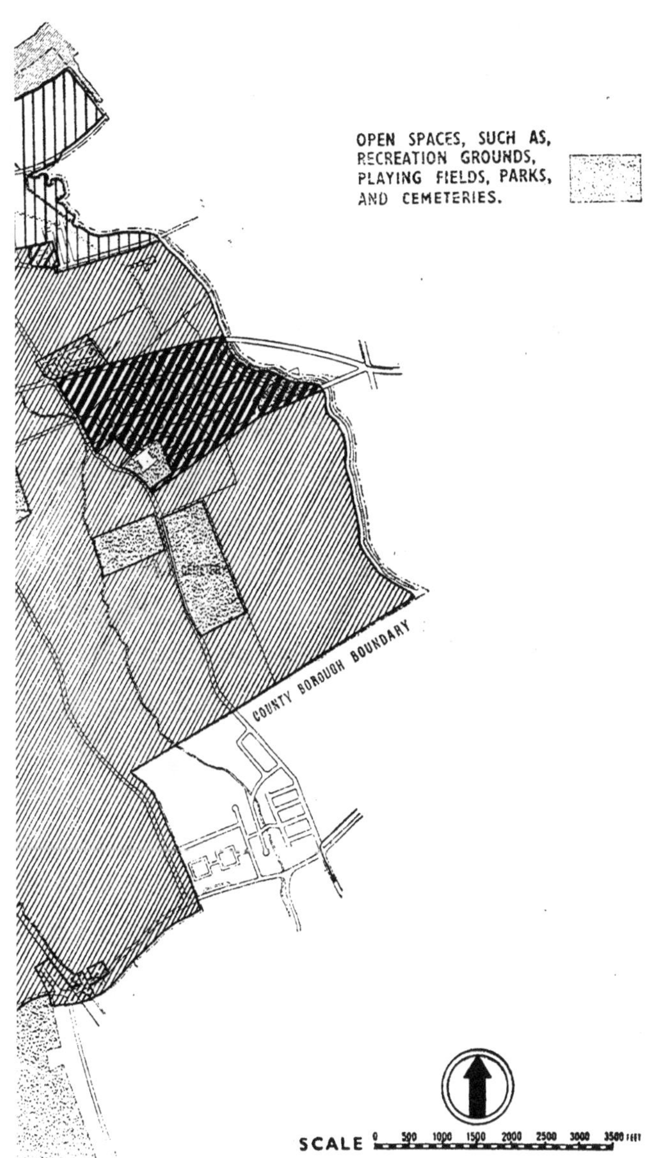

KEY

NEIGHBOURHOOD PATTERN

NEIGHBOURHOOD DESIGNATION NUMBER, e.g. .... A 9

DEFINITE BOUNDARY .... ———

INDEFINITE BOUNDARY .... —·—·—

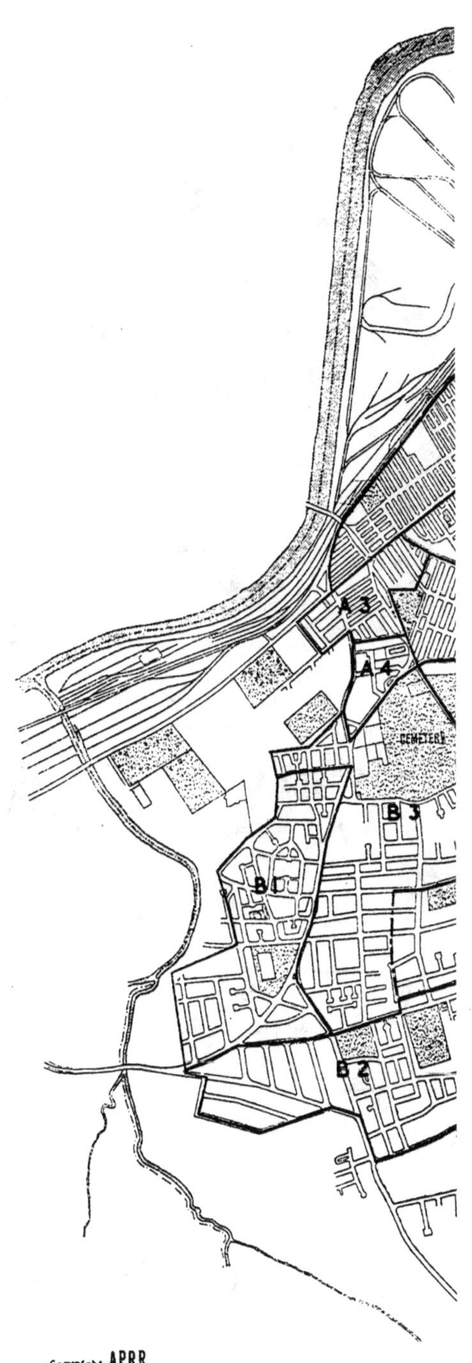
A 3
A 4
CEMETERY
B 3
B 1
B 2

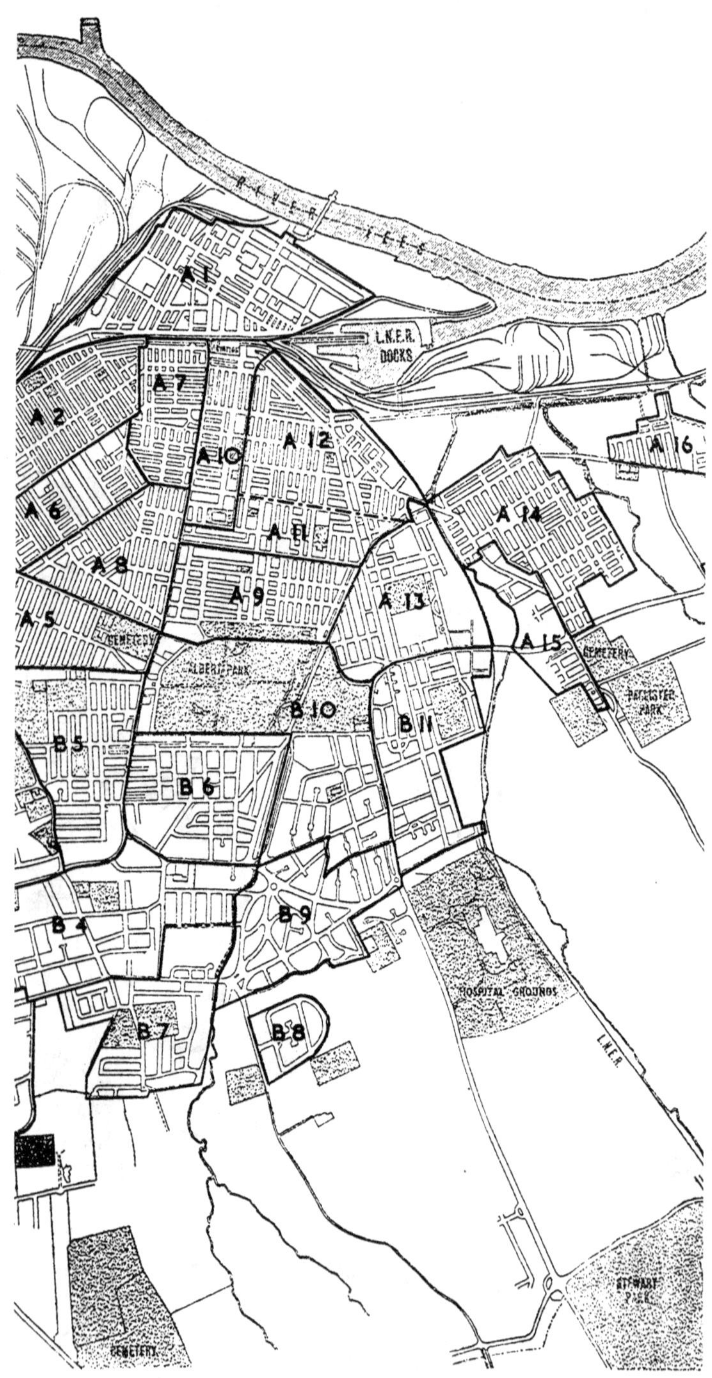

RIVER TEES
A1
L.N.E.R. DOCKS
A2
A7
A10
A12
A16
A6
A14
A11
A8
A9
A13
A5
CEMETERY
A15
CEMETERY
ALBERT PARK
PALLISTER PARK
B10
B11
B5
B6
B9
B4
HOSPITAL GROUNDS
B7
B8
L.N.E.R.
STEWART PARK
CEMETERY

MAP 2

NEIGHBOURHOODS MAP A

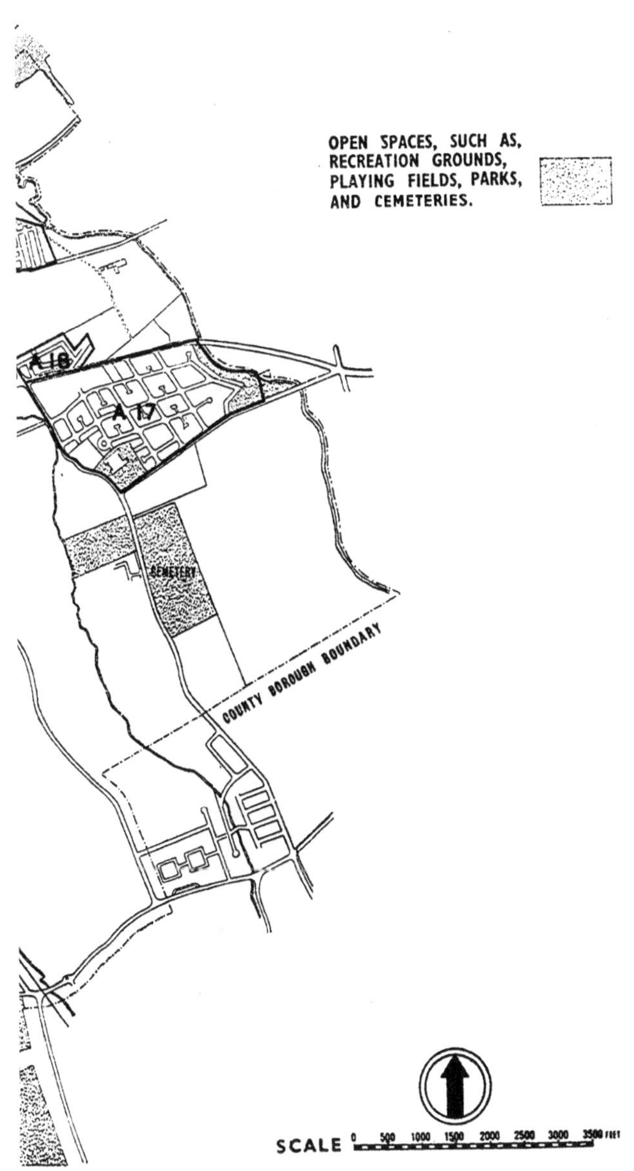

KEY

NEIGHBOURHOOD PATTERN

NEIGHBOURHOOD DESIGNATION NUMBER e.g. .... B 10

DEFINITE BOUNDARY .... ————

INDEFINITE BOUNDARY .... —·—·—·—

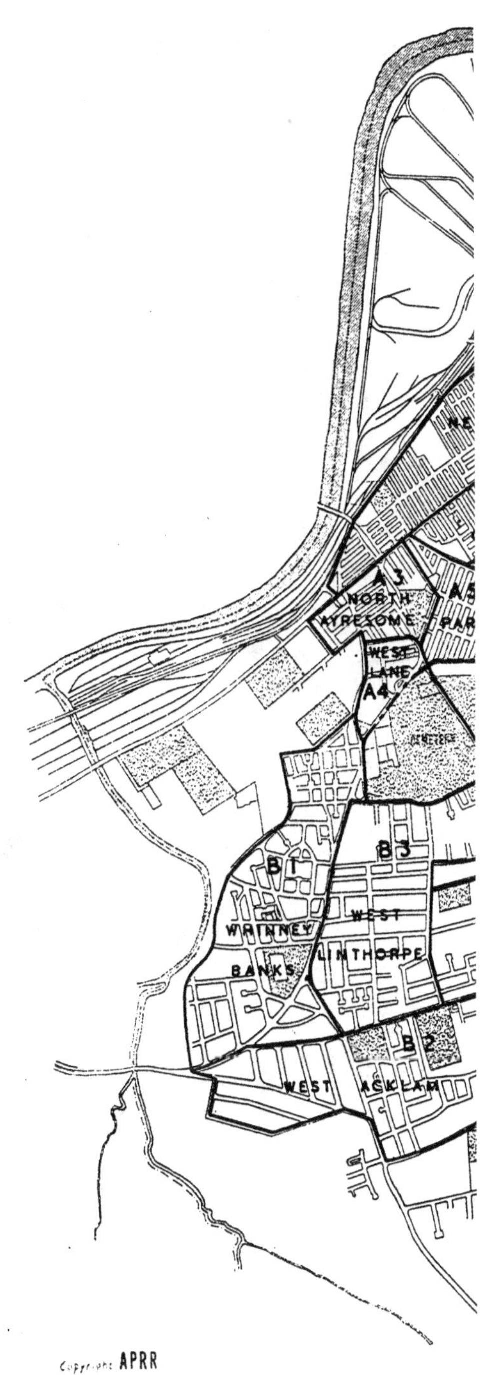
A3
NORTH
AYRESOME
WEST
LANE
A4
B1
B3
WHINNEY
BANKS
WEST
LINTHORPE
B2
WEST
ACKLAM

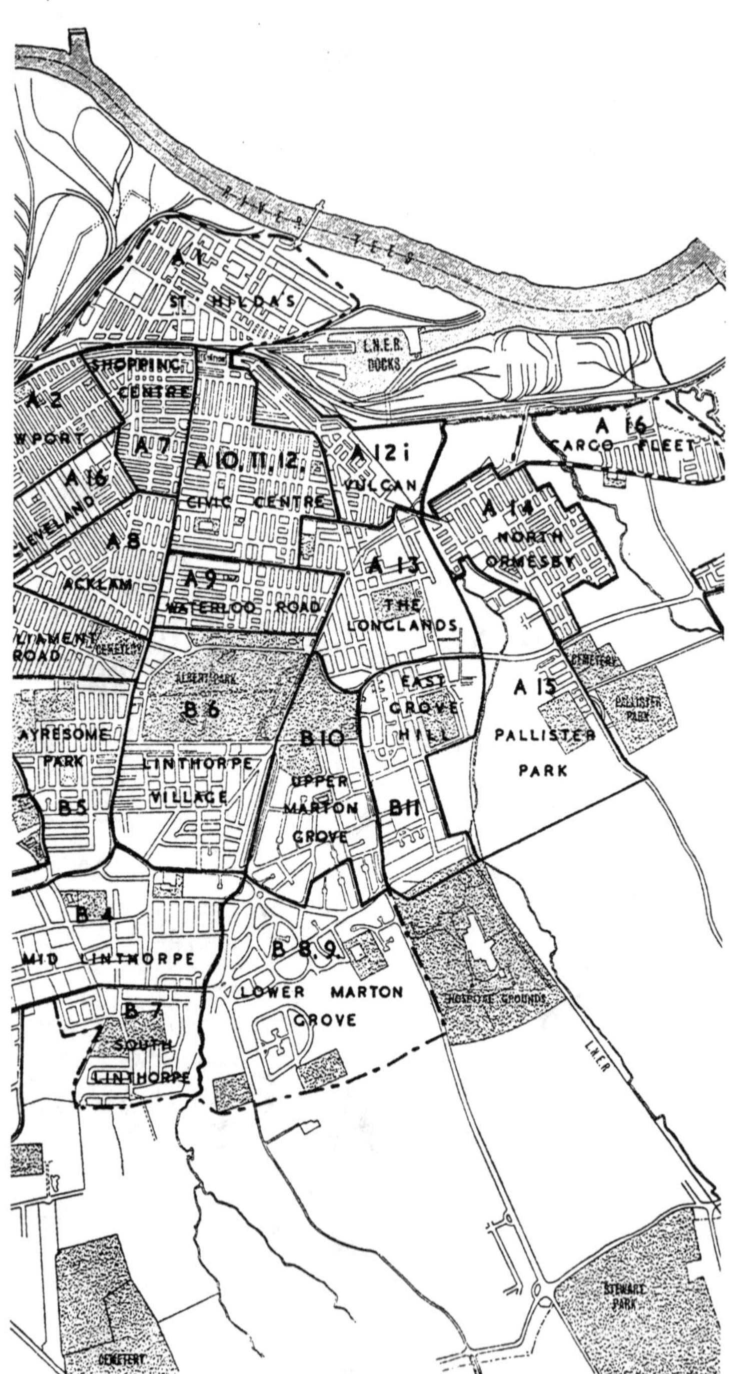
RIVER TEES
A 1
ST HILDAS
L.N.E.R. DOCKS
SHOPPING CENTRE
A 2
A 7
A 10, 11, 12
A 12i
VULCAN
A 16
CARGO FLEET
A 16
CLEVELAND
CIVIC CENTRE
A 14
NORTH ORMESBY
A 8
ACKLAM
A 9
WATERLOO ROAD
A 13
THE LONGLANDS
ROAD
CEMETERY
ALBERT PARK
B 6
EAST GROVE HILL
A 15
PALLISTER PARK
AYRESOME PARK
B 10
LINTHORPE VILLAGE
UPPER MARTON GROVE
B 5
B 11
B 4
MID LINTHORPE
B 8.9.
LOWER MARTON GROVE
HOSPITAL GROUNDS
B 7
SOUTH LINTHORPE
L.N.E.R
STEWART PARK
CEMETERY

MAP 3

NEIGHBOURHOODS MAP B

ADJUSTED BY ENUMERATION DISTRICTS

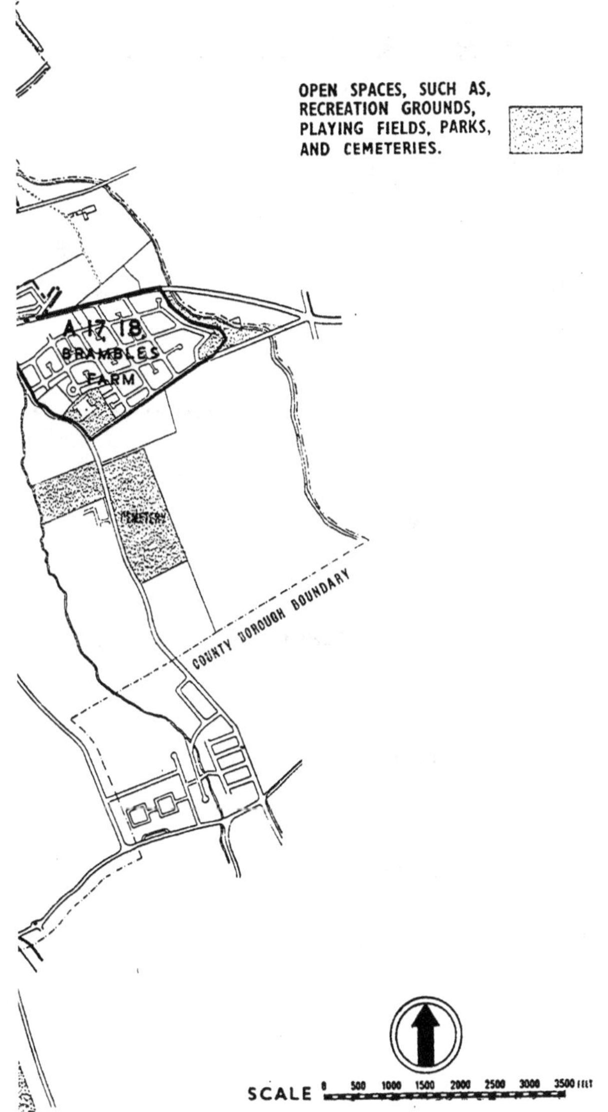

KEY

YOUTH CLUB .... ●

HOMES OF MEMBERS .... ——

ADULT CLUB .... ◉

HOMES OF MEMBERS .... -----

POST OFFICE.................................... ⊡

HOMES OF USERS ....

LOCAL AUTHORITY SCHOOL .... △

HOMES OF PUPILS................................. -—-

NEIGHBOURHOOD BOUNDARY .... ——

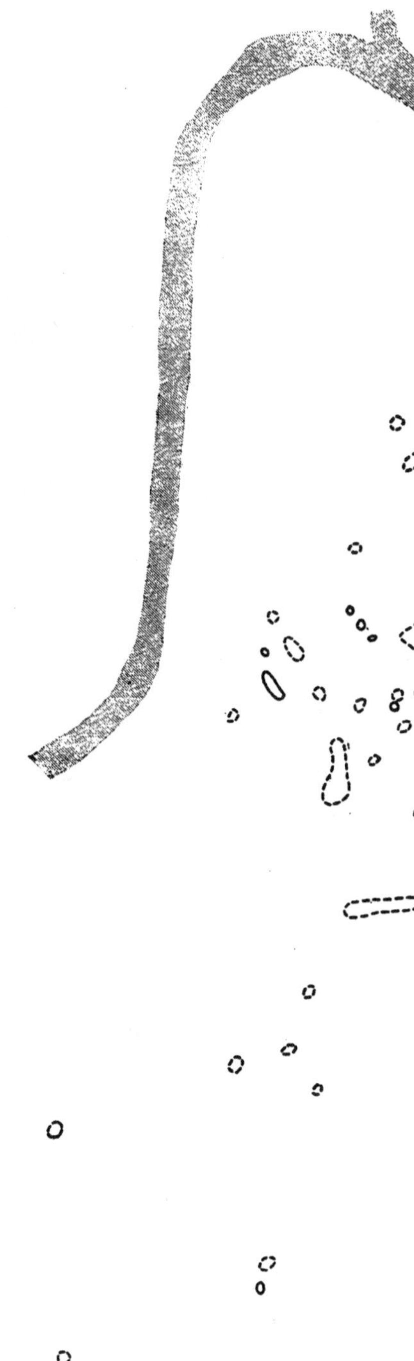

RIVER TEES

MAP 4

GENERALISED CATCHMENT AREAS IN NEIGHBOURHOOD A.9. WATERLOO ROAD.

SCALE 0 500 1000 1500 2000 2500 3000 3500 FEET

KEY

WEEKLY INCOMES OF CHIEF WAGE EARNERS

UP TO £3 12s.	●
£3 13s. TO £5 0s.	◒
£5 1s. TO £10 0s.	◎
£10 1s. AND OVER	○
NO ANSWER	×

Note :

Based on answers obtained to Wartime Social Survey Household Enquiry, July, 1944

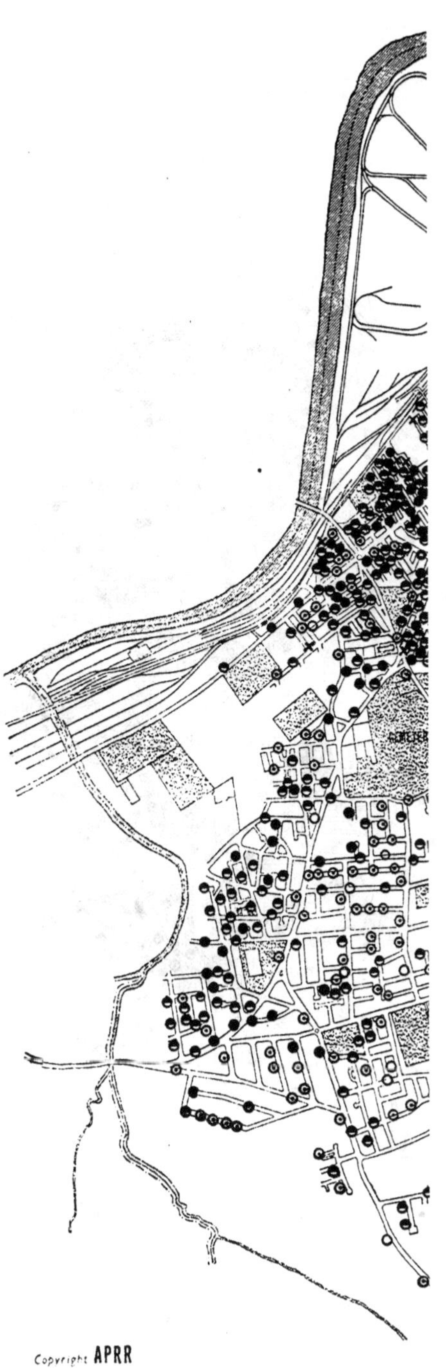

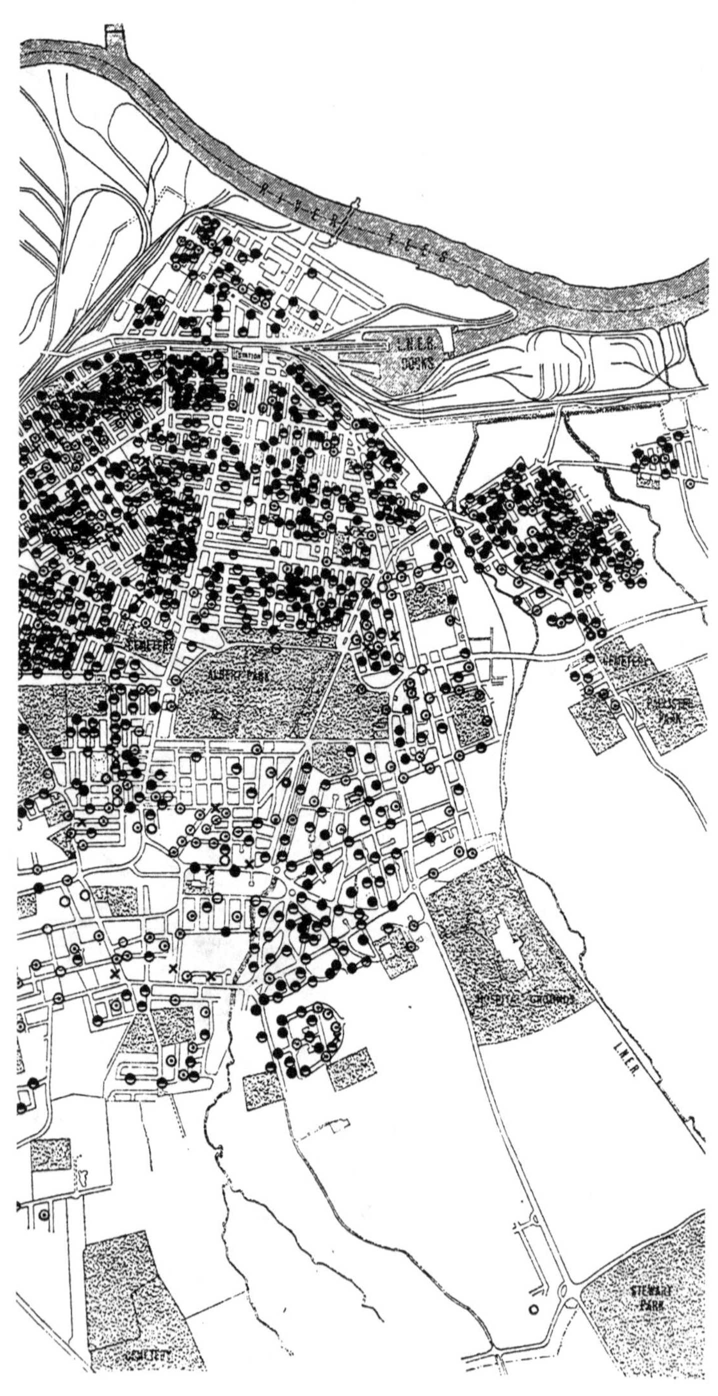
RIVER TEES
L.N.E.R. DOCKS
STATION
CEMETERY
ALBERT PARK
HOSPITAL GROUNDS
L.N.E.R.
STEWART PARK
CEMETERY

MAP 5

DISTRIBUTION OF CHIEF WAGE EARNERS BY INCOMES

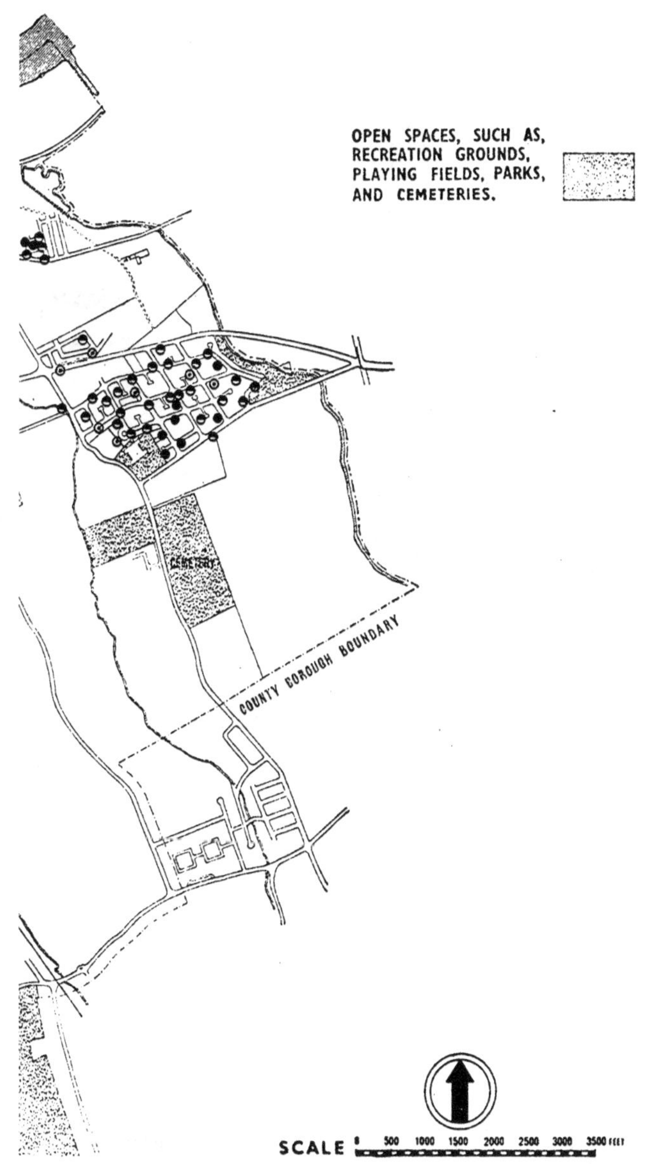

KEY

WOULD YOU LIKE TO MOVE TO ANOTHER HOUSE?

YES .... o

NO .... ●

DON'T KNOW }
NO ANSWER } .... ×

Note :

Based on answers obtained to Wartime Social Survey Household Enquiry, July, 1944

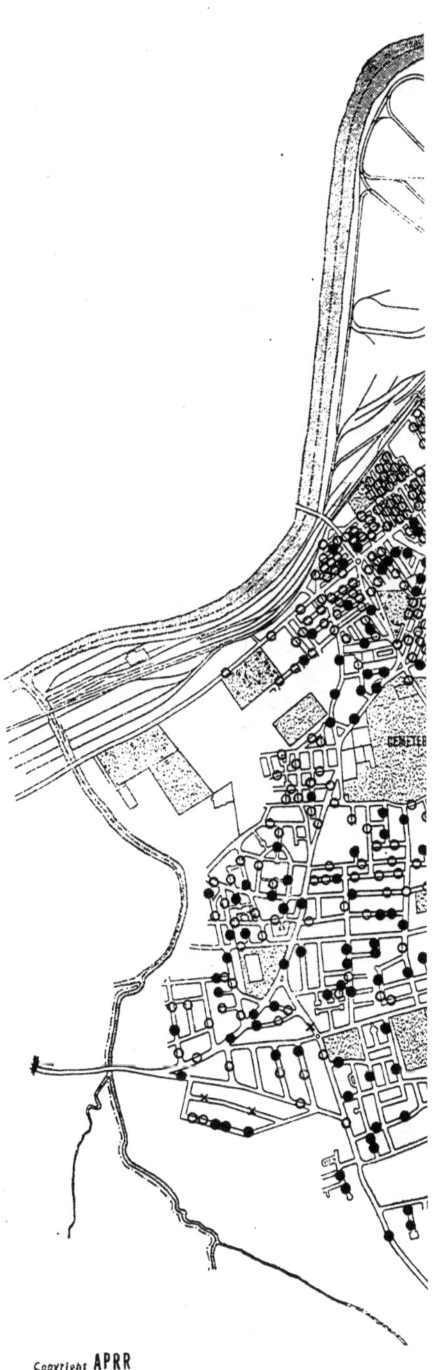

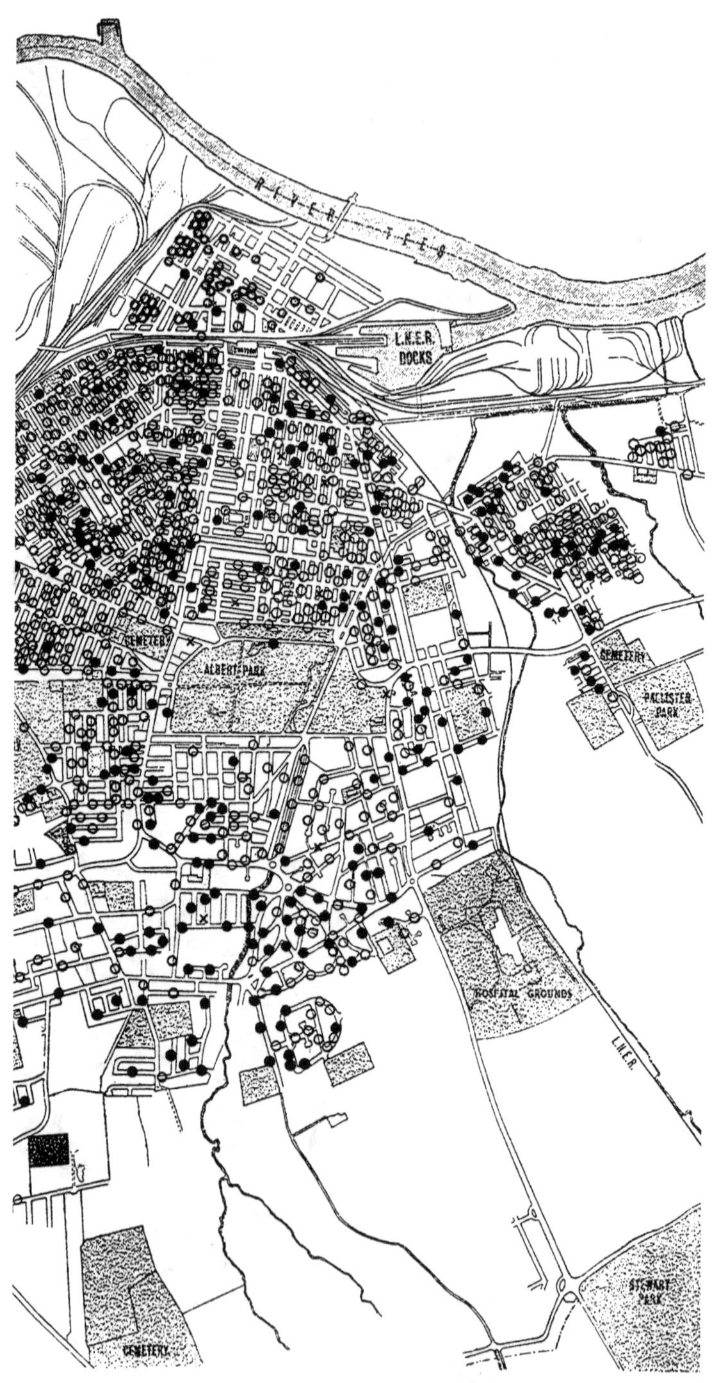

RIVER TEES
L.N.E.R.
DOCKS
CEMETERY
ALBERT PARK
CEMETERY
PALLISTER PARK
HOSPITAL GROUNDS
L.N.E.R.
STEWART PARK
CEMETERY

MAP 6

WOULD YOU LIKE TO MOVE TO ANOTHER HOUSE ?

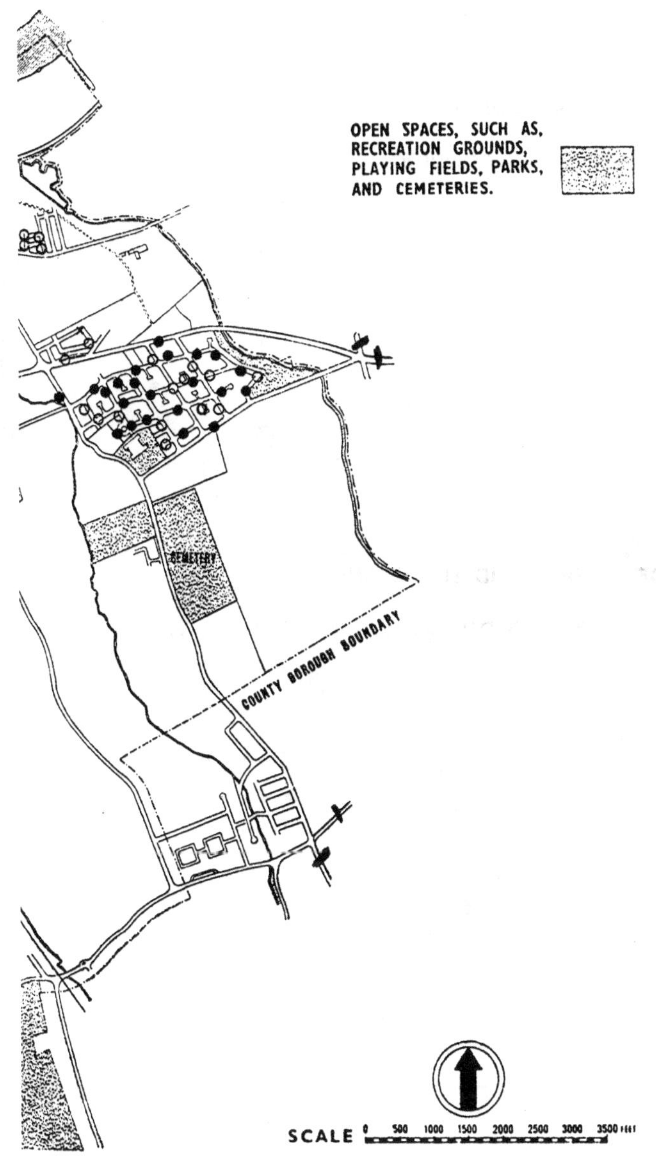

KEY

INDEX OF LIVING CONDITIONS

RATING

6 = BEST LIVING CONDITIONS

1 = WORST LIVING CONDITIONS

6   3

5   2

4   1

UNDEVELOPED LAND LEFT BLANK

NEIGHBOURHOOD DESIGNATION NUMBER e.g. A13

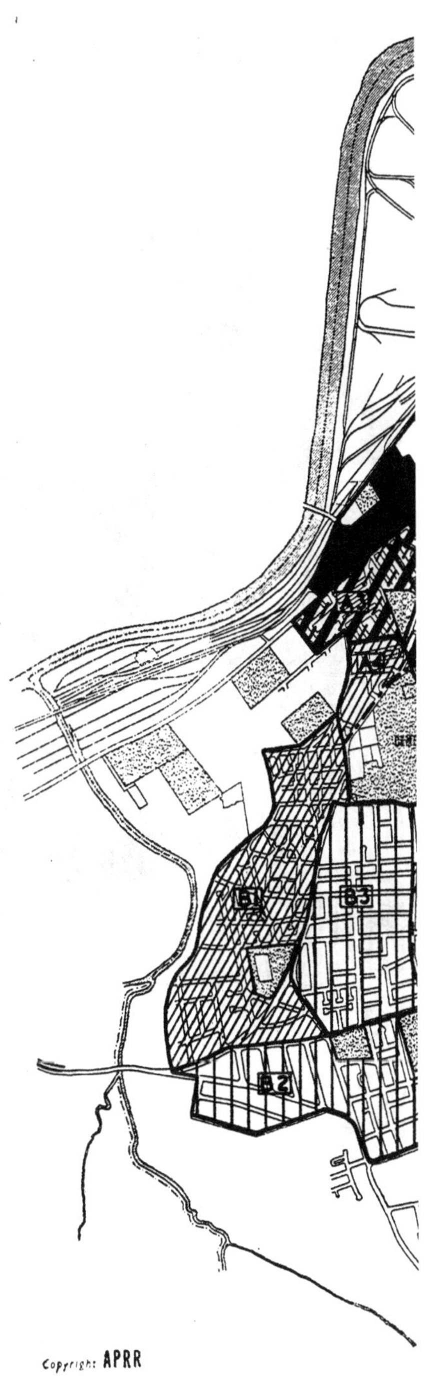
B1
B3
B2

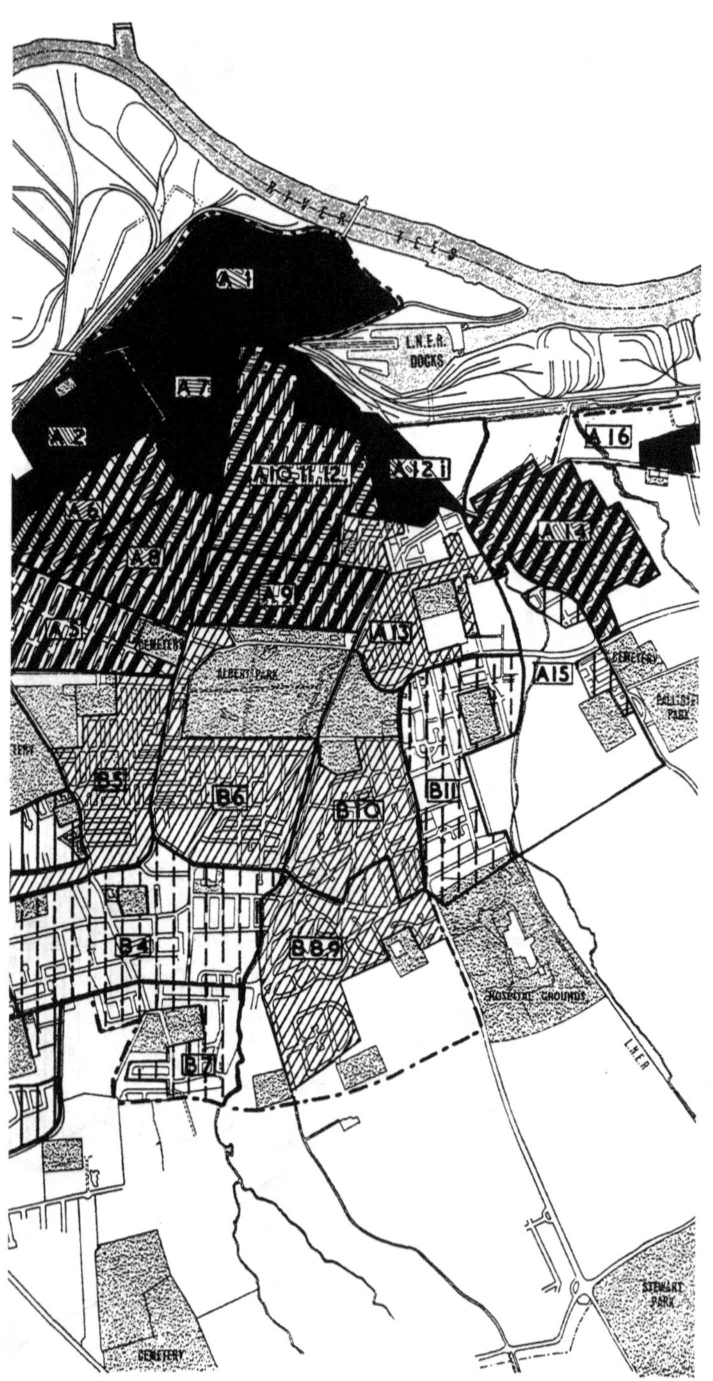

RIVER TEES
L.N.E.R. DOCKS
A7
A2
A16
A8
A9
A5
CEMETERY
A13
ALBERT PARK
A15
CEMETERY
B5
B6
B10
B11
B4
B8.9
B7
HOSPITAL GROUNDS
L.N.E.R.
STEWART PARK
CEMETERY

MAP 7

NEIGHBOURHOODS MAP C

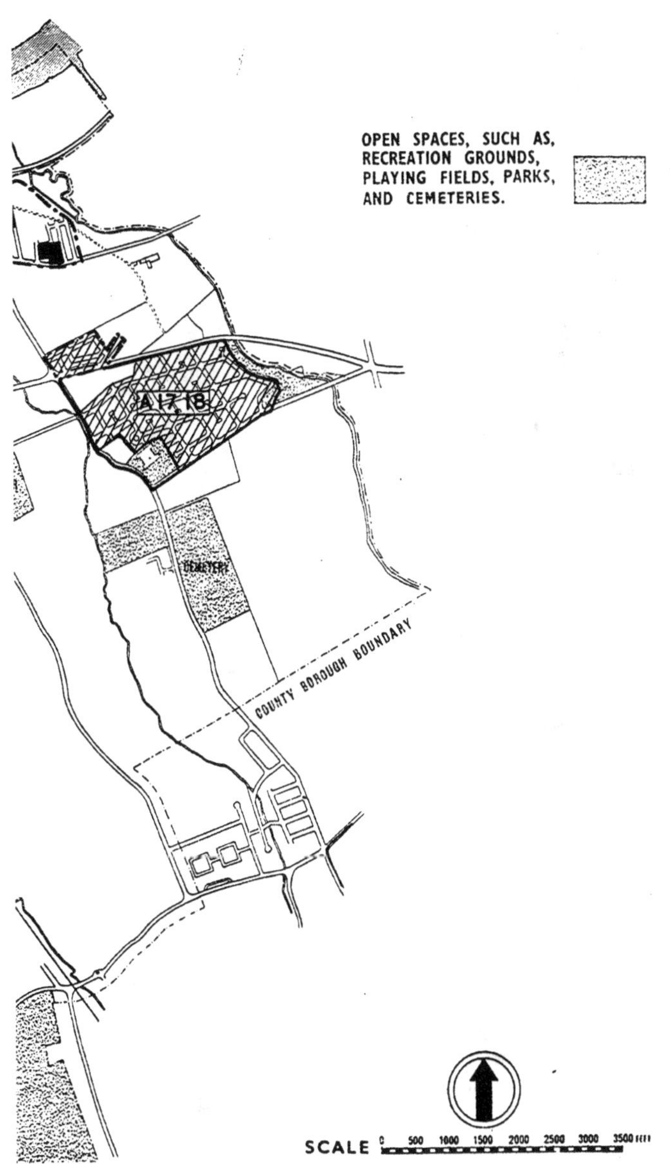

KEY

RECREATION

PUBLIC HOUSE HALLS THEATRE OR CINEMA	.... R

CLUBS

YOUTH AND ADULT CLUBS C

EDUCATION

ELEMENTARY AND SECONDARY SCHOOLS EVENING INSTITUTE LIBRARY	.... E

HEALTH

INFANT WELFARE, SCHOOL, AND PUBLIC ASSISTANCE CLINICS SURGERY WARTIME NURSERY	.... H

POST OFFICE .... ▫

CHURCH ...... †

SHOPPING CENTRE ...... ▬

NEIGHBOURHOOD DESIGNATION NUMBER, e.g. .. A.2.

Note:

This map is deliberately more comprehensive than the list of neighbourhood institutions on page 31. Some types of services have been included here which might ultimately be located in individual neighbourhoods or neighbourhood groups, but which cannot at present be classified as neighbourhood institutions, as there are as yet too few of them in Middlesbrough.

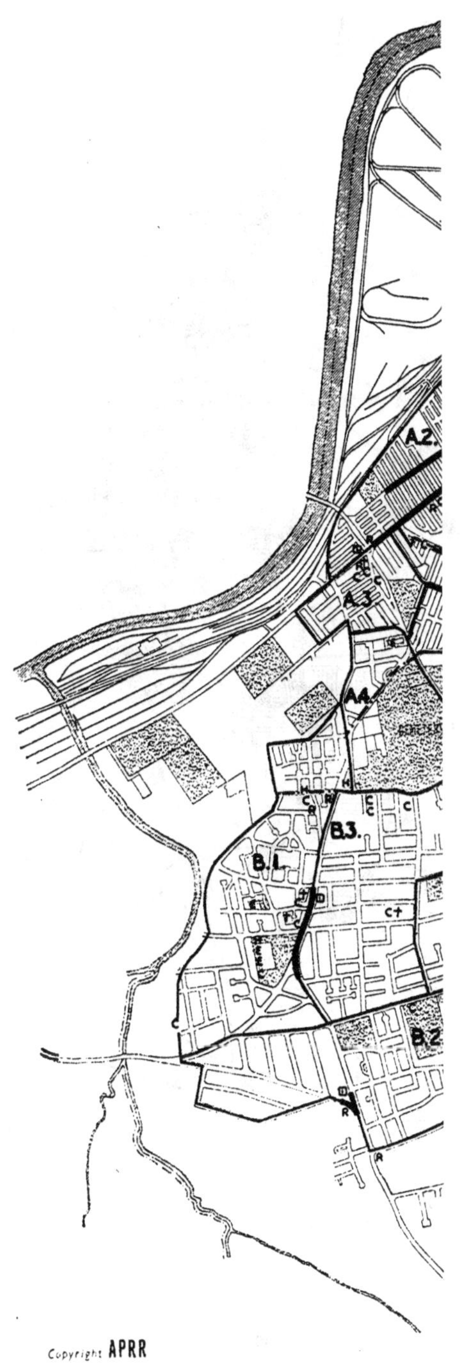
A.2.
A.3.
A.4.
B.3.
B.1.
B.2

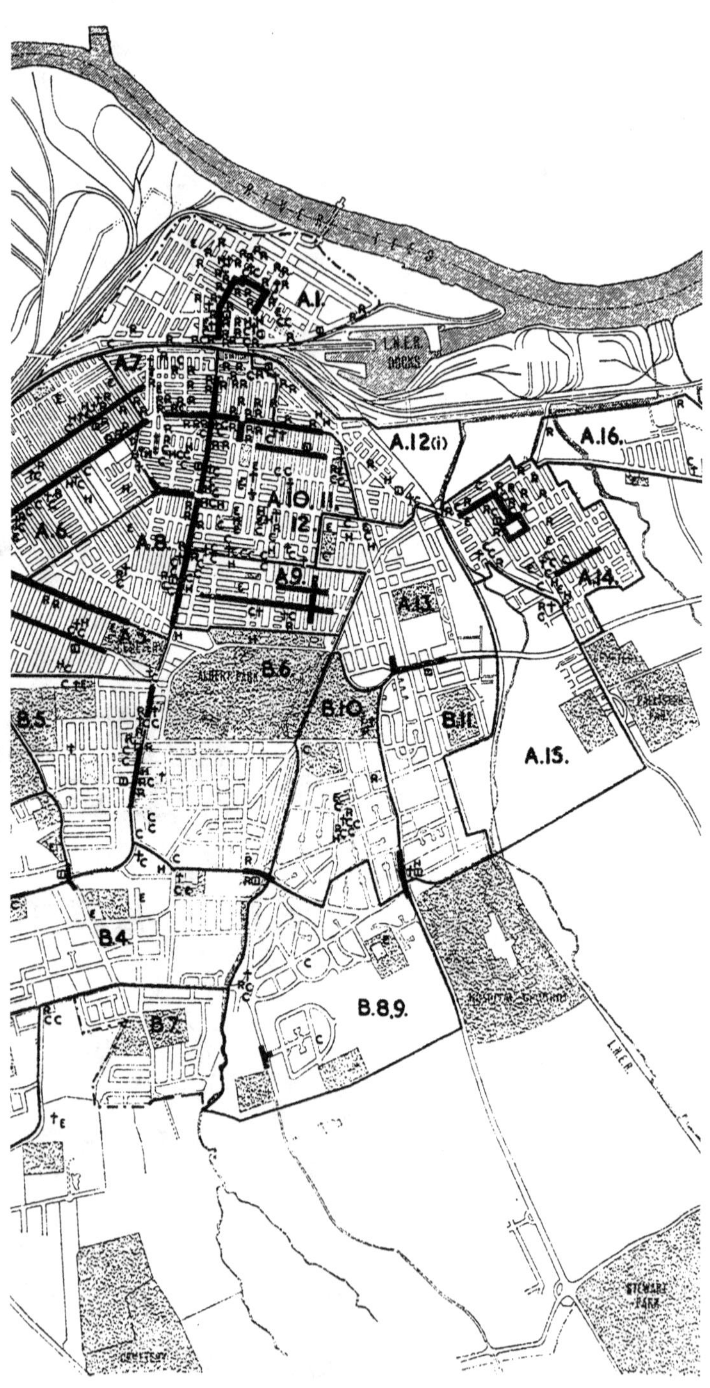
RIVER TEES
A.1.
L.N.E.R. DOCKS
A.7.
A.12(i)
A.16.
A.10.11.
12.
A.6.
A.8.
A.9.
A.14.
A.13.
A.5.
ALBERT PARK
B.6.
B.10.
B.11.
B.5.
A.15.
B.4.
B.8.9.
B.7.
L.N.E.R.
STEWART PARK

MAP 8

NEIGHBOURHOOD SERVICES

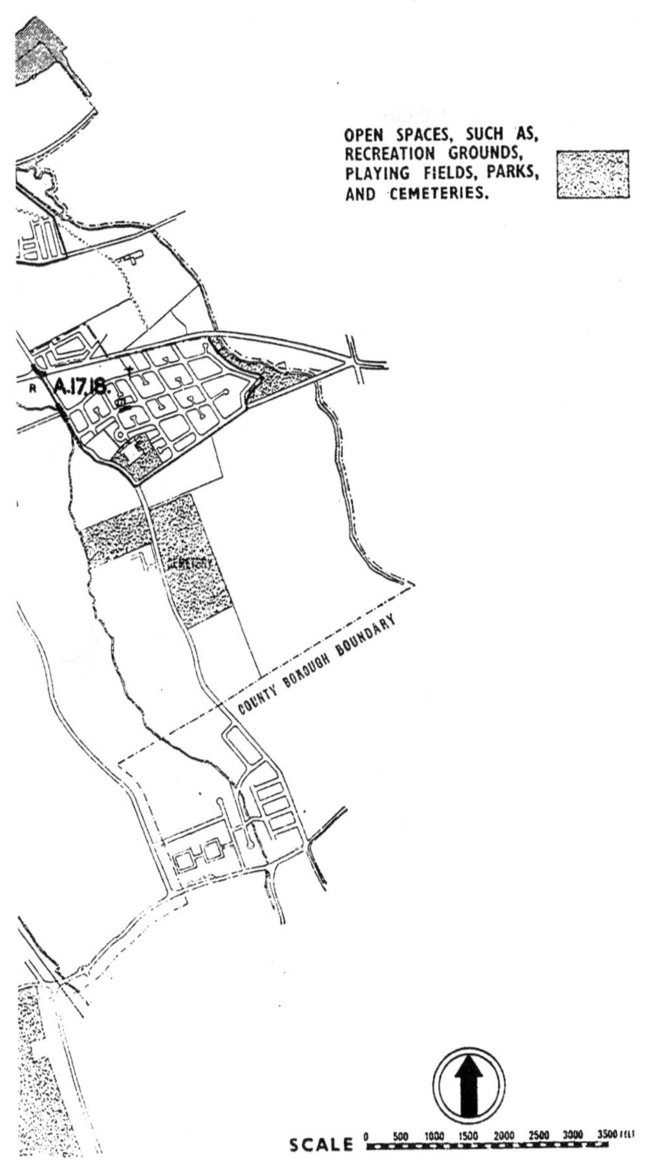

KEY

INDEX OF NEIGHBOURHOOD INTEGRATION

RATING

6=MOST INTEGRATED NEIGHBOURHOODS

1=LEAST INTEGRATED NEIGHBOURHOODS

6 | 3
5 | 2
4 | 1

UNDEVELOPED LAND LEFT BLANK

NEIGHBOURHOOD DESIGNATION NUMBER B11

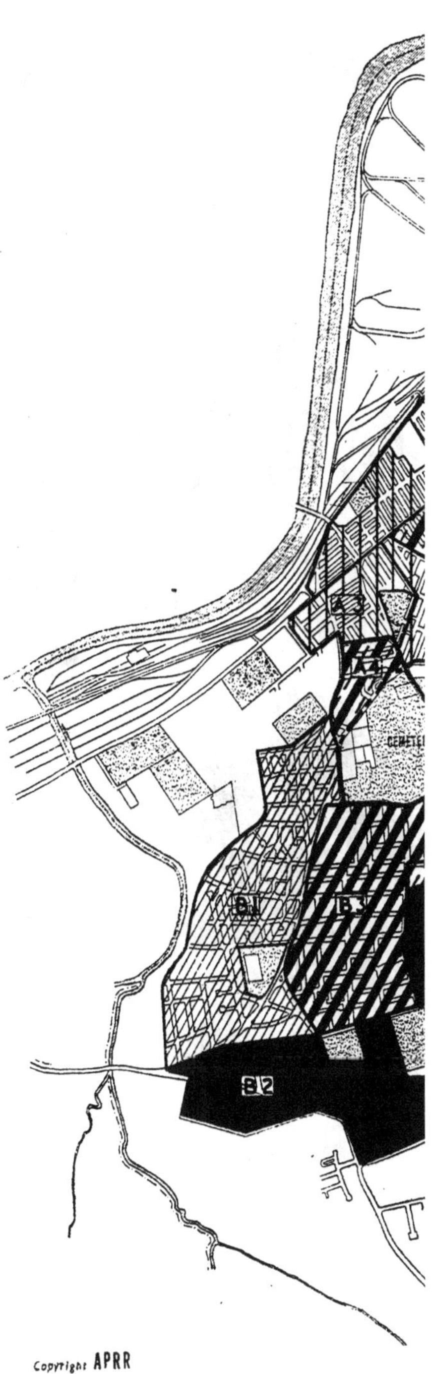
A3
A1
CEMETE
B1
B3
B2

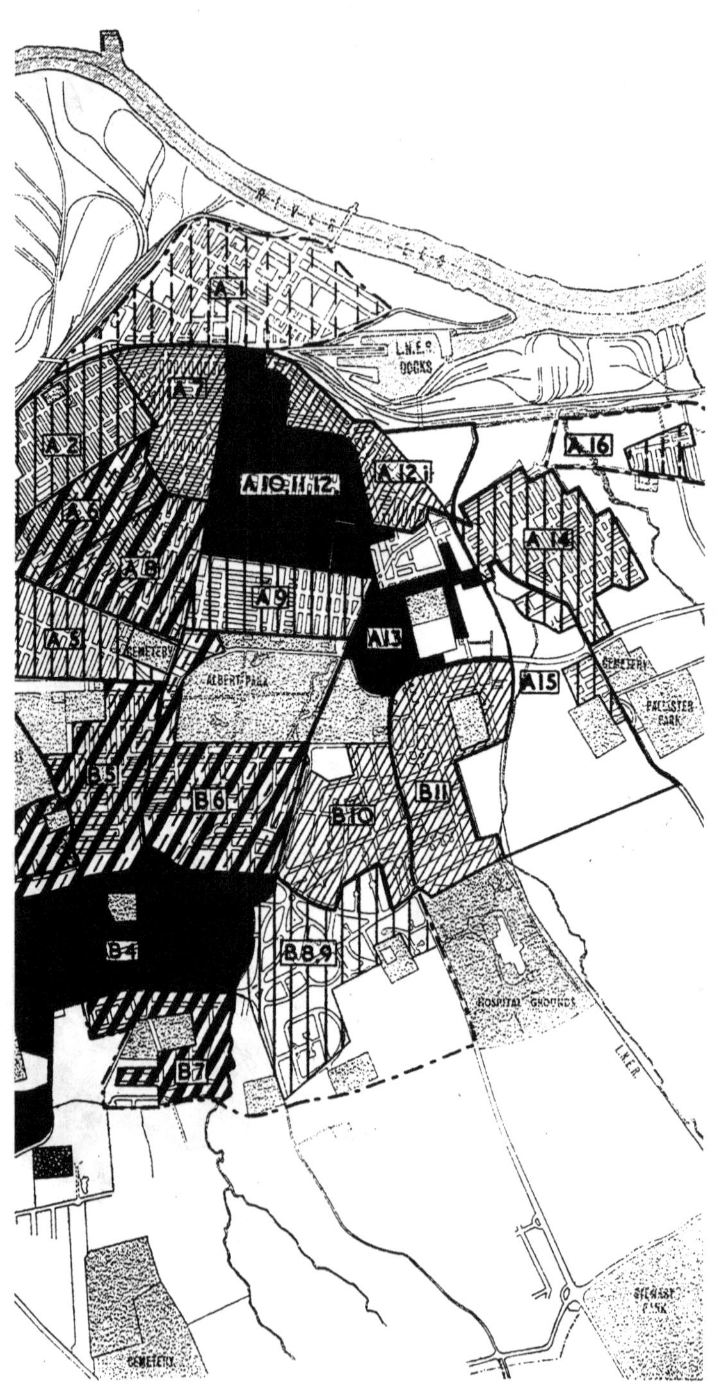

A1
L.N.E.R. DOCKS
A2
A7
A10,11,12
A16
A8
A9
A5
CEMETERY
ALBERT PARK
A13
A15
CEMETERY
B5
B6
B10
B11
B4
B8,9
HOSPITAL GROUNDS
L.N.E.R.
B7
CEMETERY

MAP 9

NEIGHBOURHOODS MAP D

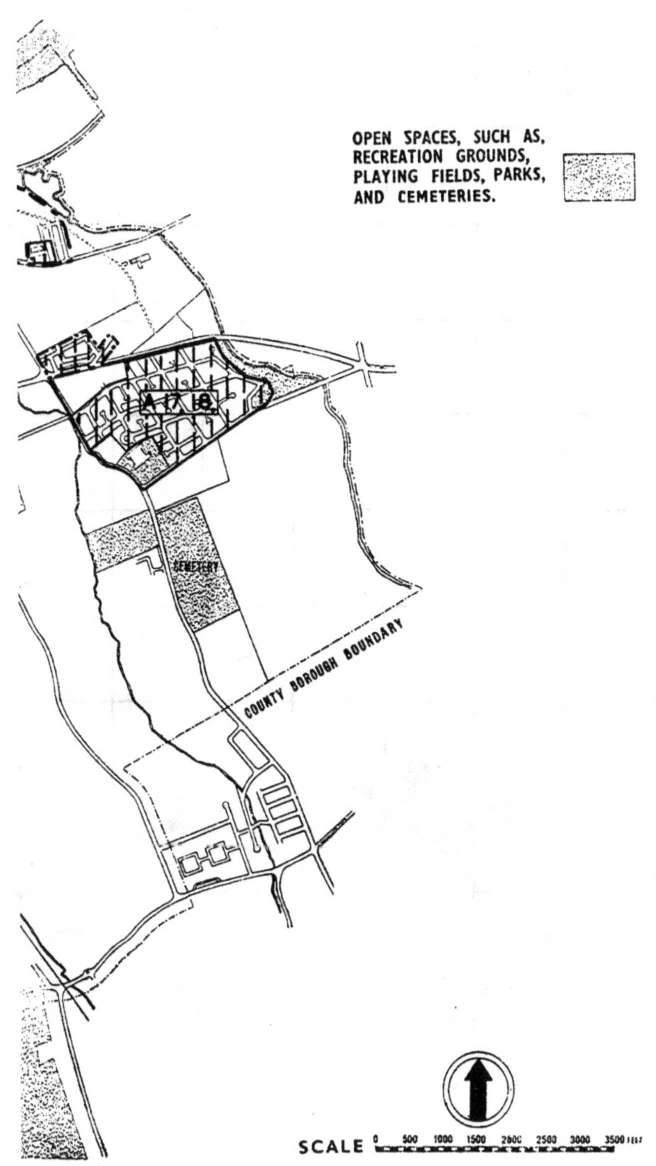

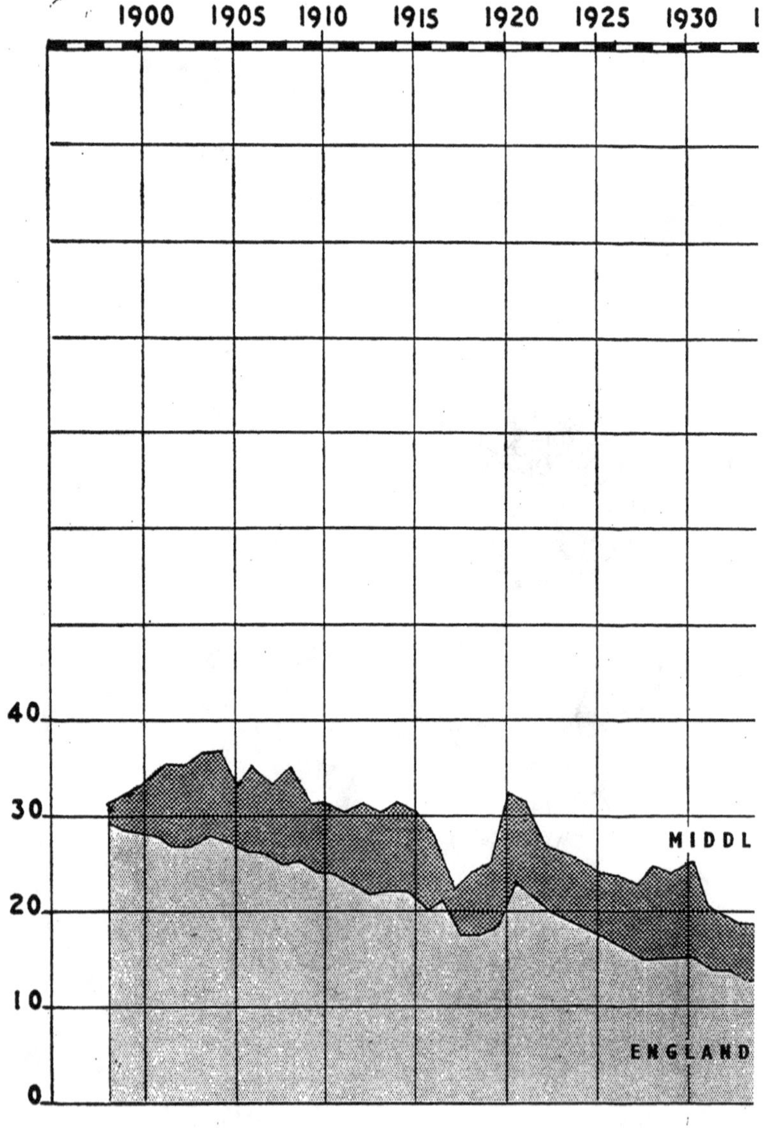

BIRTH RATE — PER 1,000 POPUl

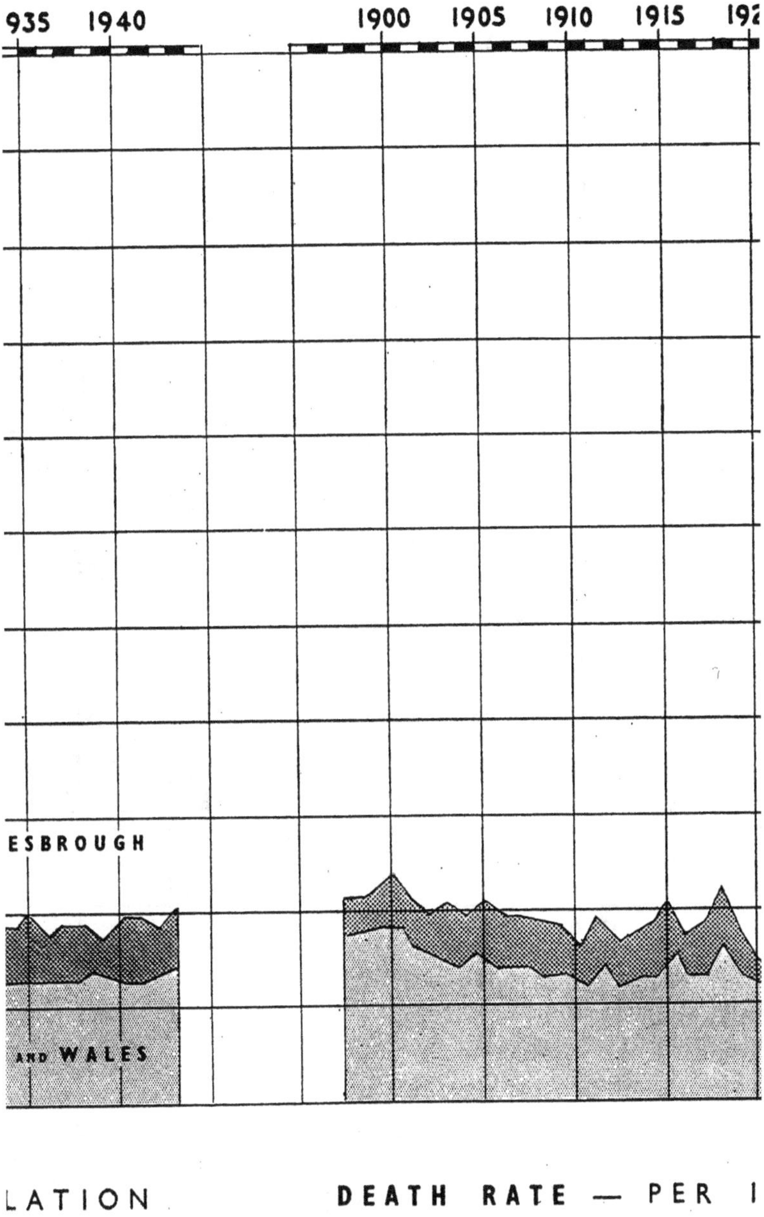

935 1940 1900 1905 1910 1915 192

ESBROUGH

AND WALES

LATION

DEATH RATE — PER I

BLIGHT FAC

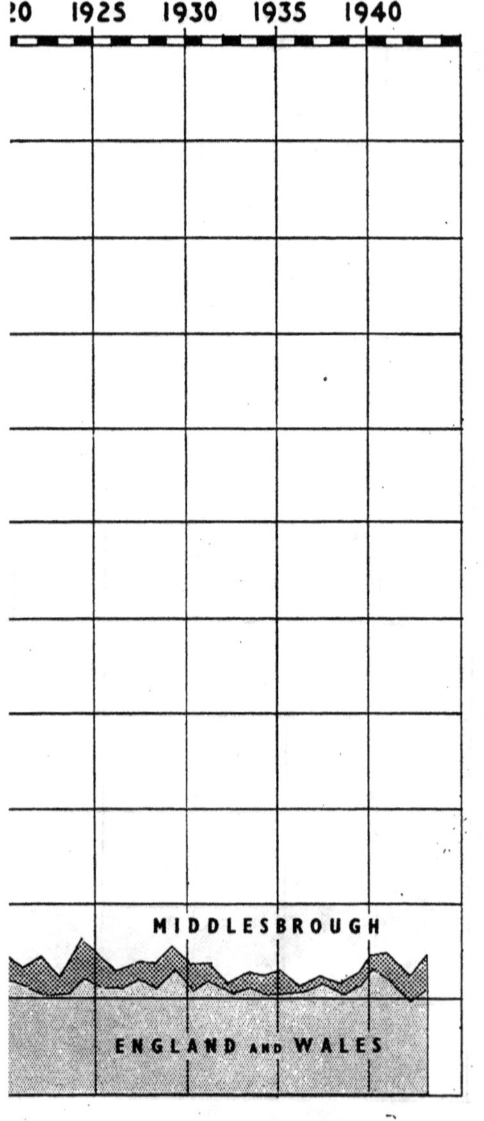

,000 POPULATION

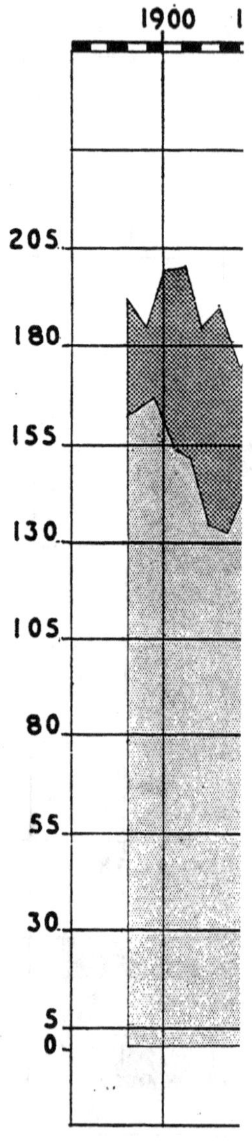

INFANT

GRAPH 10

TORS — MIDDLESBROUGH VITAL STATISTICS 1898 TO 1943

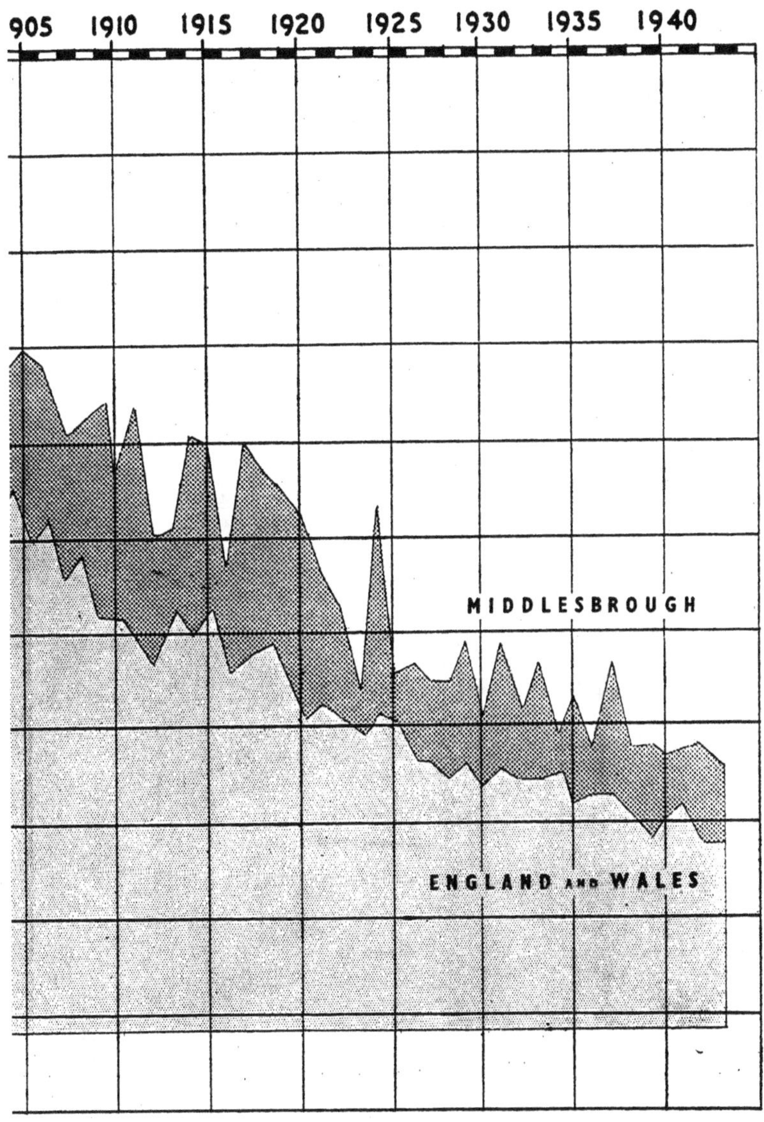

IORTALITY RATE — PER 1,000 BIRTHS

KEY

HOSPITAL .... ⊕

CLINIC

1 Tuberculosis Clinic
2 Skin Clinic
3 Public Assistance Dispensaries
} .... ⊕

SCHOOL CLINIC .... △

WARTIME NURSERY .... ■

MATERNITY AND INFANT WELFARE CENTRE .... ☒

SURGERY OF GENERAL PRACTITIONER .... O

WARD BOUNDARIES .... ∼

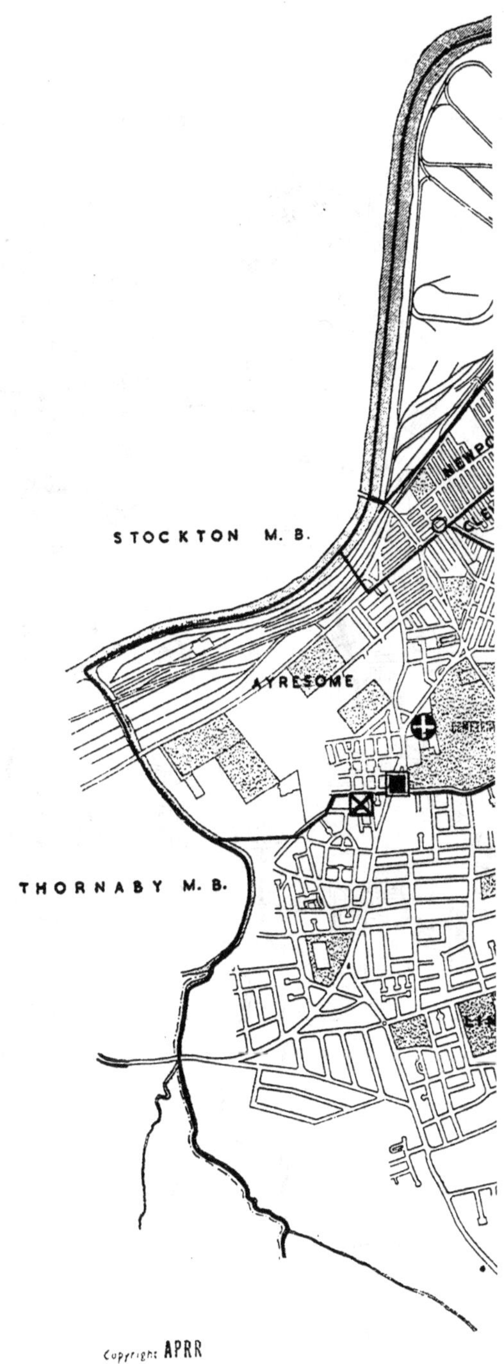
STOCKTON M. B.
AYRESOME
THORNABY M. B.

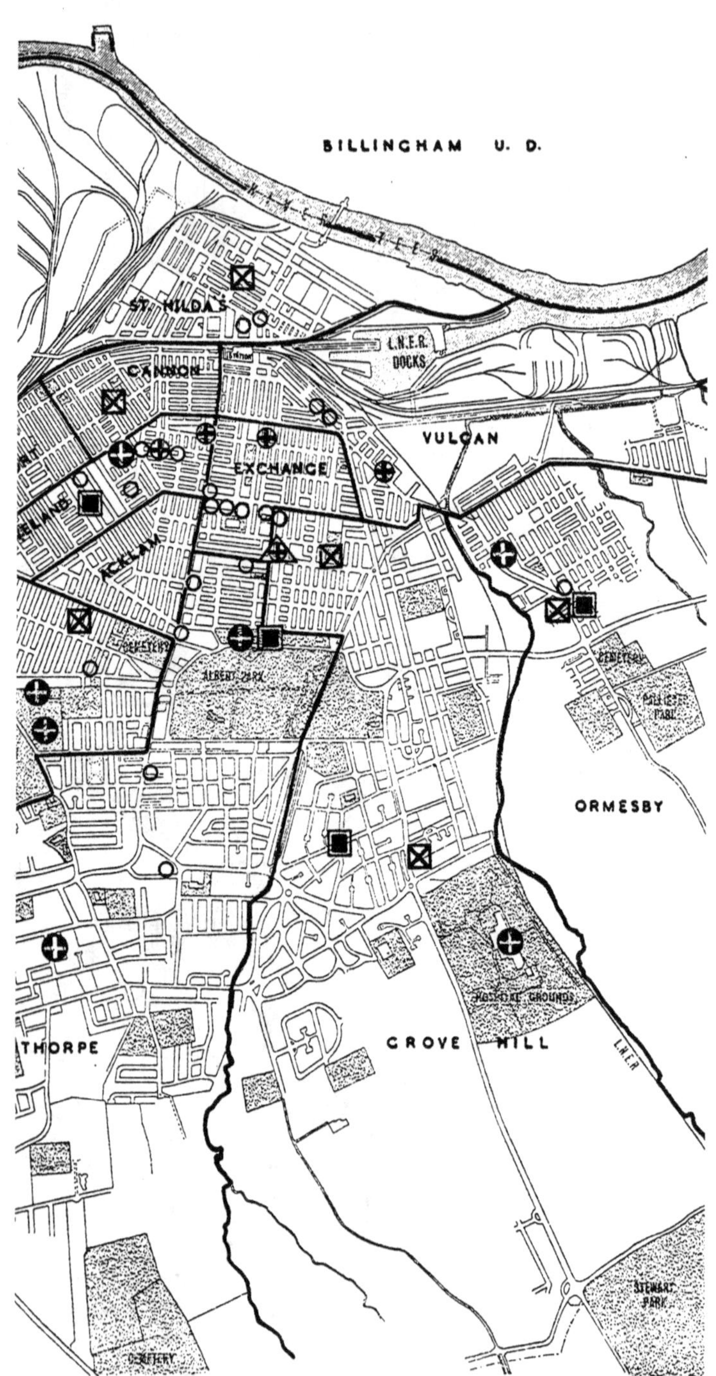

BILLINGHAM U. D.
RIVER TEES
ST. HILDA'S
L.N.E.R. DOCKS
CANNON
VULCAN
EXCHANGE
ACKLAM
ALBERT PARK
CEMETERY
ORMESBY
THORPE
GROVE HILL
HOSPITAL GROUNDS
L.N.E.R.
STEWART PARK
CEMETERY

MAP II

HEALTH SERVICES

AND ADMINISTRATIVE BOUNDARIES

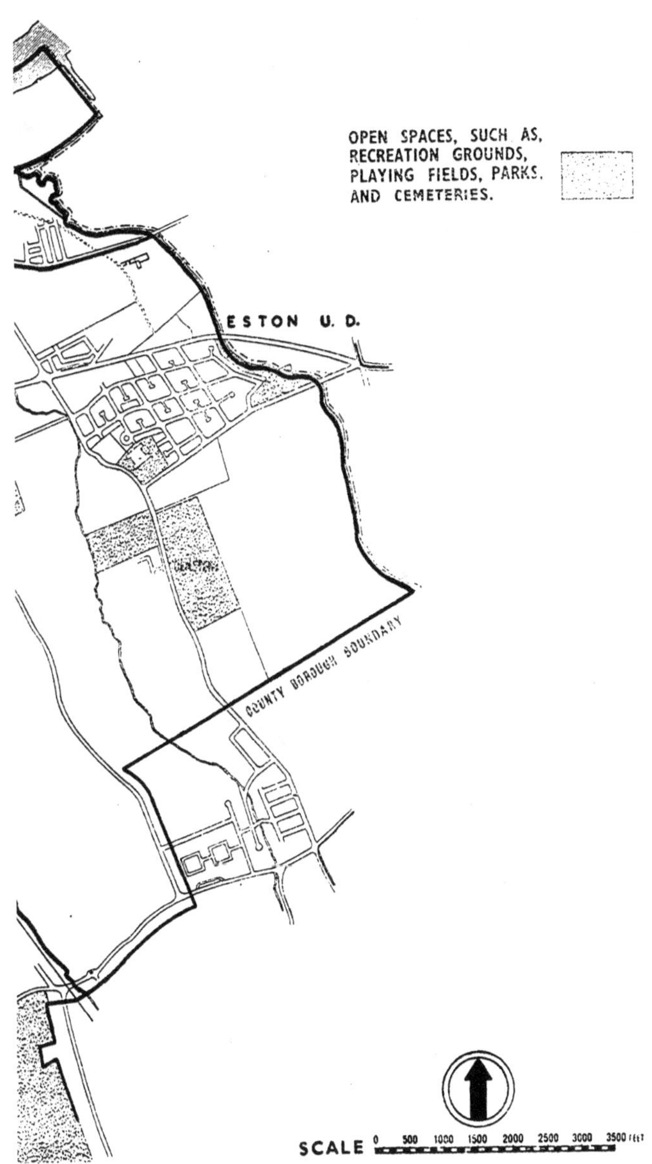

KEY

CHILD SURVIVING FIRST THREE MONTHS OF LIFE AND **NOT ATTENDING** INFANT WELFARE CENTRE DURING FIRST THREE MONTHS .... ⊙

CHILD SURVIVING FIRST THREE MONTHS OF LIFE AND **ATTENDING** INFANT WELFARE CENTRE DURING FIRST THREE MONTHS .... □

CHILD **NOT** SURVIVING FIRST THREE MONTHS OF LIFE AND **NOT HAVING ATTENDED** INFANT WELFARE CENTRE .... ●

CHILD **NOT** SURVIVING FIRST THREE MONTHS OF LIFE AND **HAVING ATTENDED** INFANT WELFARE CENTRE .... ■

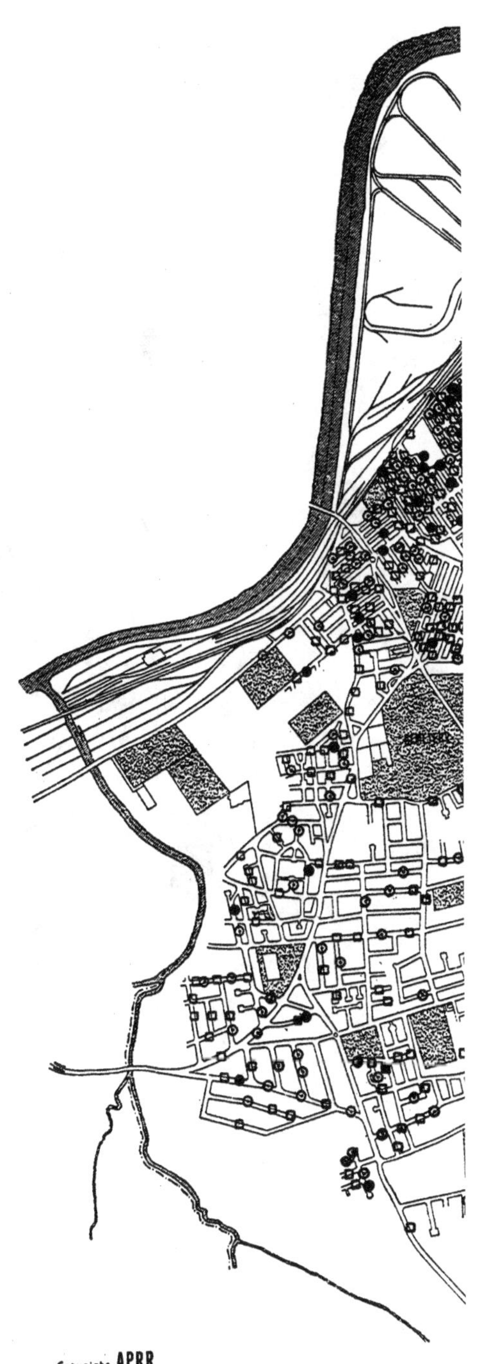

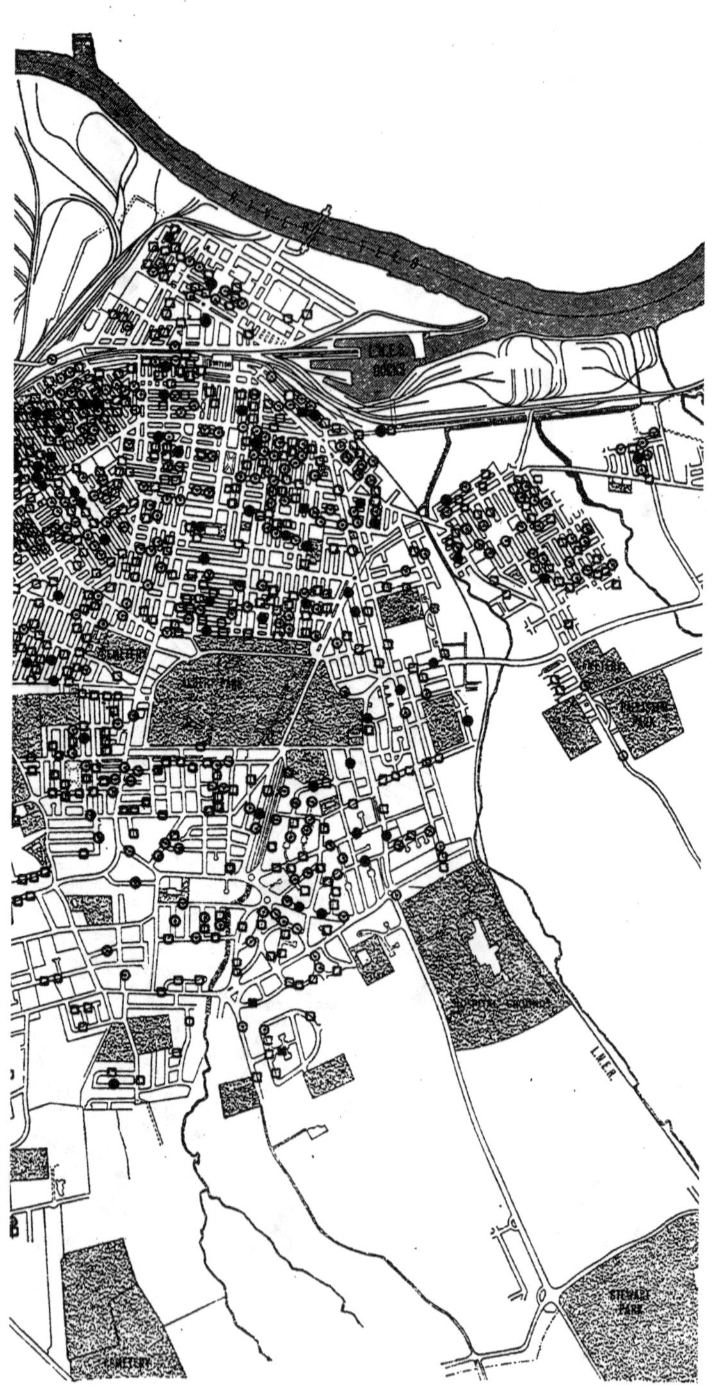
L.N.E.R.
DOCKS
L.N.E.R.
STEWART
PARK
CEMETERY

MAP 12

DISTRIBUTION OF BIRTHS

JANUARY TO APRIL 1944

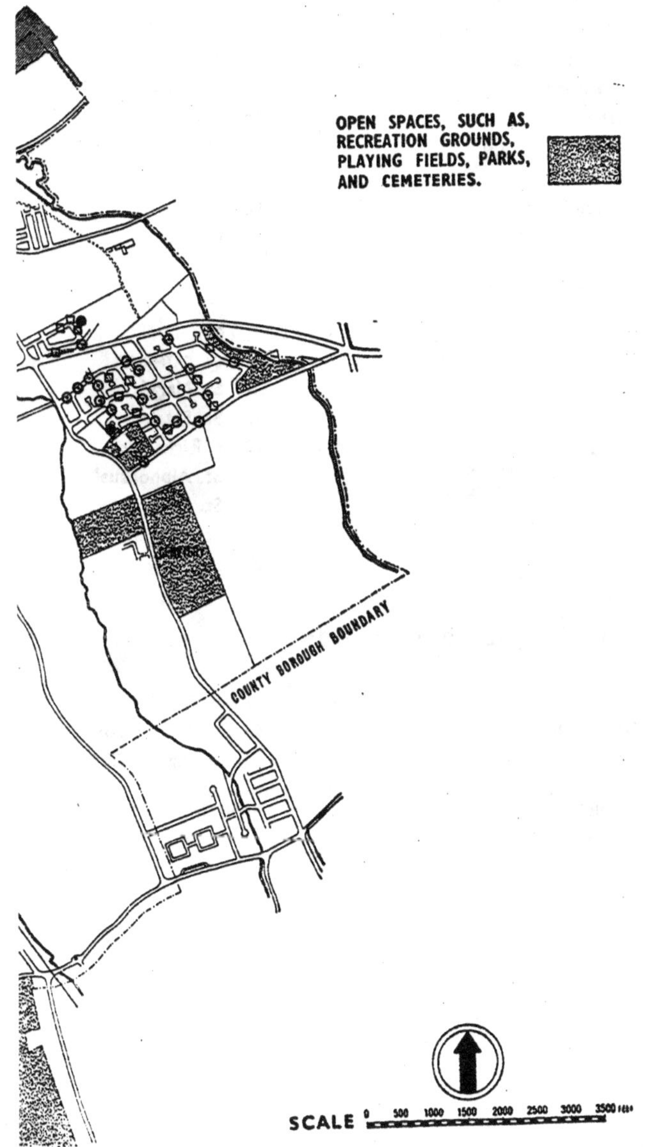

KEY TO TYPES OF SCHOOL

ELEMENTARY SCHOOLS

L.E.A. PROVIDED

1 Lower East Street
2 Southend
3 Denmark Street
4 Marsh Road
5 Fleetham Street
6 Newport Road
7 Marton Road
8 Smeaton Street
9 Derwent Street

10 Lawson
11 Victoria Road
12 Ayresome
13 Archibald
14 Linthorpe
15 Whinney Banks
16 Marton Grove
17 Beechwood
18 Brambles

36 L.E.A. Special School

L.E.A. NON-PROVIDED

CHURCH OF ENGLAND

19 St. Hilda's
20 St. John's
(St. Paul's School was destroyed in 1944. Pupils are now accommodated in part of Newport Road School)

ROMAN CATHOLIC

21 St. Mary's
22 St. Patrick's
23 St. Richard's
24 St. Alphonsus'
25 St. Philomena's
26 St. Joseph's
27 St. Francis'

SCHOOLS FOR HIGHER EDUCATION

L.E.A. SCHOOLS

28 High School
29 Kirby Girls' Secondary
30 Acklam Hall Boys' Secondary
31 Hugh Bell Central Technical and Deaf Schools
32 Preparatory School

ROMAN CATHOLIC

33 St. Mary's Boys' College
34 St. Mary's Girls' Convent

Private School

35 Loreto School

39 Constantine College

DOMESTIC SCIENCE CENTRES

37 Stockton Street
38 Borough Road

SCHOOL BUILDINGS □ PLAYING FIELDS ■

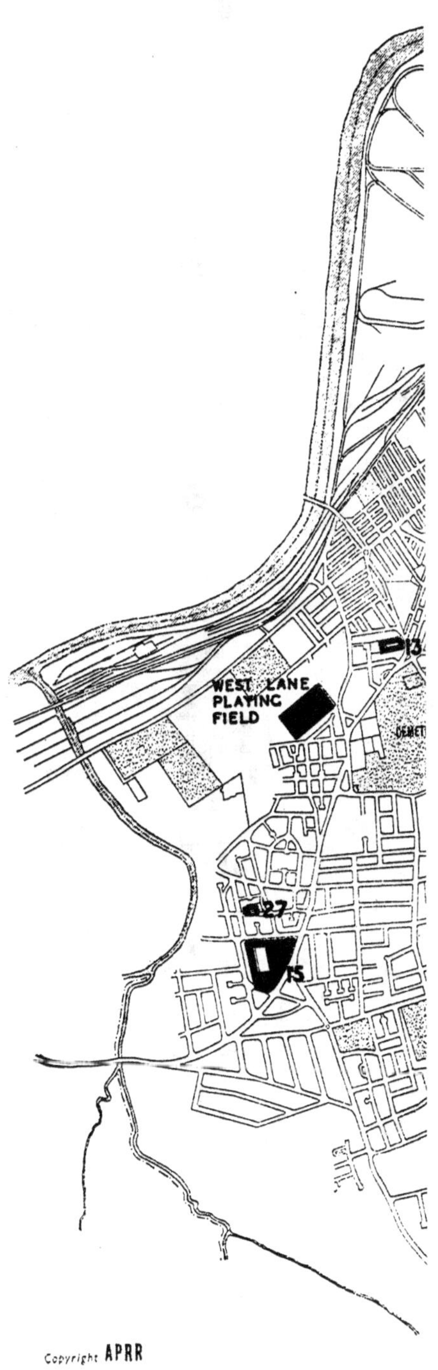
WEST LANE
PLAYING
FIELD
13
27
15

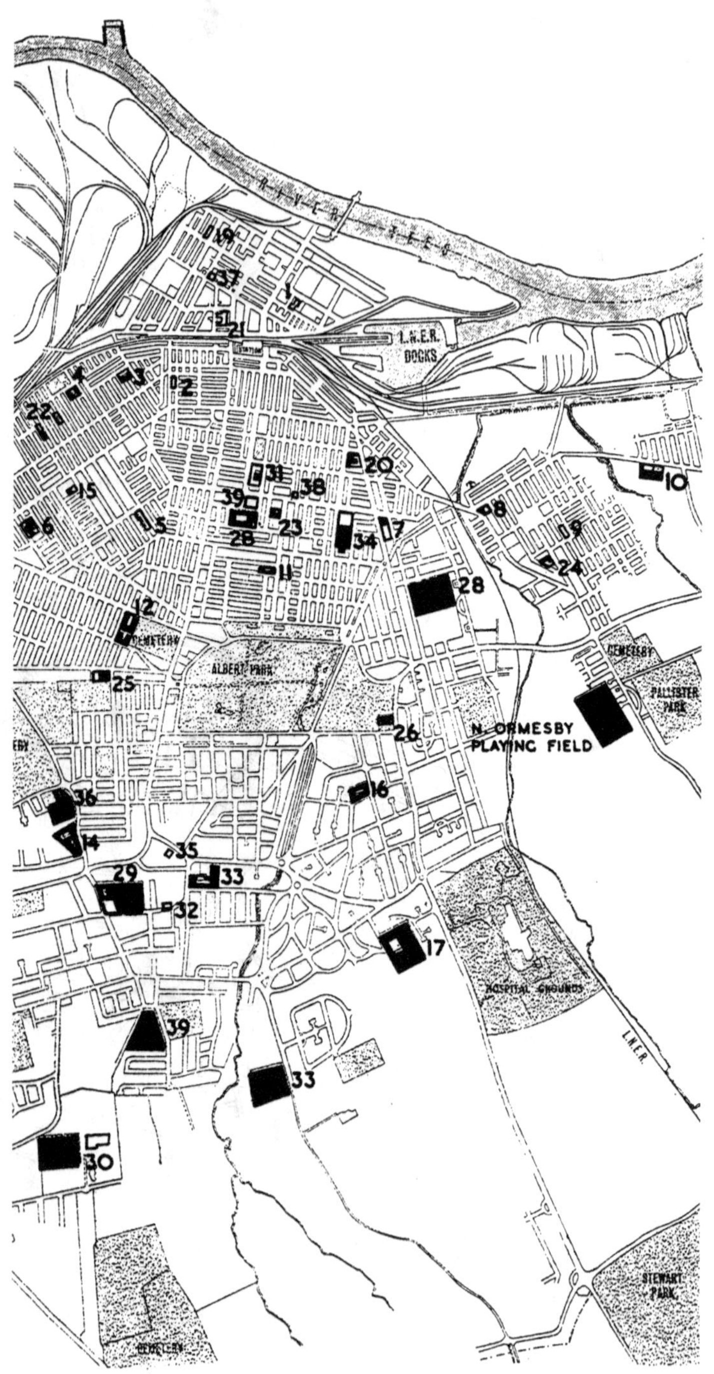
RIVER TEES
L.N.E.R. DOCKS
STATION
CEMETERY
ALBERT PARK
CEMETERY
PALLISTER PARK
N. ORMESBY PLAYING FIELD
HOSPITAL GROUNDS
L.N.E.R.
STEWART PARK
CEMETERY

MAP 13

SCHOOLS AND SCHOOL PLAYING FIELDS 1944

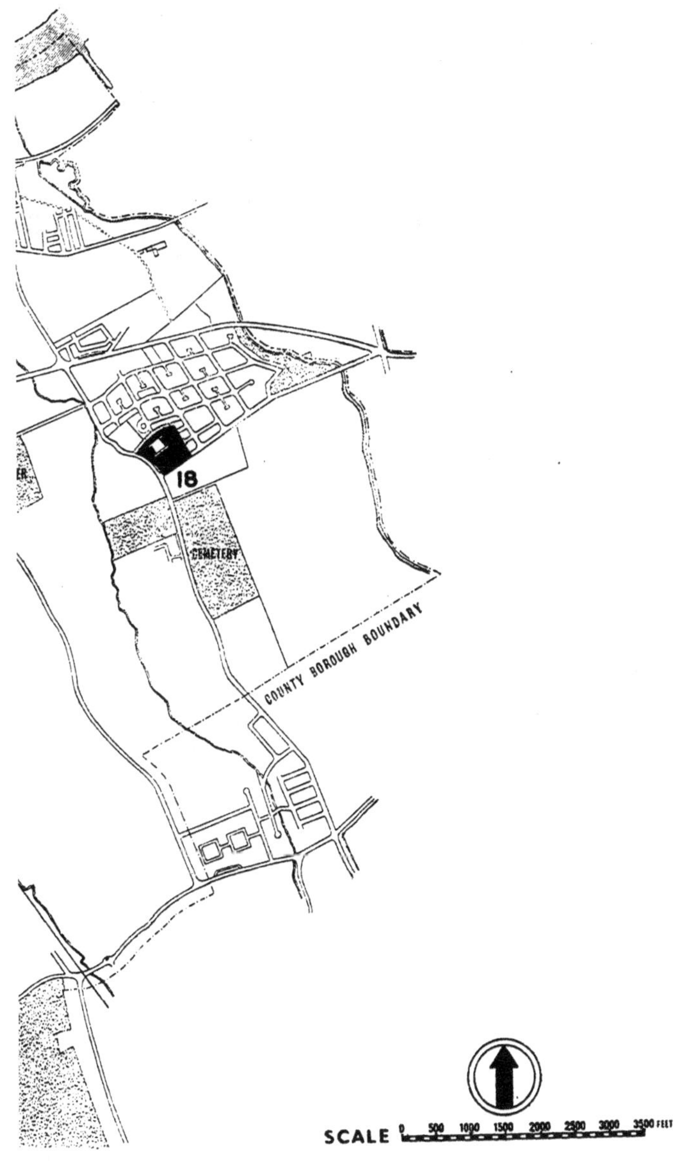

KEY

SCHOOL .... ■

PUPIL'S HOUSE .... •

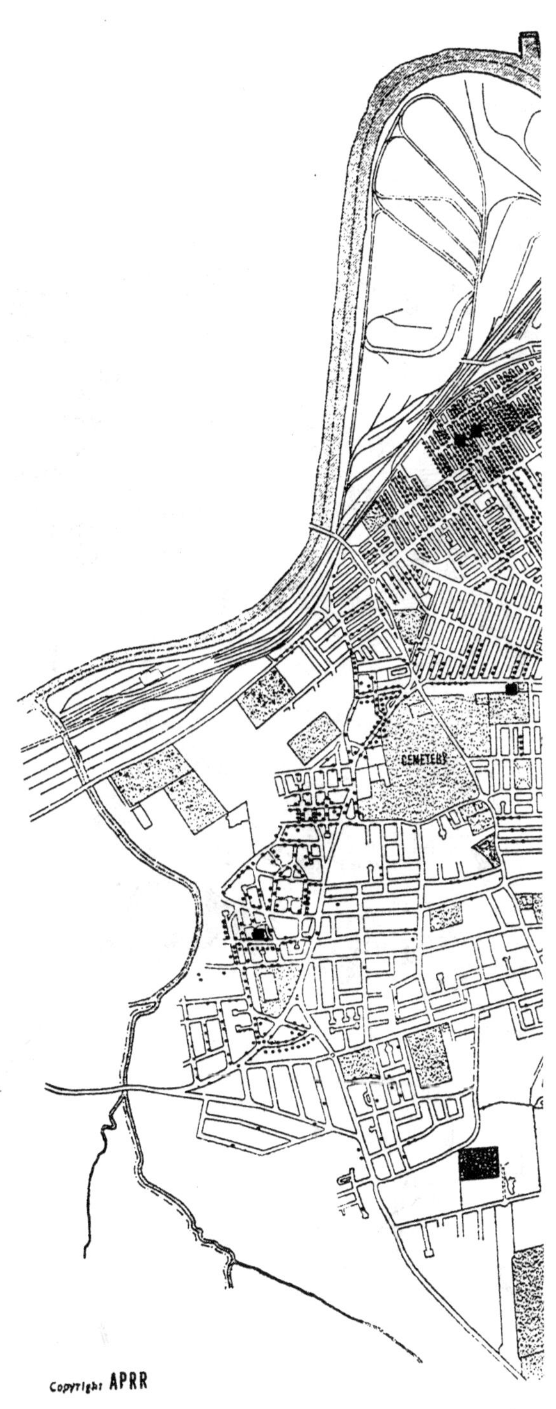
CEMETERY
Copyright APRR

RIVER TEES
L.N.E.R. DOCKS
CEMETERY
ALBERT PARK
CEMETERY
PALLISTER PARK
HOSPITAL GROUNDS
L.N.E.R.
STEWART PARK
CEMETERY

MAP 14

DISTRIBUTION OF PUPILS ATTENDING ROMAN CATHOLIC ELEMENTARY SCHOOLS JULY 1944

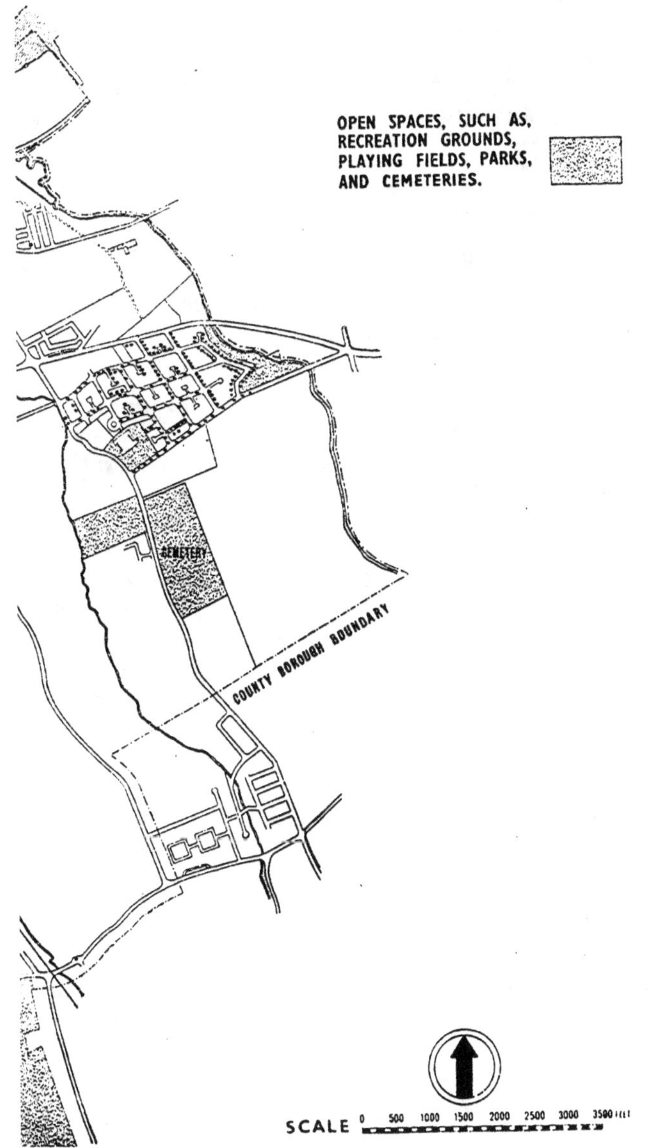

KEY

SHOPPING CENTRES

DEGREES OF PROSPERITY

PROSPEROUS ....

AVERAGE PLUS ....

AVERAGE MINUS ....

POOR ....

ISOLATED SHOPS .... •

DIVISION OF SURVEY AREA ....

CATEGORIES	NUMBER	NAME
CHIEF CENTRES	1	The Primary Centre
	2	The Secondary Centre
INTERMEDIATE CENTRES	3	St. Hilda's, North Side of Railway
	4	Newport Road
	5	Corporation Road
	6	The Park, Linthorpe
	7	The Village, Linthorpe
LOCAL CENTRES	8	Market Place, N. Ormesby
	9	Borough Road West
	10	Cannon Street
	11	Parliament Road
STRICTLY LOCAL CENTRES	12	Beaumont Road
	13	Waterloo Road
	14	The Longlands
	15	Roman Road
	16	Acklam Road South
	17	Marton Road
	18	Eastbourne Road
	19	Sutton Estate
	20	Whinney Banks
		Brambles Farm :
	21	Kestral Avenue
	22	Marshall Avenue

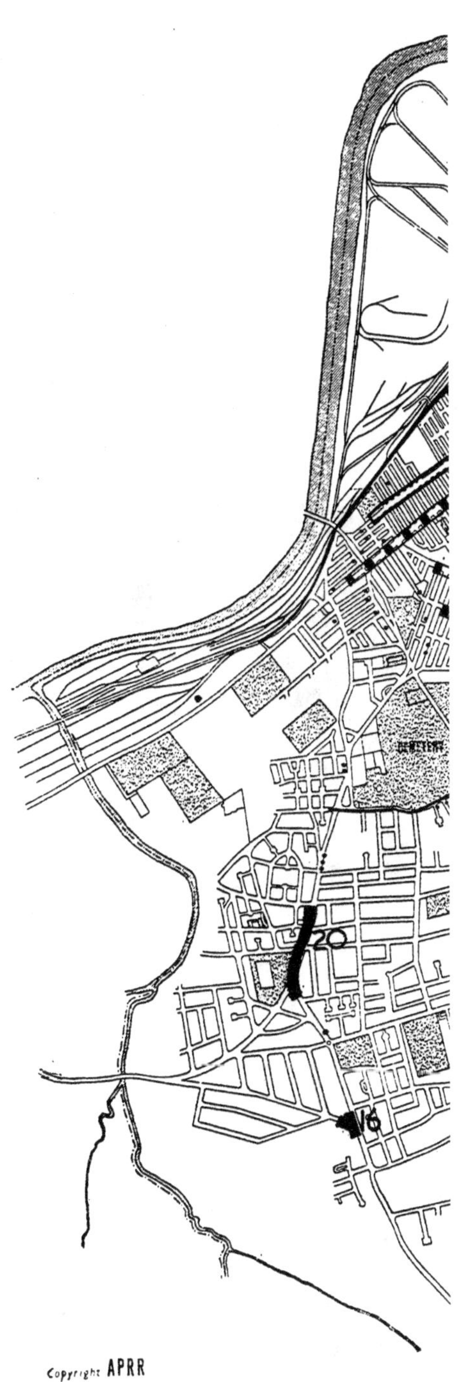
20
16

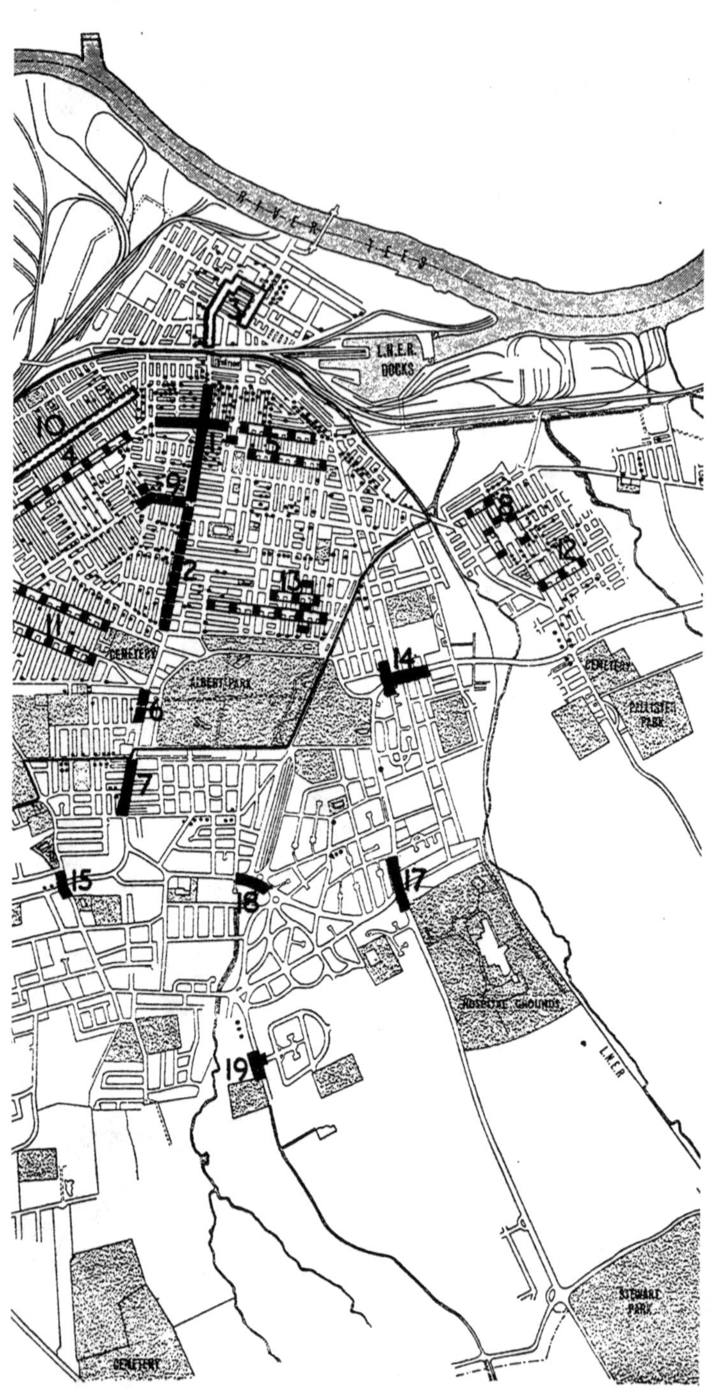

RIVER TEES
L.N.E.R.
DOCKS
10
4
1
5
9
3
8
12
2
13
11
CEMETERY
ALBERT PARK
14
CEMETERY
6
7
15
18
17
L.N.E.R
19
STEWART
PARK
CEMETERY

MAP 15

DISTRIBUTION OF SHOPPING CENTRES

SHOWING DEGREES OF PROSPERITY

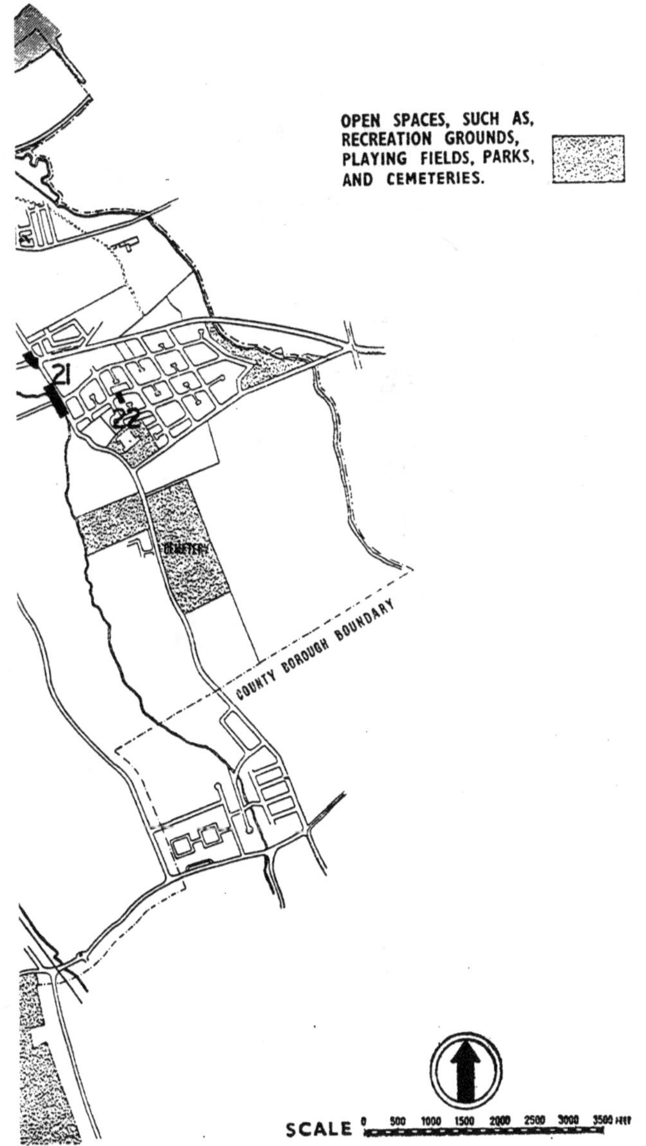

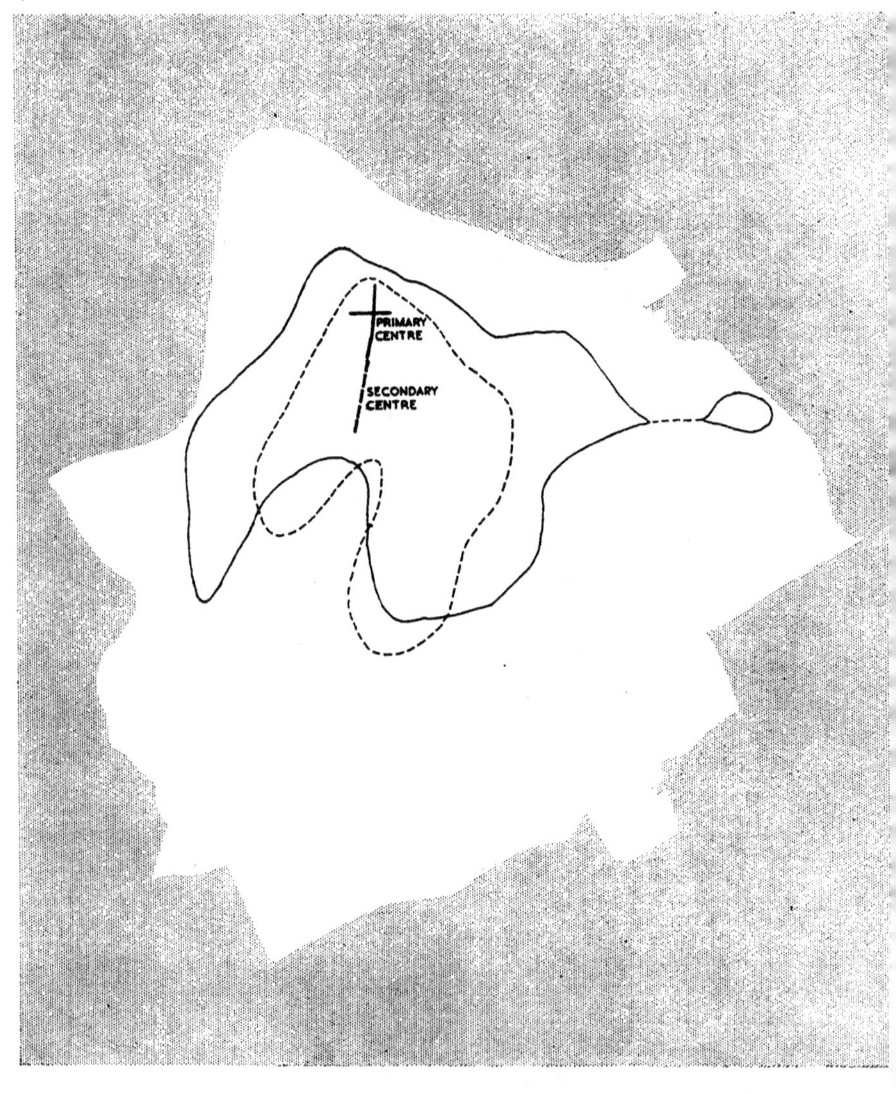

CHIEF SHOPPING CENTRES

MAP 16

GENERALISED CATCHMENT AREAS OF SHOPPING CENTRES (BASED ON SUGAR REGISTRATIONS)

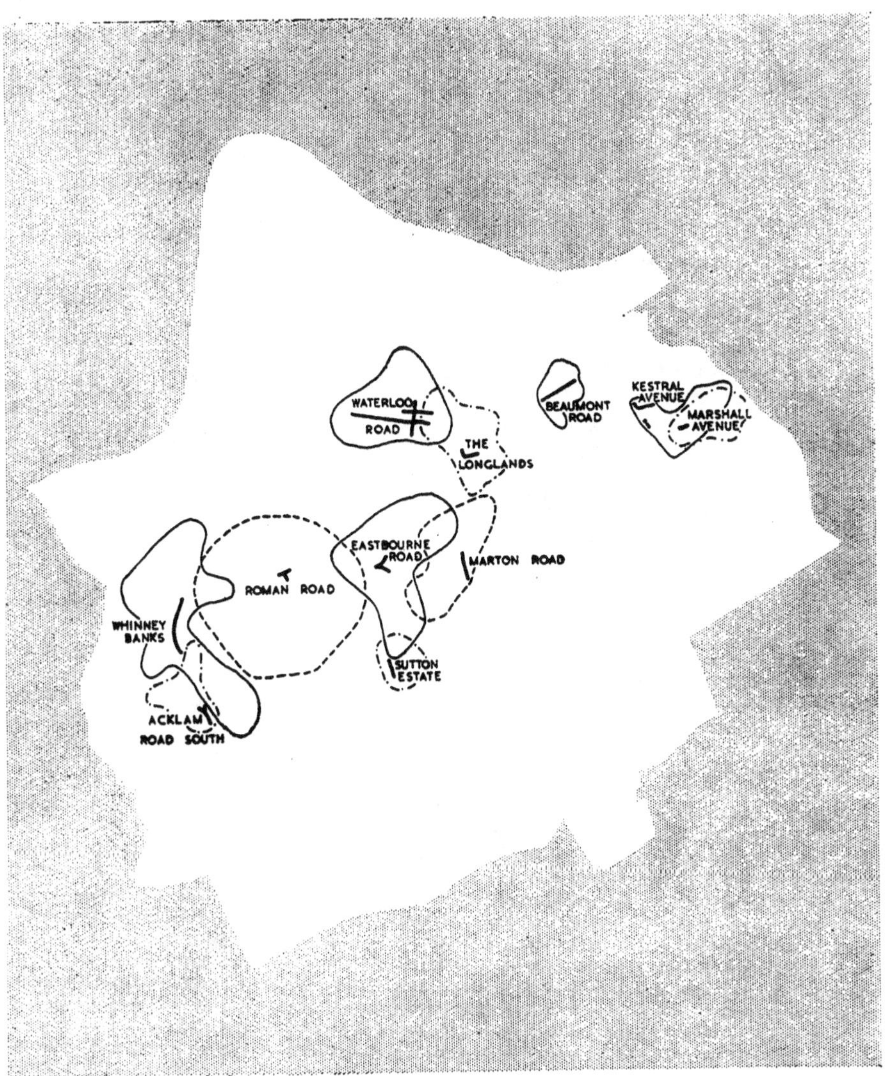

STRICTLY LOCAL SHOPPING CENTRES

KEY—MAJOR PHYSICAL FEATURES

CLIFFS OF GLACIAL DRIFT ....

ROCK CLIFFS ....

OVER 250′..

OVER 500′..

CLEVELAND ESCARPMENT..

WOODED GILLS ....

ALLUVIAL FLATS ....

HIGH SANDSTONE PLATEAU ABOVE 800′
RISING TO 1,000′..

LOW PLATEAU, 400′ TO 700′
MAINLY DRIFT COVERED..

MOOR EDGE ....

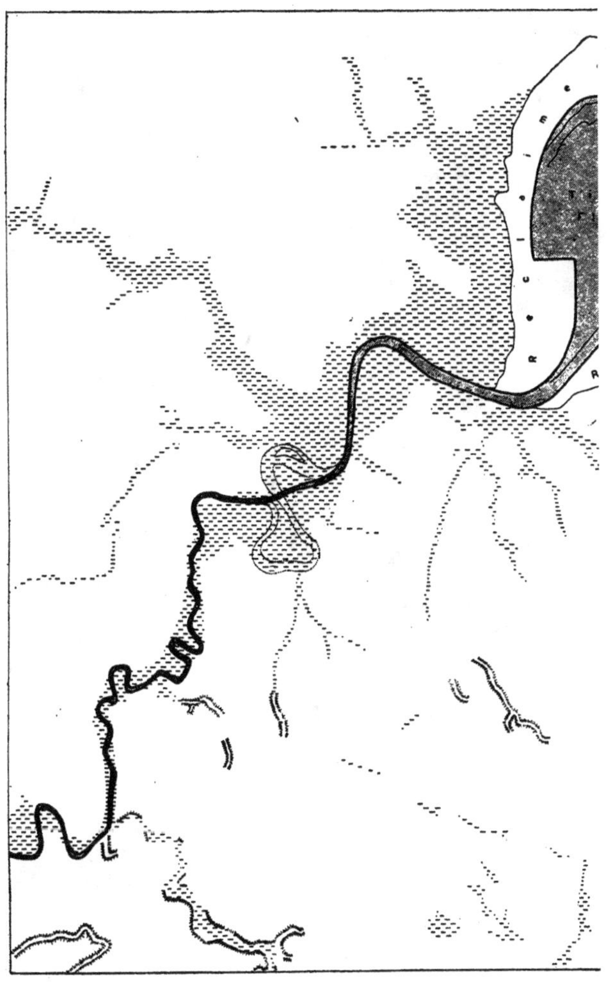

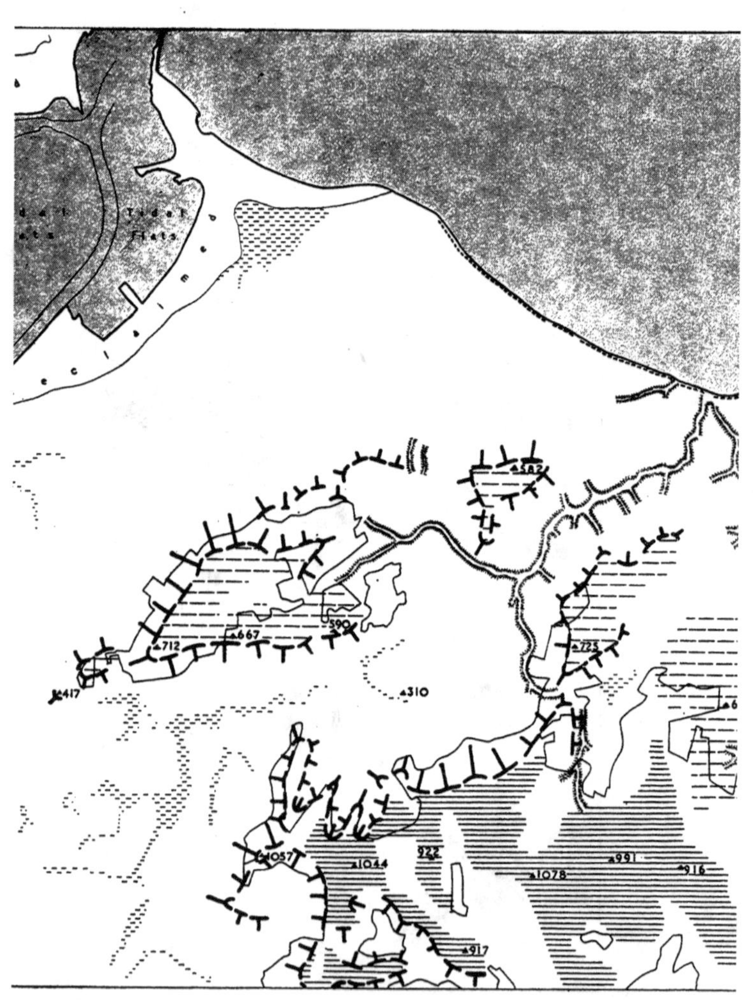

Tidal
Flats
R e c l a i m e d
712
667
590
417
310
725
1057
1044
922
991
916
1078
917

MAP 17

THE TEES-SIDE & CLEVELAND AREA—MAJOR PHYSICAL FEATURES

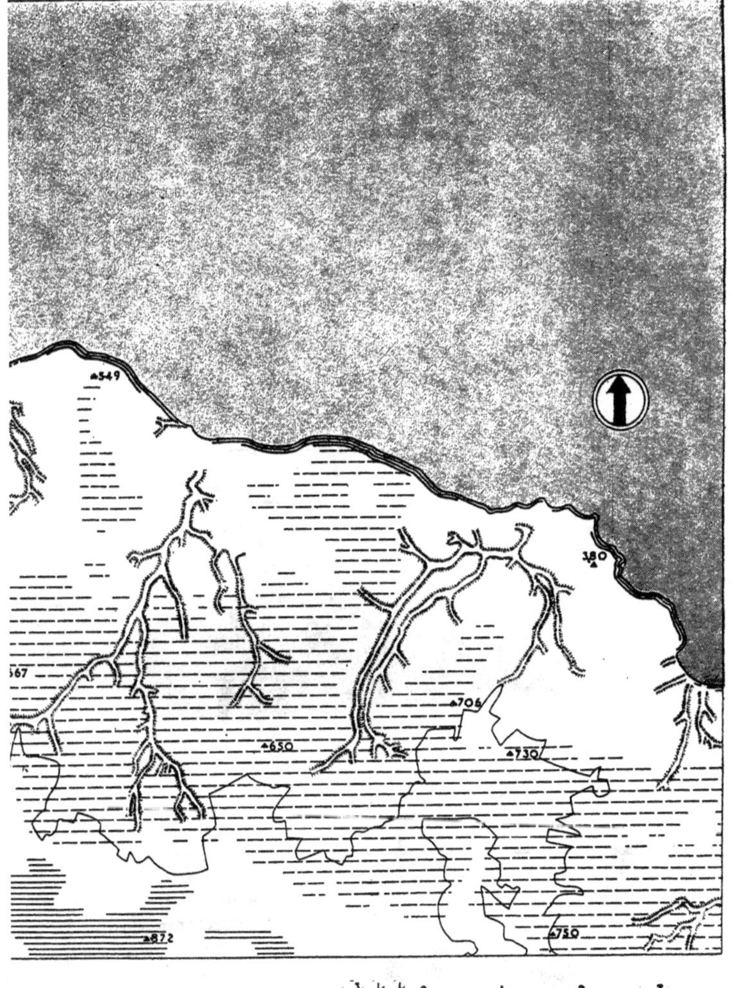

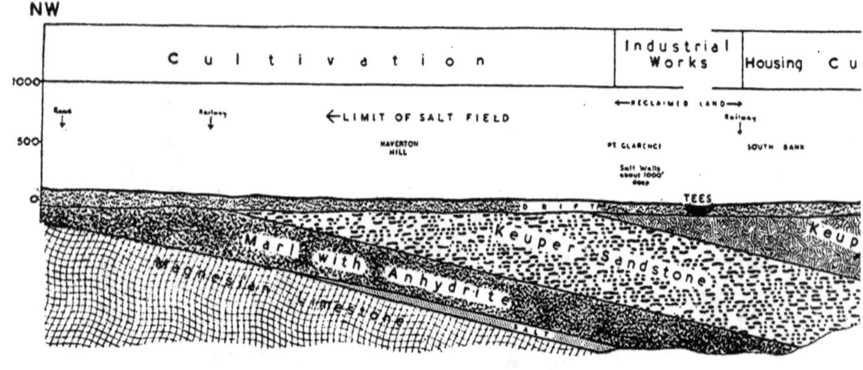
NW
Cultivation
Industrial Works
Housing
1000
500
0
←LIMIT OF SALT FIELD
←RECLAIMED LAND→
HAVERTON HILL
PT CLARENCE
SOUTH BANK
Salt Wells about 1000' deep
TEES
DRIFT
Keuper Sandstone
Marl with Anhydrite
Magnesian Limestone
SALT

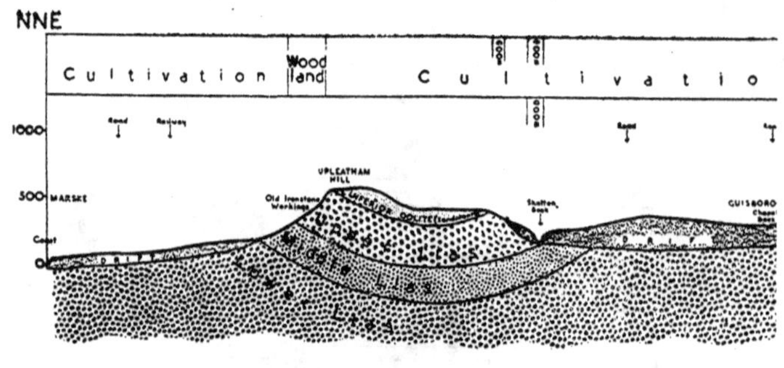
NNE
Cultivation
Wood land
Cultivatio
1000
500
0
MARSKE
Coast
DRIFT
UPLEATHAM HILL
Old Ironstone Workings
Upper Lias
Middle Lias
Lower Lias
DRIFT

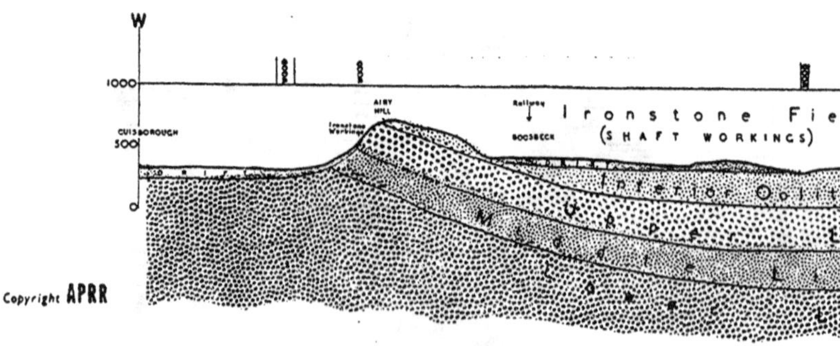
W
1000
500
0
GUISBOROUGH
DRIFT
AIRY HILL
Ironstone Workings
Railway
BOOSBECK
Ironstone Fie
(SHAFT WORKINGS)
Inferior Oolit
Upper L
Middle L
Lower L

MAP 18

CLEVELAND

TYPICAL TRANSECTS

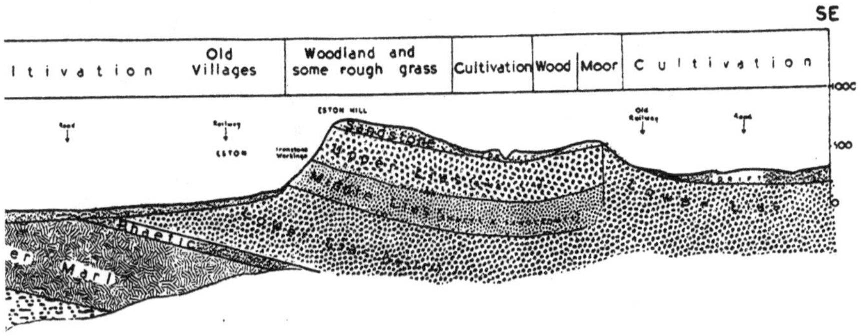

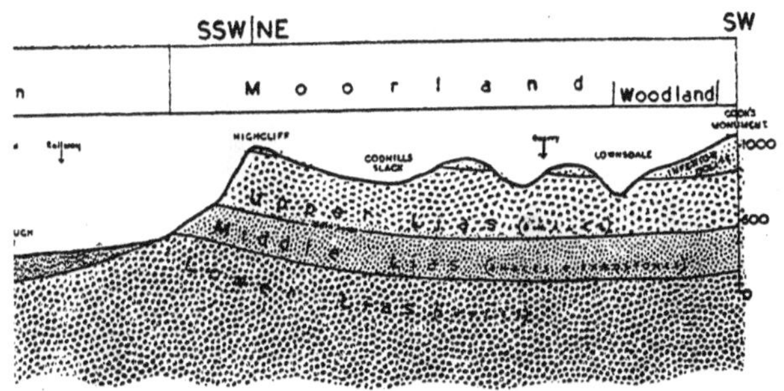

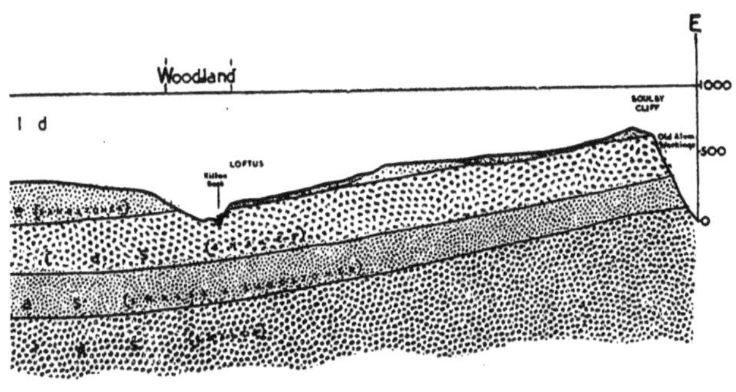

KEY

RAILWAY ....

RAILWAY STATION ....

MAIN BUILT-UP AREA ....

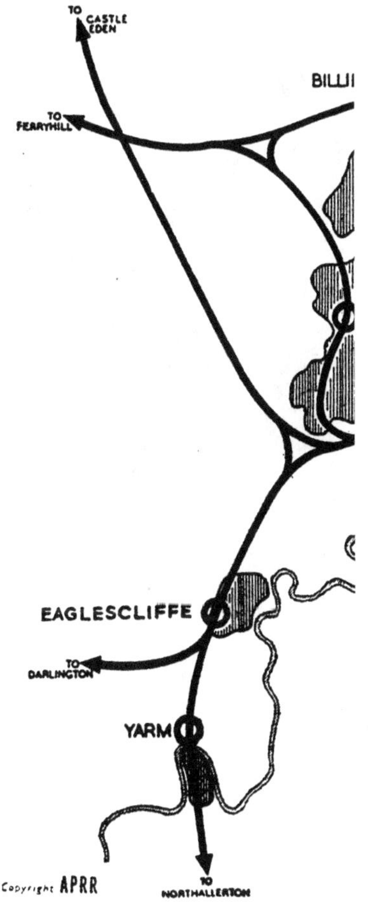
TO CASTLE EDEN
BILLI
TO FERRYHILL
EAGLESCLIFFE
TO DARLINGTON
YARM
Copyright APRR
TO NORTHALLERTON

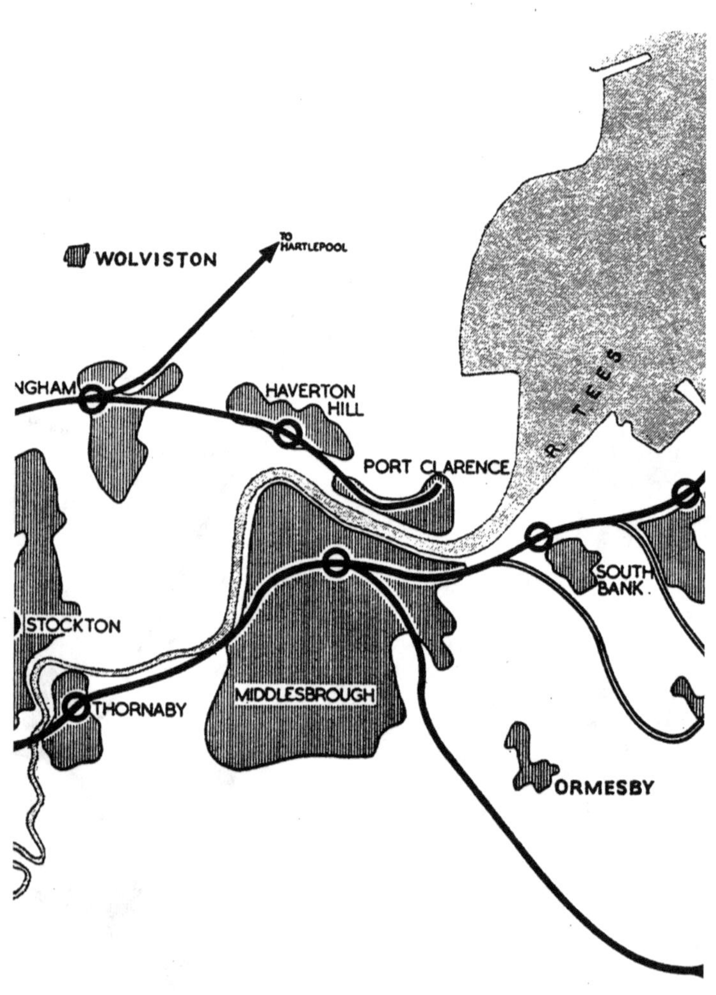

WOLVISTON
TO HARTLEPOOL
NGHAM
HAVERTON HILL
PORT CLARENCE
R. TEES
STOCKTON
THORNABY
MIDDLESBROUGH
SOUTH BANK
ORMESBY

MAP 19

RELATIONSHIP BETWEEN MIDDLESBROUGH AND OTHER TEES-SIDE TOWNS

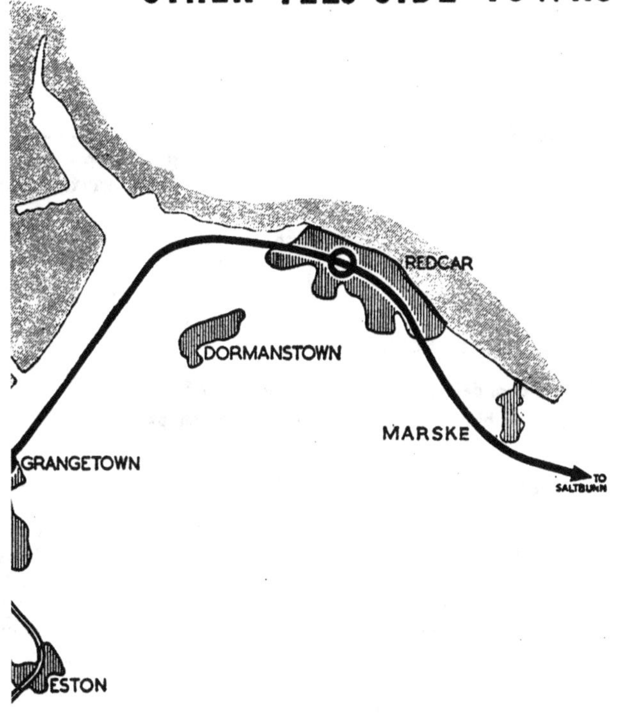

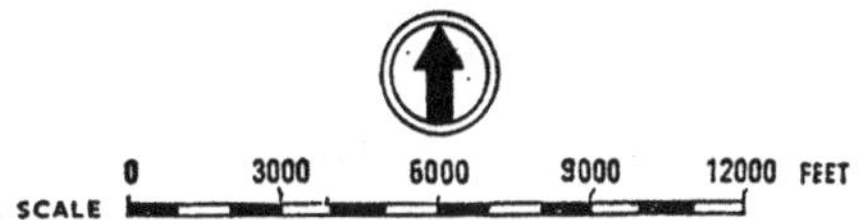

KEY TO DIAGRAMS

A WHOLESALE DISTRIBUTION AREA

Areas served by representative firms in various wholesale trades

GREENGROCERIES .... ••••••••••••••

GROCERIES .... ---------

MEAT xxxxxxxxxxxxx

BREAD AND CONFECTIONERY ....

B RETAIL DELIVERY AREA

Wartime pool deliveries by motor used by 32 firms including all big retail stores and furniture shops

DAILY ....

TWICE WEEKLY ....

WEEKLY ....

C NEWSPAPER CIRCULATION AREA

DAILY EVENING NEWSPAPER

D CO-OPERATIVE SOCIETY

BRANCHES : Single or Multiple Group .... ⑤

APPROXIMATE EXTENT OF MILK DISTRIBUTION AREA .... ---------

A From Middlesbrough Dairy

B From Redcar Dairy

APPROXIMATE EXTENT OF MILK SUPPLY AREA ....

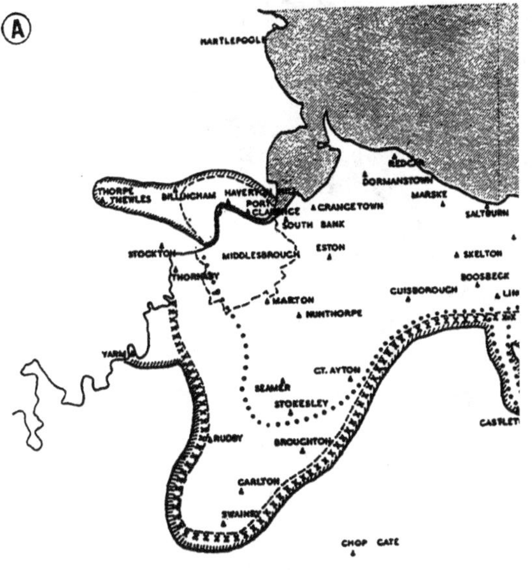

NORTHALLERTON

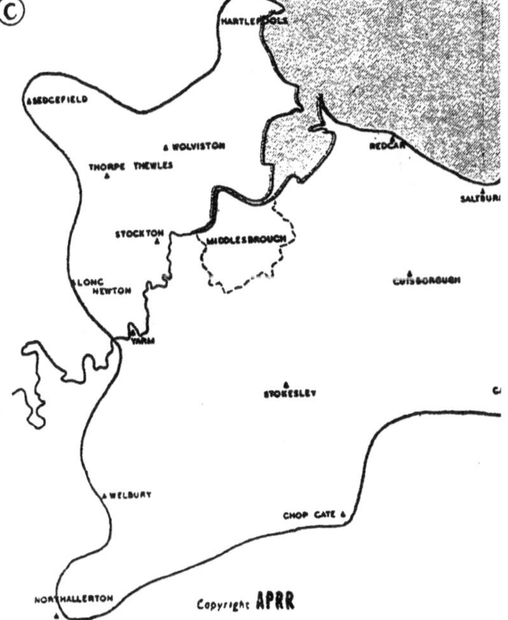

MIDDLESBROUGH —

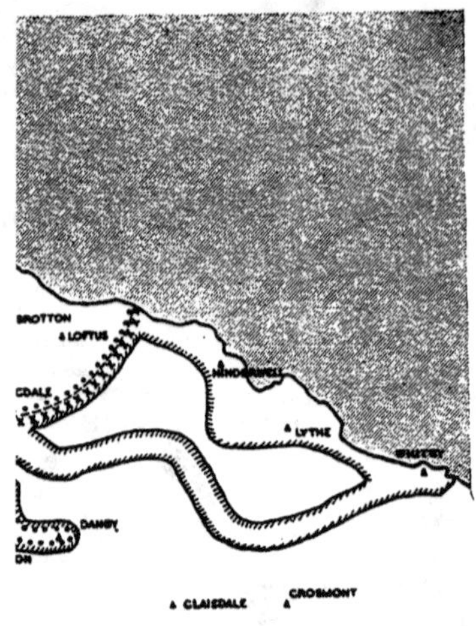

(B)

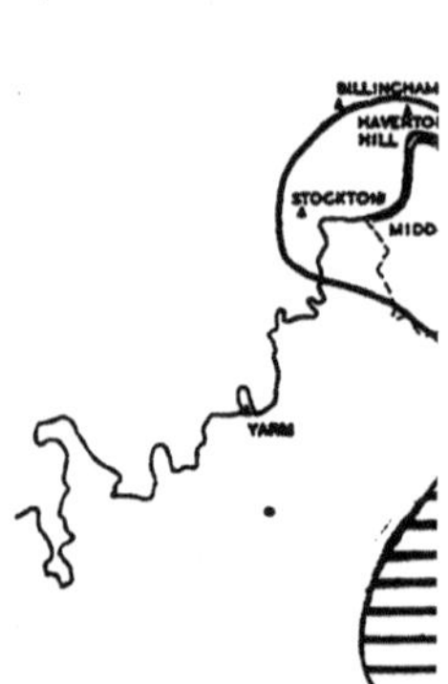

NORTHALLERTON

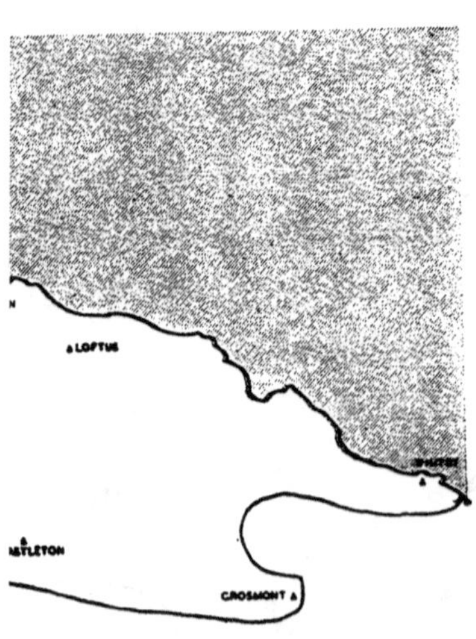

(D)

MAP 20

— SPHERES OF INFLUENCE

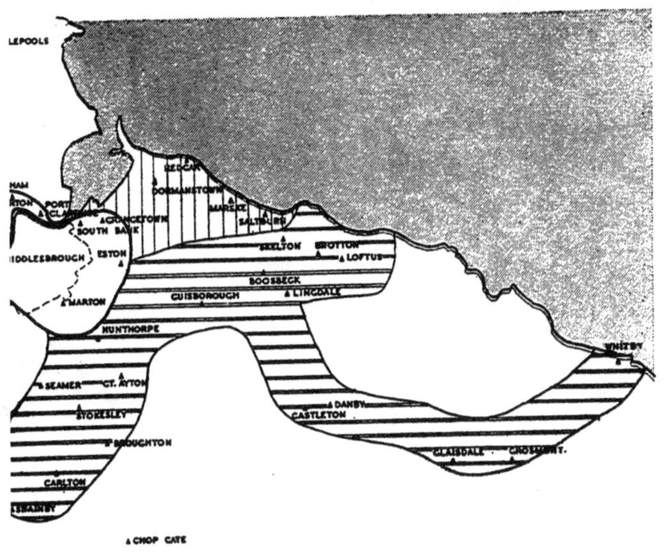

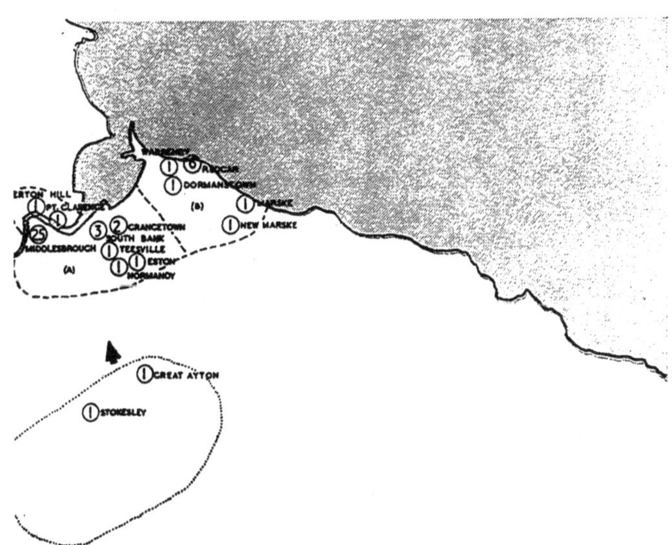

SCALE FOR ALL DIAGRAMS. ½" = 1 MILE

SCALE 0 1 2 3 4 5 6 7 8 9 10 MILES

KEY

NUMBERS EMPLOYED	TYPE OF INDUSTRY
UP TO 50	METAL
100	CHEMICALS
200	SHIPBUILDING
300	CLOTHING
400	MISCELLANEOUS
500	POPULATED AREAS
750	BOROUGH BOUNDARY
1,000	
2,000	
3,000	
6,000	
10,000 AND OVER	

STOCKTO

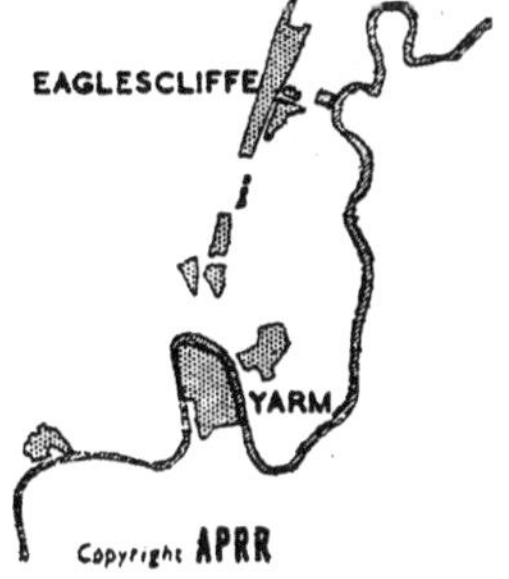
EAGLESCLIFFE
YARM
Copyright APRR

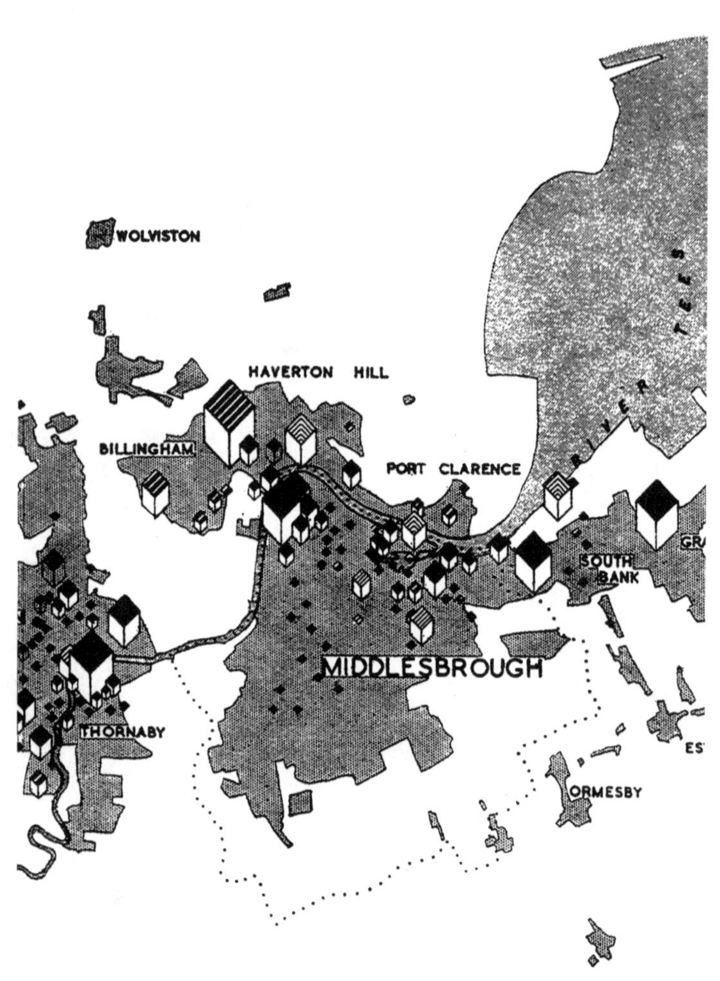
WOLVISTON
HAVERTON HILL
BILLINGHAM
PORT CLARENCE
RIVER TEES
SOUTH BANK
MIDDLESBROUGH
THORNABY
ORMESBY

MAP 21

TYPE AND SIZE OF INDUSTRY IN THE TEES-SIDE AREA

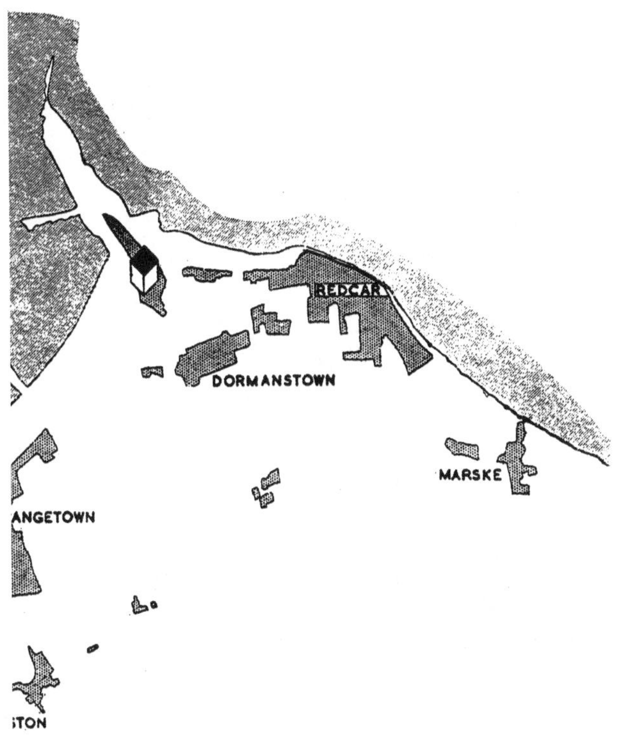

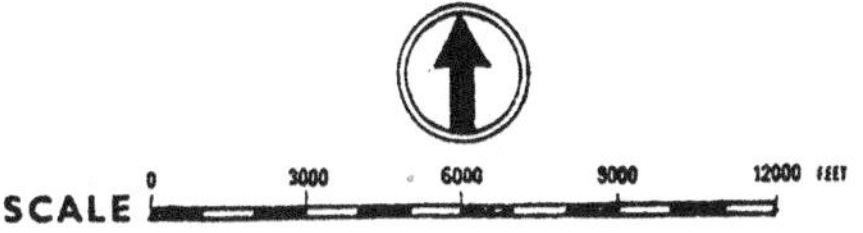

For Product Safety Concerns and Information please contact our EU representative GPSR@taylorandfrancis.com
Taylor & Francis Verlag GmbH, Kaufingerstraße 24, 80331 München, Germany

www.ingramcontent.com/pod-product-compliance
Lightning Source LLC
Chambersburg PA
CBHW070547270326
41926CB00013B/2227

* 9 7 8 0 4 1 5 8 6 8 5 5 6 *